This book focusses on the celebrated, hugely entertaining, cult 26-episode Japanese *animé* TV series *Cowboy Bebop*, first broadcast in 1998. *Cowboy Bebop*, produced by Sunrise (a subsidiary of Bandai) and TV Tokyo, is one of the masterpieces of animation of recent times.

MEDIA, FEMINISM, CULTURAL STUDIES

The Sacred Cinema of Andrei Tarkovsky
by Jeremy Mark Robinson

Liv Tyler
by Thomas A. Christie

The Cinema of Hayao Miyazaki
Jeremy Mark Robinson

The Poetry of Cinema
by John Madden

Stepping Forward: Essays, Lectures and Interviews
by Wolfgang Iser

Wild Zones: Pornography, Art and Feminism
by Kelly Ives

Global Media Warning: Explorations of Radio, Television and the Press
by Oliver Whitehorne

'Cosmo Woman': The World of Women's Magazines
by Oliver Whitehorne

The Cinema of Richard Linklater
by Thomas A. Christie

Walerian Borowczyk
by Jeremy Mark Robinson

Andrea Dworkin
by Jeremy Mark Robinson

Cixous, Irigaray, Kristeva: The Jouissance of French Feminism
by Kelly Ives

*The Erotic Object: Sexuality in Sculpture
From Prehistory to the Present Day*
by Susan Quinnell

Women in Pop Music
by Helen Challis

Detonation Britain: Nuclear War in the UK
by Jeremy Mark Robinson

Julia Kristeva: Art, Love, Melancholy, Philosophy, Semiotics
by Kelly Ives

Luce Irigaray: Lips, Kissing, and the Politics of Sexual Difference
by Kelly Ives

Helene Cixous I Love You: The Jouissance *of Writing*
by Kelly Ives

Feminism and Shakespeare
by B.D. Barnacle

FORTHCOMING BOOKS

Ghost In the Shell
Legend of the Overfiend
Fullmetal Alchemist
The Akira Book
Tsui Hark
The Twilight Saga
Hayao Miyazaki: Pocket Guide
The Pirates of the Caribbean Movies
Harry Potter
Mel Brooks
Tim Burton
George Lucas
Francis Coppola
Orson Welles
Pier Paolo Pasolini
Ingmar Bergman
Contempt

COWBOY BEBOP

THE *ANIMÉ* TV SERIES AND MOVIE

COWBOY
BEBOP

SEE YOU SPACE COWBOY...

THE ANIMÉ TV SERIES AND MOVIE
POCKET GUIDE

JEREMY MARK ROBINSON

CRESCENT MOON

First published 2015.
© Jeremy Mark Robinson 2015.

Printed and bound in the U.S.A.
Set in Book Antiqua, 9 on 14 point.
Designed by Radiance Graphics.

*British Library Cataloguing in Publication data
available for this title.*

ISBN-13 9781861714961 (Pbk)

*Crescent Moon Publishing
P.O. Box 1312, Maidstone, Kent
ME14 5XU, U.K.
www.crmoon.com
cresmopub@yahoo.co.uk*

CONTENTS

ACKNOWLEDGEMENTS

To the authors and publishers quoted.

PICTURE CREDITS

Music is the most incredible event in human history.

Ken Russell

COWBOY BEBOP

賞金獵人

又名：宇宙牛仔

6DVD

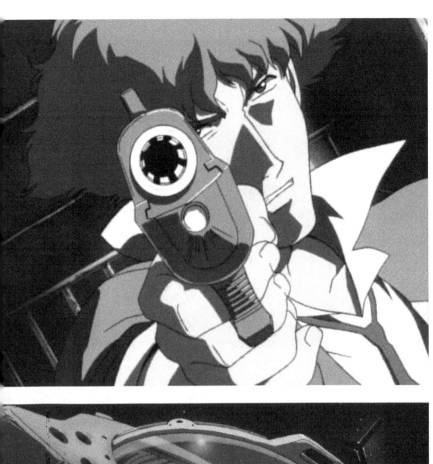
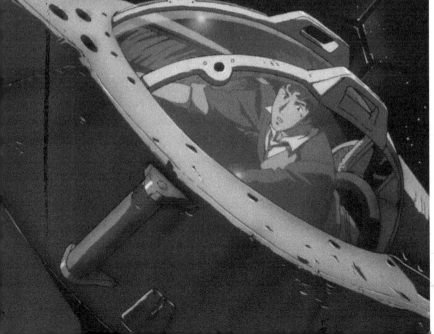

SEE YOU SPACE COWB

COWBOY BEBOP

01

OVERTURE – *OK, THREE, TWO, ONE: LET'S JAM!*

Sex + drugs + rock music + comedy + Westerns + crime + drifter lifestyles + space battles + bars + casinos + fashion – and more music – what's not to like in *Cowboy Bebop*?! – and how it wittily and cleverly mixes all of those elements, and many more. That *Cowboy Bebop* (first broadcast in 1998, and produced by Sunrise (a subsidiary of Bandai) and TV Tokyo), is a fan favourite goes without saying. It is a masterpiece of storytelling, invention, design and production on every level. It is unique. It regularly features in top ten lists of *animé* favourites, and sometimes tops the lists. Easy to see why: it's got everything, and *then some*.

This book was a total delight to write. I had written it, then rewritten it once and thought I was done. Then I watched some of my favourite episodes from the *Cowboy Bebop* series yet again (*Ballad of*

Fallen Angels, Honky Tonk Women, Speak Like a Child, Jupiter Jazz, etc), and realized there was plenty more to do! And I've gone back *again* to add to episodes I've seen for the *n*-th time! *Cowboy Bebop* is so jammed with ideas, jokes, stunts, issues, music, brilliant imagery and brilliant action, it repays *many* visits (you will find new bits to delight in every time). *Cowboy Bebop* is one of the most enjoyable TV shows ever made.

♫

Jeremy Mark Robinson
Somewhere in the Solar System

COWBOY BEBOP

02

WALTZING WITH *BEBOP*: *COWBOY BEBOP* AND THE JAPANESE ANIMATION INDUSTRY

Japan has the biggest animation industry in the world, and many would agree with me that it's also the finest. That Japan is one of the richest nations on Earth plays a part (at the height of the Bubble Economy in the 1980s, Japan had 16% of the global economic power, and 60% of real estate wealth).

The world of Japanese animation is instantly recognizable: characters with spiky hair, red hair, purple hair, long hair, hair blowin' in the breeze, giant eyes, tiny mouths,[1] snub, pointy noses, pointed chins, women with pneumatic bodies and big boobs, guys with buff, muscle-bound bodies, nerds (*otaku*

---

[1] Which're easier to animate.

and *moe*), superheroes, grimaces showing lots of teeth, elfin ears, grizzled, old guys who smoke, child-like *shojo* figures, tall, skinny villains, people who can fly, grotesque transformations, excessive violence,[2] technofetishism, robots, *mecha*, more robots, more *mecha*, mobile power suits, explosions, spaceships, jets, helicopters, motorbikes, guns, guns and more guns, characters holding guns at every opportunity, samurai swords, lightning storms, the ocean, the colours green and silver and red, headbands, silly hats, comic sidekicks like dogs or cutie critters, Tokyo, futuristic cities, dark cities, always skyscrapers and mean streets (always with the skyscrapers!), neon signs, tentacles, monsters, demons, blood and guts, and last but but least: the atomic bombs dropped on Japan by the United States of America.

The famous TV shows, OAVs, specials, videos, and movies in *animé* include: *Akira, Digimon, Pokémon,*[3] *Dr Slump, Star Blazers, Legend of the Overfiend, Escaflowne, Mushishi, Fullmetal Alchemist, Gundam, Evangelion, Astro Boy, Ghost In the Shell* and of course *Cowboy Bebop*. According to Helen McCarthy, animation in Japan accounted for 6% of films released in late 1998, 25-30% of videos, and 3-6% of television shows made in Japan.

Although the prestige *animé* movies and OAVs receive much of the media's attention (especially outside Japan), most of animation in Japan is produced for television (as well as commercials). A

2 Altho' Japanese popular culture is still regarded as pretty violent, Japanese society is actually more peaceful than many nations on Earth. Crime rates are low, guns are controlled, and the constitution forbids war. And in the years that *manga* sales boomed, crime rates fell (F. Schodt, 1997, 132).
3 The *Pokémon* movies have proved hugely popular in Japan, and rival Studio Ghibli's movies at the box office.

movie is 80, 90 or maybe 120 minutes of animation, but a big *animé* series on television runs to large numbers of 23-minute episodes. Look at the numbers of shows: *Doraemon* (over 2,000 episodes by 2004), *Astro Boy* (193 episodes x 30m – first series), *Dragon Ball* (153 episodes), *Dragon Ball Z* (291 episodes), *Galaxy Express* (114 episodes), *Mazinger Z* (92 episodes), *Gatchomon* (105 episodes), *Legend of Galactic Heroes* (110 episodes), *Maison Ikkoku* (96 episodes), *Naruto* (220 episodes), *Digimon* (205 episodes), *Pokémon* (550 episodes and counting), and *Sailor Moon* (200 episodes).

In the West, animation tends to be made for children, or regarded as for children, or it's largely comedic and throwaway, or it's produced for television (and for Saturday morning TV), or it has superheroes and action.[4] But outside of those arenas, Western animation seldom ventures.

The world of animation is vast, going back to Géorges Méliès, Winsor McCay and Edwin S. Porter, and taking in experimental and *avant garde* animation, the giants of Eastern Europe (Jan Svankmajer, Karel Zeman, Jiri Trnka, Walerian Borowczyk), to more recent proponents, such as the Quay Brothers, Michel Ocelot, and James Selick, or the use of animation in live-action cinema.

The great names of film directors in the history of animation include: Géorges Méliès, Ladislaw Starewicz, Willis O'Brien, Lotte Reiniger, George Pal, Osamu Tezuka, Tex Avery, Chuck Jones, Jiri Trnka, Paul Grimault, Ralph Bakshi, Jan Svankmajer, and Michel Ocelot. The celebrated *auteurs* in *animé*

4 Influenced not so much by the long-form films of the Walt Disney corporation but by the comedy seven-minute animated short, as Trish Ledoux and Doug Ranney point out (1997, 5).

include Hayao Miyazaki, Osamu Tezuka, Isao Takahata, and Mamoru Oshii. You can put Katsuhiro Otomo among them.

Japanese animation, meanwhile, is keyed into long-form narratives, whether it's theatrical movies, or OAVs, or long-running TV series. And *animé* is so much more *ambitious* than Western animation, according to *The Complete Anime Guide*: while Western animation churns out sequels and remakes, 'Japanese animators are forging ever forward with new techniques, new approaches, new subjects and an infinite number of new styles' (1997, 5).

THE JAPANESE *ANIMÉ* INDUSTRY

An important thing to remember about Japanese *animé* is that it is an industry that can sustain itself by producing movies and TV shows for a *domestic* audience: it doesn't need television syndication or releases overseas (but it will always take them up if available). In other words, one of the reasons that the Japanese animation industry is the biggest in the world is because there is such a large market in Japan itself for animation (and its numerous links with the *manga* industry).

That also means that Japanese *animé* filmmakers can make their movies and TV shows for a home-grown market, and don't need to pander to an international (or an American) audience. So the OVAs and TV series can reflect and explore local or national culture, and don't need to build in elements that will appeal to a global audience (no need to shift the action of their films to, say, New York or Chicago, and turn their characters into Americans).[5]

Lonely Planet's travel guide to Japan makes some useful points about contemporary Japan:

> First, Japan is an island nation. Second, until WWII, Japan was never conquered by an outside power, nor was it heavily influenced by Christian missionaries. Third, until the beginning of last century, the majority of Japanese lived in close-knit rural farming communities. Fourth, most of Japan is covered in steep mountains, so the few flat areas of the country are quite crowded – people literally live on top of each other. Finally, for almost all of its history, Japan has been a strictly hierarchical place, with something approximating a caste system during the Edo period. (C. Rowthorn, 2007)

WWII and the Occupation had enormous effects on the Japanese movie industry, which still resonate today. In *A History of Narrative Film*, still the finest single, must-have book on cinema, David Cook set the scene:

> When World War II ended on August 14, 1945, much of Japan lay in ruins. The massive fire-bombing of its sixty cities from March through June 1945 and the dropping of atomic bombs on Hiroshima and Nagasaki had resulted in some 900,000 casualties and the nearly total paralysis of civilian life. On the morning of August 15, when Emperor Hirohito broadcast to his subjects the news that the war had ended and that Japan

5 By comparison, European filmmakers can similarly make films only for their own national audience, but they tend to be much smaller (or cheaper) movies. A country such as France can sustain a huge production of movies per year because it has the largest film industry in Europe (that's one of the reasons why French movies travel outside France). And it means that France can make much bigger movies (it has more government investment than many other countries).

had lost, there was widespread disbelief. Never in their history had the Japanese people been defeated or the nation occupied, and so the circumstances of the American Occupation, 1945-52, were utterly unique. (783)

The genres of Japanese animation include pretty much all of those in live-action, as well as some genres particular to *animé*: comedy; romance; crime; action-adventure; horror; historical drama; science fiction[6] (including *mecha*, cyberpunk, war, epics); fantasy (including comicbooks; supernatural tales; myths and legends; and superheroes); animal stories; martial arts; children's stories; epics; erotica; porn; and sports stories.[7] Gilles Poitras noted in *The Anime Companion* that *animé* has more genres than exist in Western cinema (43).

Cowboy Bebop has of course wittily and imaginatively smashed a bunch of genres together, cleverly manipulating the audience's knowledge of genres. One of the captions for *Cowboy Bebop* runs:

The work which becomes a new genre in tself
shall be called
COWBOY BEBOP

In live-action, genres are divided into *jidai-geki* = period movies (typically in the feudal age), and *gendai-geki* = set in the contemporary era.[8] There are further categories within the two genres.

The Japanese film industry has been one of the most prolific historically, producing over 400 movies a year. The Japanese movie business has been

6 More people consume science fiction in Japan than anywhere else.
7 Although it is regarded as popular culture, Japanese *animé* draws on high culture, including woodblock prints, *ukiyo-e*, Kabuki theatre, painting, and classical music.
8 See G. Mast, 1992b, 410.

dominated by studio conglomerates, just like the North American system, since the 1920s (the biggies are Nikkatsu, Shochiku, Toho,[9] Toei, Shintoho and Daiei). Although the independent film sector has grown since the 1980s, the major studios continue to take up most of film production. And most Japanese film directors work for the major studios in some form or another, or for television.

In Japan, the director is king of the movie-making industry, rather than the star or producer; the director will often appear above the title, and is often used in marketing more than stars. The director is 'the paternalistic head of his own production "family"', as Gerald Mast and Bruce Kawin explain in *A Short History of the Movies*, a social structure which echoes Japanese society (1992b, 409).

Like the films of Yasujiro Ozu or Kenji Mizoguchi or Akira Kurosawa, *Cowboy Bebop* is very *Japanese*. No matter how much of Western culture *Cowboy Bebop* absorbs and reworks, the show is entirely Japanese.

Other notable filmmakers in Japanese cinema, apart from the *sensei* himself (Akira Kurosawa) include: Yasujiro Ozu, Kenji Mizoguchi, and Ichikawa Kon, and Japanese New Wave directors, such as Nagisa Oshima, Hiroshi Teshigahara, Masashiro Shinoda, Takeshi Kitano and Yoshishige Yoshida.

Among the classic films of Japanese cinema are: *Tokyo Story, The Flavour of Green Tea Over Rice, The Life of Oharu, Ohayu, Sansho Dayu, Kwaidan, Early Summer, Woman of the Dunes, Ugetsu Monogatari*, and

9 Toho, founded in the 1930s from a number of smaller companies, is best known as the studio of *Godzilla*, Akira Kurosawa and Hayao Miyazaki.

Ai No Corrida (*In the Realm of the Senses*). And of course, *anything* by Akira Kurosawa (even one of Kurosawa's minor films is finer than many film-makers' best efforts).

Gilles Poitras defined *animé* in his excellent *Anime Companion:*

> anime is not to be confused with cartoons. Anime uses animation to tell stories and entertain, but it does so in ways that have barely been touched on in Western animation. While the U.S. continues to pump out cartoons with gag stories, musicals with cute animals, animated sitcoms, and testosterone-laced TV fare, the Japanese have been using anime to cover every literary and cinematic genre imaginable in a highly compet-itive market that encourages new story ideas and the creative reworking of older ideas and themes. (vii)

It is typical for the major *animé* shows to have all of the following: (1) a TV series; (2) OAVs; (3) movie/s (often edited from the TV series, with some linking animation added); (4) merchandizing (such as video games and toys); (5) the original *manga*; (6) tie-in *manga*; (7) soundtrack albums; and (8) a bunch of websites (including fan sites). For the really big *animé* shows, like *Gundam, Patlabor, Sailor Moon, Pokémon,* and *Fullmetal Alchemist,* there will often be updated versions of all of the above (maybe with gimmicks like CGI added). Just as *manga* and merchandizing are regularly updated, so too is *animé*.

There will also be spin-off TV shows and OAVs; these might explore back-stories, or focus on new sets of charas, with the old ones appearing in cameos (and the re-boots or updates or side-stories will also have their own spin-offs). So keeping up with a big franchise can mean taking in a lot of hours of *animé* and *manga* (not difficult if you're a fan!).

Animé and *manga* are heavily merchandized, and not only in Japan. Toys of every kind are tied in with TV shows, comicbooks, video games and 'garage kits'.[10] *Animé* and *manga* merchandize includes figures, Tee shirts, handker-chiefs, posters, CDs, calendars, stationery, phone cards, candy, etc. As with Western pop culture merchandize, if there's room to put a show logo or image on it, Japanese toy manufacturers will do it.

Another area of *animé* merchandizing is sound-track albums. These tie-ins on CD and download can be very lucrative. Every big *animé* show will have not one but a number of soundtrack albums attached to it. These will include regular albums (including the main songs and cues), but also background music albums, and image albums (music inspired by the *animé*, or something relating to the *animé*).[11] The superstar composers in *animé* – Joe Hisaishi, Kenji Kawai, *Cowboy Bebop*'s Yoko Kanno – have their own followers, and are celebrated in their own right (and it's all deserved, I would say, because the music of the really great *animé* composers adds enormously to the shows and movies. *Cowboy Bebop* without Kanno's jazz and blues score or Hayao Miyazaki's movies without Hisaishi's orchestral sweep and plaintive piano not only wouldn't be the same, they would

---

10 (Model kits and figures made with cast plastic by hand in small quantities initially designed and sold in garages by fans and enthusiasts, but some have become legit companies.
11 Fans get in on the act by creating their own *animé* music videos, editing them from *animé* shows and adding their own choice of music, and sometimes uploading to website like Youtube.

have far less impact).

Japan is one of the major film markets in the world – for North American movies, yes, but also for movies from everywhere. And when it comes to animation, there is a huge appetite for it in Japan. Without that large, national market, and that enthusiastic response to animated movies and television, it would be more difficult for a show like *Cowboy Bebop* to get made.

Japanese *animé* sells in the Western world via OVAs,[12] videos and DVDs, TV shows, and related *manga* comicbooks. Animated series and movies are prepared for the Western market with English language dubs (nearly always using North American actors and American-style English), and also subtitles (there is also a subculture of fans subtitling shows). In the West, *Cowboy Bebop* has been released by Beez Entertainment in Britain, Bandai in the U.S.A., and Madman Entertainment in Oz, with Animaze providing the English language dub.[13]

MANGA AND *ANIMÉ*.

Manga (comicbooks) are certainly huge in Japan, and more so than in any other country (though they are on the increase in some places). North America doesn't have a comicbook tradition anything like *manga* culture in Japan: in Japan, a *manga* like *Shonen*

---

12 OVA means Original Video Animation (a.k.a. OAV = Original Animé/ Animation Video) – referring to sell-through videos, which may be linked to TV shows or movies, and, of course, *manga*.
13 The issue of dubbing is a thorny one, and largely to do with economics. For me, there is no question that the original language is the version to go with every time, no matter what the movie or TV show, and no matter what language the movie or show is in. If you already consume 100s of movies and TV shows in English, why would you want to see something that is utterly Japanese translated into English (American) voices? You already watch everything else in English, give yourself a change, have some variety in your life!

Jump might sell 6 million copies a week, enormous numbers.[14]

Japan has the most sophisitcated, the most varied, the funniest, the most entertaining, and by far the most imaginative comicbook culture in the world. Yes, we know that France, Germany, Spain, Italy, China, Korea, Britain and the U.S.A. (among others) have thriving comicbook industries, but none of 'em come anywhere near Japan.

In Japan, the audience for *manga* is pretty much everybody: the stigma in the West attached to comics and comicbooks simply doesn't exist: everyone reads *manga*. The Japanese *manga* market is bigger than the *animé* market. *Manga* also requires far fewer personnel to create, and is cheaper to disseminate.

In 2000 in Japan there were 15 monthly magazines, 10 twice-weekly magazines, and 12 weeklies. Some have print runs of over a million copies. *Manga* accounted for about a quarter of all publishing sales (about 550 billion Yen (there are about 100 Yen to the US dollar).) *Manga* absorbed around 40% of Japan's printed matter. The average spend on *manga* was 4,500 Yen for everybody living in Japan. According to VIZ Media, the *manga* market in Japan in 2006 was worth US $4.28 billion (and $250m in the U.S.A.).

Manga and *animé* are closely aligned commercially as well as culturally.[15] Many *animé*

14 In a 1994 speech, Hayao Miyazaki compared that 6 million with the video sales of *Beauty and the Beast* in the U.S.A.: 20 million, for a nation with twice the population of Japan. Selling 20 million in America would be like selling 10 million in Japan, Miyazaki suggested, and *Shonen Jump* sells 6 million *manga* a week!
15 The crossover between *manga* and *animé* is well-known (many animations are *manga* first, and *manga* are in turn produced from movies, including *Cowboy Bebop*, which are published by Kodakowa Shoten. They include *Cowboy Bebop: Shooting Star* and *Cowboy Bebop: A New Story*). There is also a crossover into computer games, board games, card games, pop music and online gaming.

shows are based on *manga* (and some of the big
shows have their own *manga* spin-offs). *Manga* can be
a cheaper means of testing out if a story will work
with an audience. There are many more *manga* stories
than *animé* stories. Thus, *animé* has a huge source of
stories to draw on, alongside novels, plays, TV
shows, video games [16] and all the other products than
can be adapted.

Certainly *manga* and *animé* have been important
in depicting Japanese culture overseas – and it will be
for many their first encounter with Japanese culture.[17]
Manga and *animé* are popular in many Western
markets, including France, Britain, Italy, Spain,
Germany, and into Hong Kong, South America, and
South-East Asia.[18] The U.S.A. is the primary market
outside Japan. In Europe, *animé* is most popular in
France (and France has a substantial animation
industry). Sci-fi, cyber-punk and steam-punk are also
much-loved in France, as are comicbooks and graphic
novels.

ANIMATION IN PRODUCTION

Animation is a long, hard slog – *very* labour
intensive, with projects like feature films typically
taking three or four years to complete. It requires a
particular kind of individual, then, to maintain a
high level of enthusiasm and interest, to stay focussed
on the project and not be distracted into other things.

16 Among the well-known *manga* and *animé* that were based on
computer games were *Final Fantasy, Pokémon,* and *Sakura Wars.*
17 See G. Poitras, 2001, 8.
18 H. McCarthy, 1996, 7.

Stanley Kubrick spoke of keeping hold of his initial inspiration for making a movie all the way through the long process of development, pre-production, shooting, post-production and distribution. You have to hang on to whatever it was that really excited you about doing the project in the first place (a production that doesn't have that initial spark of excitement and fascination can all too easily lose its momentum and energy).

In 1987, Hayao Miyazaki described the typical animator as young, good-natured, and poor. They made less than 100,000 Yen a month (= $1,000). They were paid ¥400 ($4) a page for theatrical movies and ¥150 ($1.50) a page for TV animation. Miyazaki reckoned there were about 2,500 in animators Japan (2009, 135). His first wage in animation was 19,000 Yen a month in 1963, Miyazaki said, when he started at Toei Animation.

THE ANIMATION PROCESS.

In the Japanese animation industry, the script comes first. Storyboards and image boards are drawn when the script is completed (but sometimes before then). The storyboards are called *e-conte* (a combination of *ei*, picture, and continuity). A complex show like *Cowboy Bebop* has a number of storyboard artists (Tensai Okamura, Shinichirô Watanabe, Yoshiyuki Takei *et al*).

Once the OAV or TV show is complete in terms of storyboards, plus indications of dialogue and sound effects, it goes to the key animators: they put the movie together as key animation (the animation at the beginning and the end of an action). In-between work means animating the movements between the key frames which the key animators have drawn, using time sheets.[19] At the same time, the drawings are cleaned up.

Once the drawings have been completed, they are transferred to cels (celluloid), and inked and painted. Finally, they are photographed (a whole complex process in itself). Photographic and special effects may be added at this stage. (However, animation doesn't always use 24 frames per second, called 'ones' or 'singles': it often goes to 'twos' or 'doubles' (12 frames a second) or 'threes' (8 frames per second). Even the most sophisticated and expensive movies use those frame rates).

♫

It is standard procedure in Japanese animation to record the voice tracks after the animation has been completed (rather as European movies dub on the voices later, as was Federico Fellini's habit). Or sometimes to work to an animatic (a.k.a. Leica reel). It's the other way around in the Western animation tradition, with animators using pre-recorded voice tracks for part of their inspiration (it is common for animators to employ video recordings of the actors performing the script, and also to draw on the actor's performances in other work).

♫

In 2005, there were 430 *animé* production studios in Japan,[20] and most of them were in Tokyo. (And that's one of the reasons why so many *animé* shows

19 Keyframes or main poses are drawn by the animators or animation directors; assistant animators will usually draw the halfway poses between the keyframes; in-betweeners are animators (often trainees) who draw the frames in between the keyframes.
20 Animation studios themselves become the centre of attention for *animé* fans, and fans will follow particular animation houses and their work. The famous ones include Production I.G., Bandai, Studio 4°C, Gainax, Madhouse, Sunrise, Pioneer, Tezuka, Gonzo, Clamp, Toei, and of course Studio Ghibli.

are set in Tokyo – and even when *Cowboy Bebop* is exploring the outer reaches of Mars or Ganymede, it's still all about Tokyo in the end). The *animé* market was worth about ¥20 billion ($200m) in 2004.

The typical 30 minute (= 23 mins) *animé* TV show cost 10 million Yen (= $100,000). Thus, prestige shows like *Cowboy Bebop,* at ¥20m (= $200,000) per episode, are costly in Japanese *animé* terms, not only compared to TV shows, but also compared with animated feature films (but *Cowboy Bebop* was always designed for consumption on a TV screen, not a movie screen).

Comparing animation production in the West with Japan isn't as simple as doing a straight comparison. Budgets in TV and cinema are notoriously difficult to check accurately: no one wants to admit how much money something *really* cost, or *exactly* how much they're earning (and Hollywood studios routinely exaggerate figures like budgets and grosses). But you know that if the budgets are one hundred million dollars or more, then *somebody somewhere* is making a lot of money. As William Goldman noted, there's a lot of money to be had in simply *making* a film, regardless of whether it's released or seen or not. And some people make a living out of producing movies, including existing on development deals and other deals, and many of those films aren't shot, and some that *are* filmed aren't released.

It's hard to believe that movies like *Home On the Range* or *Tarzan* from the Mouse House could have cost over $110 million or $115 million, but there are all sorts of economic factors to consider. The piecework labour of Japanese *animé* is going to be cheaper than hiring staff on a permanent basis that occurs more in North American animation.[21] Living costs, unions and working conditions in Japan and America are further factors (altho' Japan is far costlier to live in than, say, India or Egypt). The much longer production schedules of American animated movies must contribute to the higher costs too: Disney and Pixar movies can take 3 or more years. However, the large crews of hundreds of workers aren't hired for all of those years, but it's safe to say that the production teams in Western feature animation are larger than those in the Japanese animation industry, and that they are hired for longer periods. All of which drives costs up (at the same time, Western animation companies farm out work to outfits in countries such as Korea, Thailand and India, just as the Japanese animation industry does).

Animé shows typically run for 13 or 26 or 39 or 52 episodes, in TV seasons, and sometimes much longer. Shows such as *Mushishi, Ghost In the Shell: Stand Alone Complex*, *Samurai Champloo, Evangelion* and *Escaflowne* are in 26 episode runs. Quite a few of the classic *animé* shows only ran for six or so episodes: *Gunbuster, Space Battleship Yamato, Dominion: Tank Police* and *Patlabor*.

♫

One of the delights of *animé* is definitely its running time: as movies, animations rarely top the two-hour mark (compared to far too many live-action movies which bloat beyond two hours). And most *animé* movies are 75-90 minutes. Among OAVS,

---

21 Hayao Miyazaki often complained about the piecework system of producing animation in Japan, which turned out work like an assembly line, instead of the hand-crafted and personal, artistic approach that Miyazaki favoured.

30 to 45 minutes is typical. And of course for television *animé* is nearly always in roughly 23 minute blocks, to be shown in half-hour slots with commercials (and the more recent *animé* made for outlets like streaming, online or cell phones tend to be even shorter). So on TV, animation has to make an impact very quickly: you've got to use those 23 minutes wisely, as well as hit the immovable commercial breaks with a suitable break or pause.

The finest *animé* shows for television know exactly how to exploit the 23 minute format to the max, with their pre-credits teasers, their artful main titles, and the cliffhangers at the ad breaks: *Cowboy Bebop*, *Ghost In the Shell: Stand Alone Complex*, *Samurai Champloo*, *Escaflowne*, *Moribito*, *Fullmetal Alchemist*, etc. However, there is still some terrible animation around, no matter if it's made for a 6 minute short, a 23 minute TV show, a 45 minute OAV or a 95 minute feature. You still get recycled junk, shows that're repetitive, unimaginative, and plain *dull*. It's just that, with TV, those 23 minutes fly by, and you're into the next episode before you know it. (Japanese television prefers longer opening credit sequences – which not only allows for a long chunk of the promotional tie-in songs, but also cuts down on the animation required. And it leads to celebrated sequences, such as the credit sequence for *Cowboy Bebop*).

As well as short running times, Japanese animation for television also tells stories very quickly and economically yet, and this is extraordinary, they don't feel rushed or thin. But if you go back to contemporary Hollywood cinema after watching Japanese animation for a while, you're struck by how *slow* it is. *So slow*! Not the *editing* (which obscures a funereal pace with 'flashy', gimmicky cutting), but the *pacing* and the *storytelling*. *Animé* speeds along at a rapid pace, yet there is also time for interludes, for plot points, characterization and conversations. As storytelling, *animé* is *far* in advance of Western television or Western movies.

CELS VERSUS COMPUTERS

Like most of Japanese animation, *Cowboy Bebop* is traditional cel animation, but computers and computer-generated effects and devices are employed from time to time. *Cowboy Bebop* utilized digital technology to build 3-D models, and used particle systems to drive animation. But cel animation is already as supremely *technological* and *industrial* as computers or digital technology. *Everything* in movies is *technological*, everything is fake, everything is a highly sophisticated cultural form created by humans for mass entertainment. So whether it's done with machines/ tools like cameras or pencils or paint-brushes or computers isn't really the point – you're just talking about different forms of fakery. But it's all *fakery*.

However, the sci-fi environment of *Cowboy Bebop* suits a computer-generated approach: the plasticky look of computer-generated imagery, or the 3-D look of computer animation, or the floaty appearance of computerized additions to scenes, aspects of digital animation which many audiences don't like, work fine in a space opera setting.

The animation industry has since *Cowboy Bebop* embraced 3-D animation (all of Pixar's output, plus *Ice Age, Shrek, Robots, Chicken Little*, etc), as well as releasing animation in 3-D. If *Cowboy Bebop* was made today, it would probably go the 3-D route (my plea to filmmakers everywhere: please *do not* re-make *Cowboy Bebop!*).

But using computers is just another tool out of many that animation employs: a common view, still being voiced by critics who should know better, is that: *cel animation = good, computer animation = bad.*[22] It's rubbish – *all* animation is *already* highly techno-logical. Film critics really should visit film studios from time to time, to dispel the falsehoods that they perpetuate. For instance, that some movie sets look made out of cardboard: actually, *all* movie sets are constructed from bits of wood or foam or cardboard and painted, then they're torn down as soon as shooting stops on them.

If you visited an animation house in Tokyo, London, or Hollywood (or the many out-sourced centres in, say, India or Korea), and including the studios used by Sunrise, the makers of *Cowboy Bebop*, you'd find tons of technology and machines, with computers being just one among multitudes. For instance, the cameras employed to photograph the cels are very sophisticated. And they always have been: have a look at the famous multiplane camera designed by William Garity at the Walt Disney Company in Burbank in the 1930s, which required a group of technicians to operate it.

---

22 The cel vs. CGI argument merely trots out the ancient oppositions between old and new, or tradition and modernism.

Illustrations

Some *animé* shows and movies.

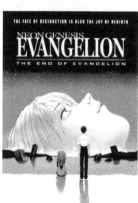

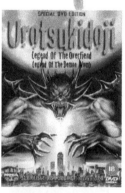

Some animé products released 1980s-2000s. Only a few have a theatrical release (either in Japan or elswhere).

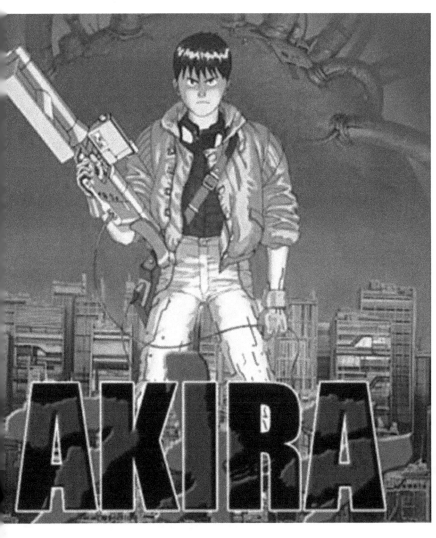

Akira, 1988

Ghost In the Shell, 1995

Escaflowne, 1996

(© Aniplex/ Funimation/ Square Enix)

Mushishi (2005-06)

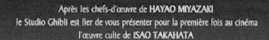

(© Toho/ Studio Ghibli, 2013)

COWBOY BEBOP

03

COWBOY BOOGIE WOOGIE: THE PERSONNEL AND PRODUCTION OF *COWBOY BEBOP*

Cowboy Bebop (1998) is a hugely entertaining Japanese animated series of 26 episodes of 30 minutes (actually around 23 minutes), produced by Sunrise (a subsidiary of Bandai) and TV Tokyo.[1] Shinichiro Watanabe directed; Keiko Nobumoto, Michiko Yokote, Ryota Yamaguchi, Sadayuki Murai and Dai Sato wrote the scripts; Toshihiro Kawamoto and Kimitoshi Yamano were the designers; and Yoko Kanno composed the music. Only 12 episodes were shown on TV Tokyo (one of the backers) during *Cowboy Bebop*'s first run; it was shown in full in Japan

---

[1] Among the companies involved in the production of *Cowboy Bebop* were Studio Cockpit, Studio Takuranke, Studio Deen, Anime World Osaka, Maki Pro and Asahi Production (G. Poitras, 2001, 54).

on WOWOW (World Wide Watching) after midnight. It was a big success when it was broadcast in the New World in 2001 (on the Adult Swim[2] slot on Cartoon Network – it remained on air for many years).

PRODUCTION.

Cowboy Bebop was produced by Kazuhiko Ikeguchi and Masahiko Minami. The distributors were Bandai Entertainment in Japan, Beez Entertainment in Britain, Bandai in the U.S.A., and Madman Entertainment in Oz. Toshihiro Kawamoto was a vital contributor: he was the character designer *and* the chief animation director. Art director was Junichi Higashi. *Mecha* designer was Kimitoshi Yamane. Yoichi Ogami was DP. Shihoko Nakayama was colour coordinator. Backgrounds were by Easter, Kusanagi and Pinewood studios. Tomoaki Tsurubuchi was editor. Effects were by Shizuo Kurahashi. Toshiaki Ohta, Shiro Sasaki and Yukako Inoue were the music producers. The shows cost about ¥20 million per episode (= $200,000 – some of the best money ever spent on animation, television or entertainment of any kind!).

To single out a couple of people is silly in the complicated production of animation, which involves so many people slogging away for months and years. But the person who came up with the concept has to be credited. In fact, the story for *Cowboy Bebop* is by

2 Adult Swim and Cartoon Network are owned by the Turner Broadcast Network; programming on Adult Swim was by Williams St Studios (who also did most of the commissioning). Apart from *Cowboy Bebop*, other shows on Adult Swim included *Aqua Teen Hunger Force* (Dave Willis and Mat Maiellaro, 2000), *Robot Chicken* (Seth Green and Matthew Senreiche, 2005), *Harvey Birdman* (Michael Ouweleen and Erik Richter, 2001), and *The Venture Brothers* (Jackson Publick, James Urbaniak and Patrick Warburton).

Hajime Yadate – a pseudonym for the group at the Sunrise Studio used for copyright reasons (the *animé* industry is full of credits which are dubbed 'committees' or 'planning committee'. So there isn't a single *auteur* behind *Cowboy Bebop* like there is behind *Akira*, say, or *Spirited Away*).

And also Keiko Nobumoto (b. 1964,), the chief screenwriter of *Cowboy Bebop*: she deserves much of the credit for making it such as stellar series. Nobumoto also has writing credits on episodes 1, 3, 6, 12-13, 15, 22, 25 and 26.

One of the more unusual things about *Cowboy Bebop* is that the chief writer Keiko Nobumoto was a woman, as was the second chief writer, Michiko Yokote.

Among Keiko Nobumoto's writing credits are *animé* such as *Macross Plus* (1995), *Wolf's Rain* (2003) and the wonderful *Tokyo Godfathers*, a stunning 2003 *animé* comedy, and live-action such as *Give Me Good Love*, *World Apartment Horror*, *Nurse Call* and *LxIxVxE*. She was born in Hokkaido in North Japan, and has also written novels. Nobumoto was a protegé of Takao Koyama's writing school,

The other chief writer, Michiko Yokote, wrote episodes 2, 5, 7-8, 11, 16-17 and 24 (however, it appears that Michiko Yokote is a pseudonym for three writers. Yokote's credits are huge, so that may be the case).

The other writing credits on *Cowboy Bebop* are: Akihiko Inari (episodes 10, 18-19), Aya Yoshinaga (18), Dai Sato (9, 14, 23), Ryota Yamaguchi (3), Sadayuki Murai (4, 20-21), and Shoji Kawamori (18). Director Shinichiro Watanabe has writing credits on one episode, 21: *Boogie Woogie Feng Shui*. Most of the storyboards were drawn by Tensai Okamura (7 episodes) and director Shinichiro Watanabe (7 episodes).

Episode directors were Hirokazu Yamada (4 episodes: 10, 14, 19, 24), Ikuro Sato (7 episodes: 2, 6, 9, 13, 16, 21, 25), Kunihiro Mori (6 episodes: 3, 7, 11, 15, 17, 22), Yoshiyuki Takei (8 episodes: 1, 4, 8, 12, 18, 20, 23, 26) and Tetsuya Watanabe (episode 5).

Many *anime* television shows, including many of the famous ones like *Ghost In the Shell*, *Fullmetal Alchemist*, *Escaflowne*, *Naruto* and *Bleach*, were first of all *manga* stories which were optioned and adapted in animation. Not *Cowboy Bebop*: it is a project that originated in television animation.

And, whaddya know?, *Cowboy Bebop* is also not a remake, a 're-boot', a 're-imagining', an update, a spin-off, a side-story or a sequel. And it's not based on a TV show, a theme park ride, a cereal box, a computer game, a board game, a set of cards, a book, a play, an opera, a ballet, a fairy tale, a poem, letters, a diary, a musical or a biography.

However, there were, inevitably, *manga* versions[3] of *Bebop* which tied-in with the TV series (some *anime* shows start off as *manga*, and later have new *manga* published that're inspired by the TV series, with one medium feeding into the other. It's typical for stories to continue or to end in the other media).

Television *anime* series like *Cowboy Bebop* are complex, lengthy and expensive productions involving many companies: those who helped to produce *Cowboy Bebop* included Nakamura Product-

3 Including *Cowboy Bebop* (1999-2000, 3 vols), with art by Yukata Nanten, and *Cowboy Bebop: Shooting Star* (1998, 2 vols), with art by Cain Kuga. Both were published by Kadokawa Shoten, with stories by Hajime Yadate and Sunrise.

ion, Satelight (for 3-D animation), Studio Easter, Sunrise D.I.D., Kusangi, Studio Pinewood, M.I., Jay Film, Studio Live, Anime-ya, Anime R, MARIX, and 3DCG.

Sunrise, one of the companies behind *Cowboy Bebop*, was founded in 1972[4] (as Sotueisha),[5] and is now owned by Namco Bandai. It produced shows such as *Escaflowne, Mobile Suit Gundam, Dirty Pair, City Hunter, Outlaw Star, Mai-Hime, Gasaraki* and *Inuyasha* (thus, many in the *Cowboy Bebop* team, including director Shinichiro Watanabe, have worked on those shows). TV Tokyo (or 'TX'), another company behind *Cowboy Bebop*, was founded in 1964 (as Television Tokyo Channel 12). Its big successes include *Pokémon, Naruto,* and *Evangelion*.

The production company behind *Cowboy Bebop*, Bandai, was originally a toy company (founded in 1950), that moved into *animé* via the sponsorship of kids' shows. Among Bandai's productions were *Gundam, Transformers, Brave Saga* and *Mighty Morphin Power Rangers* (all shows with strong links to toys). Sunrise, which produced *Cowboy Bebop*, is one of Bandai's subsidiaries (others include Ashi Pro and Happinet). In 2005, Bandai merged with Manco (another toy manufacturer, founded in 1955).

There were also video games based around *Cowboy Bebop*.[6] In the game *Smoke Too Much!*, you have to smoke your way thru five packs of cigarettes without gasping and expiring. In *Handcuffs-a-Go-Go!*, everybody is handcuffed: who escapes quickest (and

---

4 Sunrise was renamed Nippon Sunrise in 1977, then Sunrise in 1987.
5 Many of the founders were from Mushi Production, which had recently hit the skids.
6 As with many major *animé* franchises, there have been *Cowboy Bebop* computer games (such as for Playstation 2 in 2005).

in the coolest manner) is the winner. In *Where's the Food?!*, you battle moldy four course meals which come alive.

Cowboy Bebop has been released a few times on home entertainment formats: the Perfect Sessions,[7] the Best Sessions, individually, and the best of the lot, the Remix release (2008), which has many extras, including some wonderful audio commentaries by the Japanese actors (there's also a Blu-ray version, 2012).

MORE *COWBOY BEBOP*? YES PLEASE!! BUT NOT IN LIVE-ACTION.

I would imagine that many people who've met director Shinichiro Watanabe or other members of the production team of *Cowboy Bebop* have asked about sequels or follow-ups. But Watanabe has always resisted. And, to their credit, the TV Tokyo, Sunrise and Bandai companies behind *Cowboy Bebop*, have also declined. Because, let's face it, many (most) other companies, who have a hit on their hands, immediately order up more. It's also classy that the producers didn't simply chop up and re-edit the 26 episodes to make a movie, as most *animé* houses would do (putting the Spike 'n' Vicious episodes together – 5, 12, 13, 25 & 26 – would be one obvious choice). Instead, they cooked up a new movie.

Inevitably, there were rumours of a Hollywood live-action version of *Cowboy Bebop* (apparently in development at Fox or Columbia). Oh, for fuck's sake, why do these people bother? (Oh yeah: *$$$$$!*). And, yes, Keanu Reeves was put forward as a possible

---

7 The episodes are also called 'sessions' – from the music world, of course. Note that it's *Cowboy Bebop*, not *Cowboy Rock,* or *Cowboy Rock 'n' Roll,* or *Cowboy Jazz* – or the title that might've been second choice: *Cowboy Blues.* What is bebop? It's a form of jazz.

Spike Spiegel. Oh fuck me, how fucking predictable is that?! (And Kee-aaa-noo was also being suggested for the role of Togusa in the live-action adaption of *Ghost In the Shell*, or for Kaneda in *Akira*. Listen to the fans: *nooooooo*!!!).

THE VOICE CAST.

The voice cast for *Cowboy Bebop* is simply brilliant, one of the finest casts in all *animé*. It is headed up by Kôichi Yamadera as Spike Spiegel, Unsho Ishizuka as Jet Black, Megumi Hayashibara as Faye Valentine, and Aoi Tada as Radical Ed.

Kôichi Yamadera (b. 1961) is a veteran of numerous *animé* and TV shows – *animé* fans will know him as expertly playing Togusa in the *Ghost In the Shell* movies and TV series (he's also Nikki in *Urotsukidoji* and the hero Jubei in 1993's *Ninja Scroll*).[8] Yamadera can do serious drama, but he is also accomplished, as all of the voice actors in *Cowboy Bebop* need to be, to play comedy. Yamadera captures Spike's slickness, super-cool and wise-ass dialogue, and also his lassitude and laziness.[9]

The voice of Faye Valentine in *Cowboy Bebop*, Megumi Hayashibara (b. 1967), is a veteran of numerous shows, and rightly one of the *seiyu* superstars. Hayashibara is a singer, songwriter (she's a pop idol in J-pop), a DJ, has a radio show, and has appeared, like the other two adult actors in the cast, in everything. It doesn't hurt that she's also very attractive. Hayashibara's other voice work includes *Blue Seed, Paprika, Evangelion, Ranma 1/2, Slayers, Saber Marionette, Video Girl Ai, Tenchi Muyo,* and

---

8 In live-action, Yamadera has voiced Tom Hanks, Jim Carrey, Eddie Murphy and Robin Williams.

9 Yamadera also supplies the voice of the dog Ein.

Gundam.

Megumi Hayashibara contributes so much to the character of Faye Valentine – she can do the kookiness, the fury, and the sassiness and sexiness, but also the whispered resignation, and the world weariness.

Jet Black is played by Unshô Ishizuka (b. 1951), another veteran of an enormous amount of *animé*, including *Samurai X, Gundam, Pokémon, Fullmetal Brotherhood, Hellsing, Dragonball Z* and *Macross Plus* (where he plays Guld). Ishizuka is terrific at voicing the many grunts or 'uhhs' that Jet Black makes, often in bemusement at what the crew of misfits get up to.

Singer-songwriter Aoi Tada (b. 1981), 17 at the time of recording the show, was the voice of Radical Ed. She brings an appealing child-like charm to Ed, adding babyish babble and nonsensical songs and giggles. (How do you direct Tada to perform Ed?!).

Among the secondary characters, the voice cast included:

> Norio Wakamoto (Vicious),
> Gara Takashima (Julia),
> Kenyu Horiuchi (Gren, a.k.a. Grencia Mars
> Elijah Guo Eckener),
> Hikaru Midorikawa (Lin),
> Miki Nagasawa (Judy),
> Nobuyuki Hiyama (Shin),
> Takehiro Koyama (Bull),
> Tsutomu Taruki (Punch)

All the *seiyu* are wonderful,[10] and particularly adept at the ensemble scenes (which also tend to be the funniest in *Cowboy Bebop*). The writing and

---

10 The voice casts (*seiyu*) in *animé* sometimes become stars in their own right (they have their own *animé* magazines, such as *Voice Animage*). Voice actors in *animé* may be stars, but they still have to take other work, such as commercials, dubbing live-action, or regular acting on TV, to make a living (J. Clements, 2009, 59).

filmmaking are incredible, but the voice actors come along and take it to the next level. Also worth noting are the many non-verbal cues the voice actors deliver, in those parts of the script where 'ad lib' is written. In a TV show with so many moments of apathy, chilling on the couch and shrugging, the voice actors deliver many ways of saying 'yeah, whatever' without using the words.[11] (The voice director, Katsuyoshi Kobayashi, should be noted, too, for coaxing out those terrific performances from the voice cast.)

DIRECTOR SHINICHIRO WATANABE.

Shinichiro Watanabe's (b. May 24, 1965, Kyoto) credits include two parts of *The Animatrix*,[12] a segment in *Genius Party* (from Studio 4°C), and *Samurai Champloo* (2004-05), a 26-episode TV *animé* series (see appendices).[13] Watanabe has also worked on many other shows, like many directors and animators in Japanese animation, from storyboard-ing to music producing. Watanabe co-helmed *Macross Plus* (1995), a fan favourite outing of the *Macross* franchise; he drew storyboards for part of the classic *Escaflowne* series; Watanabe has also

11 Japanese voice actors (*seiyu*) have their voices recorded while watching an animatic (which's called a Leica reel). And they have voice work recorded after the animation is complete.
12 The *Animatrix* project was a collection of 9 short animated movies made primarily by Japanese filmmakers drawing on *The Matrix* (1999). It became enormously successful overseas. Some of the team behind *Final Fantasy* produced the first animated *Animatrix*, employ-ing the same sort of digital animation in *Final Fantasy*. Shinichiro Watanabe provided two shorts: *Kid's Story*, about an alienated teenager (it featured the voices of Keanu Reeves and Carrie-Ann Moss from the *Matrix* movies), and *Detective Story*, set in his beloved 1940s *film noir* world (and featuring a 'tec chasing down a hacker, *à la Cowboy Bebop*).
13 In Japanese animation, terms like 'director' and 'designer' don't have the same meaning as in the Western film industry. 'Director' might refer to a 'wide range' of different jobs (H. McCarthy, 1996, 9). It's customary, for instance, for designers to have a speciality, and to be brought onto a production to exploit that gift.

worked as a music producer, and has directed music promos. Other credits include: *Eureka Seven, Kids On the Slope, Mind Game, Mobile Suit Gundam 0083: Stardust Memory, Mobile Suit Gundam Wing, Star Driver* and *Baby Blue*.

Shinichiro Watanabe was one of the co-founders of Studio Bones, founded in 1998 by a group of filmmakers from Sunrise (including Masahiko Mikami, producer and Toshihiro Kawamoto, animator). Bones' work included *Fullmetal Alchemist, Escaflowne* and *RahXephon*.

Shinichiro Watanabe is a passionate lover of music (who isn't?), and it runs throughout his work, and is foundational to two of the big shows he helmed, *Cowboy Bebop* and *Samurai Champloo*. Indeed, if the budget was unlimited (ah, if only!), and allowed for the legal rights to any amount of music, you can bet that Watanabe would stuff *Cowboy Bebop* with wall-to-wall music, like *American Graffiti* or *A Hard Day's Night*. There would be every famous Rolling Stones song, plus the Beatles, B.B. King, John Lee Hooker, Parliament, Bob Dylan, the Grateful Dead, the Doors, the Velvet Underground, Elton John, David Bowie, Led Zeppelin, the Beach Boys, Frank Sinatra, and so on.

But who needs all of those acts when you've got something even better? – Yoko Kanno composing the music.

COMPOSER YOKO KANNO.
Cowboy Bebop includes probably the most accomplished and marvellous soundtrack in all *animé* for television, composed by Yoko Kanno (*Macross Plus, Please Save My Earth, Jin-Roh, Ghost In*

the *Shell: Stand Alone Complex* and *Escaflowne*) and her team, mixing jazz, blues and rock. Only *Ghost In the Shell: Stand Alone Complex*, also composed by Kanno, covers such an astonishing variety of music.[14] (Kanno has also written music for computer games, commercials, and television).

Yoko Kanno and her band the Seatbealts (formed for the *Cowboy Bebop* show) created what is for many fans and critics *the* great *animé* soundtrack[15] (the 1998 TV series and the 2001 movie). There's nothing else like it in Japanese animation. Kanno is a genius, without question, one of the top composers in Japanese animation, alongside Joe Hisaishi and Kenji Kawai. (Kanno is rumoured to be an inspiration for the character of Ed in *Cowboy Bebop*).

Yoko Kanno (b. March 19, 1964, Miyagi, Japan) is a superstar of *animé*. Make no mistake, Kanno may look (and sound) like a little pixie, but she is one of the great talents of film music, the equal not only of *any* of the great composers for the screen thru cinema history, but also most contemporary classical and new music composers.

Yoko Kanno sold her first composition in 1985 (for a computer game). She played keyboards in the band Tetsu 100%. For Helen McCarthy, writing in *500 Essential Anime Movies*, Kanno 'is the best composer working in anime today' (18), and 'Japan's greatest living composer'.[16] She might well be: simply on the basis of three TV series, *Cowboy Bebop, Escaflowne* and *Ghost In the Shell*, Kanno is up there with the finest (and she was only 34!).

---

14 Kanno's extraordinary score for *Ghost In the Shell: Stand Alone Complex* would also be a close runner for the finest *animé* soundtrack.
15 It's 'the most colourful music score ever heard in anime' (Brian Camp, 79).
16 In J. Clements, 2006, 409.

But Yoko Kanno has also composed soundtracks to *animé* TV and movies such as *Escaflowne, Macross Plus, Record of Lodoss War, Wolf's Rain, Gundam, Earth Maiden Arjuna, Genesis of Aquarion, Sakamichi no Apollon, Brain Powerd,* and the incredible *Magnetic Rose* episode in *Memories*, among many others. Kanno also produced her own albums,[17] as well as composed and arranged songs for other artists, has written for television, for movies, and made music for video games. Have a look at Kanno's CV: it's hugely impressive (how Kanno finds time to sleep in the midst of producing all that music, arrangements, and lyrics is incredible).

For commercials and companies, Yoko Kanno has written music for Nissan, Fuji Xerox, Canon, DoCoMo, Seven-Eleven, Microsoft, Toyota, Shiseido, Avon, AGF Maxim, Avon, Cosmo Oil, Daio Paper, Daiwa House, FamilyMart, Japan Medical Association, Japan Railways, Japan Telecom, Microsoft, Mister Donut, Mitsui Home, Nikon, Nintendo, Ono Pharmaceutical, Pioneer, Pola, Sharp, Shimura, Sony, Tokyo Gas, Tokyo Metro, and Mastercard. And she has composed music for plenty of video games (such as *Genghis Khan, Napple Tale, Cowboy Bebop, Ragnarok Online* and *Nobunaga's Ambition*).

Yoko Kanno's other film soundtracks include: *Tokyo: Sora, Mizu no onna, Say Hello!, Surely Someday, Honey and Clover, Asalto, Su-ki-da* and *Elegant World* (*The Show Must Go On*). Her TV work includes: *Chichi ni Kanaderu Merodi, Camouflage, Kaze ni Mai Agaru Vinyl Sheet,* and *Mayonaka Betsu no Kao* (*The Other Side of Midnight*).

Yoko Kanno has worked with directors such as

---

17 There are rumours that the singer Gabriela Robin is a pseudonym for Kanno.

Kenji Kamiyama, Yoshiyuki Tomino, Shinichiro Watanabe and Shoji Kawamori. Kanno was married to fellow composer Hajime Mizoguchi (until their divorce in 2007).[18]

Yoko Kanno has composed and arranged music for numerous Japanese pop and rock acts, including: Maya Sakamoto, Akino Arai, Kyoko Koizumi, Miki Imai, Akino Arai, Chiyono Yoshino, Crystal Kay and Kyoko Endo.

Yoko Kanno and co. deliver absolutely stunning music cues for the *Cowboy Bebop* TV show, running from heavy rock (in *Heavy Metal Queen*), thru dance and pop to jazz, folk and world music (there are thumping drums for some action sequences, fr'instance). The music cues in *Cowboy Bebop* include: rapid, rhythmic handclaps out of a children's game; a brilliant *hommage* to Ennio Morricone's Spaghetti Western scores; North African *rai* (featuring Turkish drums); soft grand piano cues for emotional scenes; a striking reworking of the kind of guitar-blues music Henry Mancini composed in the 1960s (reminiscent of 'Peter Gunn'); an extraordinary post-Pink Floyd electronic pulse; tons of American, bluesy slide guitar *à la* Ry Cooder (in the *Paris, Texas* style); and plenty of electronically-based atmospheres familiar from sci-fi cinema.

There are many allusions to genres of music in the titles of the *Cowboy Bebop* episodes, too: funk, folk, blues, elegy, waltz, ballad, samba, serenade, shuffle, jamming, heavy metal, boogie woogie, and of course jazz.

The confidence with which the music is deployed in the *Cowboy Bebop* TV series is one of many

18 As well as Mizoguchi, Kanno sometimes works with Steve Conte, Akino Arai and Tim Jensen.

indicators to the audience that they are watching an incredibly accomplished piece of work. You've got be *very* skilled to be able to pull off a music score which includes Egyptian drums as well as European rock, Ennio Morricone *hommages* and science fiction mood music.

When Yoko Kanno's music gets going, it adds 95% to the effect of the piece. Sometimes I wonder if animators would prefer it if they could have Kanno's music playing continuously throughout their shows, losing the dialogue and the sound effects. Because Kanno's music is perfectly suited to animation.

The opening theme in *Cowboy Bebop* is called 'Tank', and is played by Yoko Kanno and the Seatbelts band (it's a Kanno composition, with lyrics[19] by Yuho Iwasato). It is a full-on, big band jazz arrangement, filled with brass instruments (trombones, trumpets, horns), and driven along with a punchy rhythm (it includes a saxophone solo by Masaoto Honda). The feel of 'Tank' is of the 1960s, something that Henry Mancini or John Barry might've composed for a glossy TV show aimed at the international market, or a movie starring Roger Moore, James Coburn, or Elliot Gould. A voice's heard at the start saying (in English): 'I think it's time to get everybody and the stuff together. OK, three, two, one, let's jam!'

The end credits features Mai Yamane performing with the Seatbelts in 'The Real Folk Blues' (Yamane appears on other pieces in *Cowboy Bebop*).

---

19 You can find the lyrics to the songs in *Cowboy Bebop* online.

COWBOY BEBOP AND *MACROSS PLUS*.

Some of the key members of the team that produced *Cowboy Bebop* contributed to *Macross Plus* (1995), an *animé* classic of four OAVs (each 40 minutes) which updated the 1982-83 series.[20] Yoko Kanno, Keiko Nobumoto, Shinichiro Watanabe[21] and Shoji Kawamori worked on *Macross Plus*. If you enjoy *Cowboy Bebop*, have a look at *Macross Plus*: you'll see the same American West and desert settings, the same sorts of aerial dogfights,[22] similar rivalry between macho guys,[23] pop music references, a stellar soundtrack from Yoko Kanno, and eccentric pop culture references (the skateboarding kids in the first episode, for instance).

(For more on *Macross Plus*, see the appendix).

COWBOY BEBOP AND DISNEY.

We don't think of the *Cowboy Bebop* series as having any relation to the Walt Disney corporation (animation fans would probably spot the references to Warner Bros. cartoons, or the Fleischers, or Tex Avery and Chuck Jones). But there're numerous affinities with Disney's output – the allusions to the history of cinema, the trashy Americana, the comic sidekicks (the dogs!), the suppressed and unexpressed eroticism, the recycling of genres, the theme parks, the broad comedy and action, the emphasis on music, etc.

Of course, the Mouse House would *never* have

---

20 There was also a 1996 movie, edited, as usual, from the OAVs.
21 *Cowboy Bebop*'s director, Shinichiro Watanabe, co-directed *Macross Plus* with director Shoji Kawamori (b. 1960), a veteran of numerous *animé* shows, including *Patlabor, Transformers, Escaflowne,* and *Dangaioh*. Kawamori also co-wrote one of the episodes of *Cowboy Bebop* (18: *Speak Like a Child*).
22 Including pilots arguing loudly as they dogfight, a staple of *Cowboy Bebop*.
23 Isamu in *Macross Plus* also lies on his back on the ground, as Spike does quite often in *Cowboy Bebop*.

produced *Cowboy Bebop* – not with shoot-outs and drug-taking in the first five minutes of the opening episode! The lawlessness, the laziness, the weariness and the ultra-violence of *Cowboy Bebop* are distinctly *not* Disney's cup o' tea. (And even U.S. satellite and cable channels might find plenty in *Cowboy Bebop* to unsettle them. Some shows, such as *True Blood*, aim towards 'NC-17' material in their deseperation to be cool and trendy, with depictions of drugs, sex, 'bad language', violence, etc, but they're actually utterly conventional and traditional when you look closer. Also, no North American comedy-drama TV show has anything like the wildness of style, the endless invention, and the ecstatic sense of freedom of Japanese animation and *Cowboy Bebop*).

Illustrations

Images of some of the personnel behind the
Cowboy Bebop series.

Kôichi Yamadera, the voice of Spike Spiegel

Unshô Ishizuka,
the voice of Jet Black

Megumi Hayashibara,
the voice of Faye Valentine

Aoi Tada, the voice
of Radical Ed

Shinichiro Watanabe, director of Cowboy Bebop (above).
Keiko Nobumoto, chief writer of Cowboy Bebop (below).

Yoko Kanno

Make no mistake, Yoko Kanno may
look (and sound) like a little pixie, but she is one of
the great talents of film music, the equal not only of
any of the great composers for the screen thru cinema
history, but also any contemporary classical and
new music composers.

COWBOYBEBOP

04

JAMMING WITH *BEBOP*: THE WORLD OF *COWBOY BEBOP*

INGREDIENTS IN *COWBOY BEBOP*

Each episode in the *Cowboy Bebop* series is a stand-alone episode. Some of the stories are too long for a single 23 minute show, however, and are split into two episodes (episodes 12 and 13, *Jupiter Jazz*, and episodes 25 and 26, *The Real Folk Blues*). However, there is some narrative progression running thru the individual episodes (the development of the relationships between the family of misfits, for instance, and their characterizations, and the parcelling-out of back-story info on what happened to Planet Earth). But it doesn't matter too much which order you watch them in.

The recipe for *Cowboy Bebop* includes:

- countless references to pop, rock, jazz and blues music
- countless allusions to cinema and television
- money (Woolongs)
- debts
- food
- hunger
- death (Spike is repeatedly 'killed')
- sex
- gambling
- multi-cultural, multi-racial communities
- the past – you can't escape it, but gotta deal with it
- hacker culture
- computers
- cyberspace
- crime syndicates and gangsters
- a family of misfits
- big cities
- episodes climax with a fight in space btn space craft
- episode titles use musical forms
- episode titles allude to pop songs
- each commercial bumper/ 'eye-catch' is different, often with quotes inserted
- each episode closes with the phrase 'SEE YOU SPACE COWBOY' or summat similar
- there's always a scene where a new setting is lovingly evoked in spectacular images
- flashbacks (some in b/w or sepia)
- spaceships in hyperspace and at the hyperspace gates
- guns (inc. guns vs. samurai swords)
- scenes where one character stands still while

someone shoots at them

• classic Hitchcockian MacGuffins (money/
drugs/ software)

• references to *film noir* and detective movies of
the 1940s

• countless references to 1960s and 1970s pop
culture

• villains or guest stars get their own introduction scenes

• youths who get over their heads in crime

• *mecha* and gadgets

• cigarettes (Spike with bent cigs in his maw)

• Faye Valentine always runs away

• Faye Valentine gets tied up or handcuffed

• dressing up and crossdressing

• male homosexuality and gay culture

• zero gravity gags

• three old coots who re-appear[1]

• scenes where Spike follows up leads on foot
detective-style

• scenes in bars, restaurants, diners, casinos

• fashion – great clothes

• characters in mock shock who freeze in a pose

THE CHARACTERS

SPIKE SPIEGEL.

Cowboy Bebop was about a group of bounty hunter
misfits led by Spike Spiegel (voiced by Kôichi
Yamadera). Spike drew primarily on the well-known

1 The running gag of three old coots playing poker crops up
throughout the *Cowboy Bebop* series (and they appear in the movie,
too).

Japanese actor Yusaku Matsuda. Spike also clearly draws on Lupin III[2] with Jet Black as Jigen and Faye as Valentine Fujiko (as well as Humphrey Bogart, *film noir* detectives, and James Coburn in his *Our Man Flint* persona). Spike is an ultra-cool, gangly, spindly ex-crime operator, 27 years-old, emotionally wounded (yes, it was a girl! She left him!), with a past. He sports dark suits (often blue) with open, white shirts, spiky, dark hair, pointed, angular features, walks with his hands in his pockets, hunched over, and has a cigarette dangling from his mouth.

Spike Spiegel's philosophy is classic drifter, bohemian, Beat Generation and Existential stuff: 'whatever happens, happens'. Spike goes with the flow: he's not a hero, not in a hurry to get all heroic and brave and determined – in fact, he's not in a hurry to do anything: if Spike had enough dough to live on, he'd quit tearing around and chill out (but of course he *does* do loads – well, he is the main character, after all).

Spike Spiegel lazes around a lot: he's not in a hurry to wash the dishes or hang out clothes to dry (tho' he will rinse down his beloved *Swordfish* space-craft). He resembles your older brother who borrows your favourite clothes without asking (and rips them), who crashes your motorcycle and hasn't got the dough to pay for repairs, and who steals your girlfriend (without trying. Arrgh!). He's the guy at high school who was always irritatingly witty, made everyone laugh, was great at sports, and who on top of it all wasn't a dickhead jock.

Although one word defines Spike Spiegel – *cool*,

2 Lupin's yellow car appears in episode 15.

of course! – he often loses his cool. No matter how hard he tries, some people – principally Faye Valentine – wind him up summat rotten. Faye has an innate knack of pissing off Spike without even trying. Her very existence perplexes and irritates him, yet he can't keep away from her either. In fact, the more 'cool' Spike tries to be, the more desperately uncool he becomes. Simmering just below the surface of that super-cool, street punk exterior, under that brilliant-at-everything-including-smoking-cigarettes veneer, there is plenty of rage and resentment and angst and emotional woundedness.

JET BLACK.

Jet Black's the burly 36 year-old ex-cop (with the I.S.S.P., Inter-Solar System Police), blunt, no-nonsense, gruff (and wears dark vests to show off his muscular bulk, has a beard, is bald – and has shades, of course). Jet has a mechanical arm, from the betrayal of a colleague (related in *Black Dog Serenade*).

Jet Black (voiced by Unsho Ishizuka) is both the father and the mother to the family of misfits and vagrants; there's a heart of gold beneath that crusty, seen-it-all-before exterior. It's Jet who keeps the *Bebop* ship running, who does the paperwork, checks the bills, looks after the food, does the cooking, and hangs out the washing.

FAYE VALENTINE.

Faye Valentine (voiced by Megumi Hayashibara) is an *animé* super-babe in the Tank Girl mode, show-ing lots of skin (she wears yellow short shorts, a croptop, designer jewellery – and has large boobs, of course). The filmmakers exploit many opportunities for Faye to display her body (putting her in a bikini, for instance).

Spike Spiegel and Jet Black on their own would be enough for an action comedy cartoon smashing together the American Western genre and the space opera genre within a cop/ crime show format, but the introduction of Faye Valentine into the mix is a stroke of genius. There's always an edge of spontaneity and unpredictability about Spike – it's one of the elements in his personality that make him so appealing – but Faye is equally reckless and out-there. Bringing a sensational super-babe like Faye into the show creates all sorts of tensions that can be explored – comic as well as dramatic.

One of the intriguing aspects of Faye Valentine's character is just how she transformed from being the rather shy, bemused and uncertain young woman (born in 1994) who woke up from cryogenic sleep to become the spunky super-babe who can wield guns, fly spaceships, and beat up bad guys.

A recurring gag has Faye Valentine always running away – and always getting tied up with rope or handcuffs. Escape and flight are Faye's default mode: she is a nomad, like all of the *Bebop* crew, but it takes a long time for her to realize that the place she feels most at home is on the *Bebop*.

Faye Valentine completely perplexes Spike Spiegel and Jet Black. They simply don't understand her at all. Sometimes they agree, two men together, that women are irrational and don't make sense, but their bafflement goes way beyond gender issues. Faye would confound them whatever gender she was (and she is very tomboyish and masculine anyway). She's way beyond gender.

And Faye Valentine treats the *Bebop* crew pretty badly when she runs away repeatedly – including robbing them or scuppering their spaceship! Yet they always take her back. Why? For a number of reasons, some of which are unspoken. A bond forms in this bunch of misfits which is mysterious but instantly recognizable (Jet Black ruminates on the concept of 'family' in the series).

RADICAL ED.

Voiced by Aoi Tada with a bold, out-there quirkiness, Radical Edward Wong Hau Pepelu Tivruski the IV (a.k.a. Ed or Edo)[3] is a hacker and computer expert girl (she calls herself a 'net diver'), cute, off-the-wall eccentric, with a high-pitched baby voice, and curiously wavy, floppy limbs. Edo has spiky, orange *animé* hair, goes barefoot everywhere, and wears lycra shorts. Ed makes up nonsense rhymes which she sings. She carries her computer on her head. She has a big cheesy cartoon smile as her personal logo (it pops up and giggles). There's also a sweetness and tenderness to Ed, underneath the kooky exterior.

Ed can sleep anywhere, and is often depicted either asleep, or waking up and yawning. When the filmmakers're stuck for summat for Ed to do, they either have her sleeping in a bizarre pose, or walking thru a scene singing a silly song.

Ed is, in short, *play*, the spirit of play – not only the play of being a kid who's free as a bird, but the spirit of play which everybody needs. For the writers, one of the challenges of a truly out-there character like

---

3 The name Radical Ed is reminiscent of Presuming Ed in the cult classic comedy *Withnail & I* (1987), a movie with many similarities with *Cowboy Bebop*.

Radical Ed is how to integrate her into the series. It requires a particular kind of story for Ed to flourish in. (Like Tetsuo in *Akira*, or Ed Elric in *Fullmetal Alchemist*, or Lupin III, a wildly expressive character like Ed is gift to an animator, and the animators play Ed very broad, in the cutie, *kawaii animé* style).[4]

And there's even a sweet mutt, a Welsh corgi called Ein (it's not *animé* unless there's a dog in there somewhere; the dog is also a super-computer). It's a classic misfit band of renegades, self-consciously quirky and out-there, and it works.

THE *BEBOP* CREW AS A BAND OF MISFITS.

You wouldn't want to hang out with the crew of the *Enterprise* in *Star Trek* (too strait-laced and uptight), or the emotionally-inept oddballs on the *Millennium Falcon* in *Star Wars*, or the Vietnam grunts or dull engineers in the *Alien* movies, but you would want to hang out with the *Bebop* gang.

And the default pose of the *Bebop* crew – lounging around in their living room occasionally watching TV and perpetually wondering where the next meal is coming from – mirrors segments of the *animé* audience.

One of the appealing aspects of *Cowboy Bebop*, and a large part of its success, is the group of misfit characters.[5] Spike Spiegel would be super-cool enough to have a series on his own, maybe with a sidekick, and an on-off love interest. But placing him as just one of a band of misfits or outsiders works

---

4 Cute characters – *kawaii* – are a staple of Japanese animation: Pikachu in *Pokémon*, for example, or young women in *manga* and *animé*.
5 'These are affectionately drawn characters with enormous appeal, who keep us interested even when the going gets incomprehensible', remarked Brian Camp (80).

beautifully (Spike may be the hero, for instance, but he's not the leader or the chief, so to speak: Jet Black reminds one and all that it's *his* spaceship they're living in. Besides, each of the bounty hunters works *alone* very often – they simply go off and do their thing, sometimes going after the same target at the same time!).

Japanese movies are often about communities and families rather than individuals, and *Cowboy Bebop* depicts a central group, with charas 'who make different choices, take different paths in life, and thereby come to different ends', but are united by a common theme, as Gerald Mast and Bruce Kawin note of the typical Japanese film.

Cowboy Bebop is of course yet another 'character team' (*sentai*) show, which are everywhere in Japanese animation (*Gundam, Macross, Patlabor, Gatchaman, Evangelion, Escaflowne, Gunbuster, Ghost In the Shell,* etc). Obvious forerunners of the team in *Cowboy Bebop* include *Lupin III, Dominion: Tank Police,* and *Patlabor.*

The next stroke of inspiration in *Cowboy Bebop* has these guys working as bounty hunters, but not always successful bounty hunters. So they're often only just getting by, and food is a big consideration: they are always looking for the next meal. That makes 'em even more appealing: they are not superheroes, brilliant at everything, with no flaws except Kryptonite. They just want to get by and eat (empty stomach noises are frequent, as in *Fullmetal Alchemist*). A lot of TV shows (and movies) have left food as a plot device far behind – it's just not 'big' enough, 'tragic' enough, 'epic' enough for filmmakers and TV producers. They want plots where the world has to be saved from aliens or terrorists. And if food is employed, it'll be as the basis of watering-hole scenes, where characters get together and talk. Or there'll be a fat, comic sidekick who thinks about nosh all the time. But *Cowboy Bebop* makes grub more central, because it is: wherever there are humans, they gots to eat (and food is a big deal in the Japanese media, and in *anime*).

Another vital ingredient is the *tone*: *Cowboy Bebop* hits the spot: exciting and full of action, but not deadly serious about it (only sometimes). In fact, it's essentially a comedy drama, or an action comedy. It's not like one of those cynical TV cop shows where everybody's snippy and sarky, and the undercurrent of resentment and loathing is barely suppressed. *Cowboy Bebop* is much warmer than that; it's upbeat, it's optimistic, and it's laid-back.

The *Bebop* misfits are together partly for the sake of practicality: it's a relationship that works for the time being. But they are often on the verge of leaving, or they grudgingly respect and care for each other, and somehow they stay together. It's not a family unit, as Jet Black muses in the 2001 movie (though the presence of the youngster Ed leans towards that, and Jet does play mother and father at times).

It's endearing too that the gang of bounty hunters in *Cowboy Bebop* are not tied to each other to the point where they do everything together. In fact, they often pursue a prize or goal on their own, coming back to the spaceship *Bebop* to compare notes. They are not an efficiently organized SWAT team or CIA team; they're more like a band of outlaws in a 1940s or 1950s horse opera, and if one of them strikes lucky, they're not going to share it with the others (echoes of

The Treasure of the Sierra Madre, 1948).

THE *BEBOP* MISFITS AS A FAMILY.

Another key theme in the *Cowboy Bebop* universe is *family*. True, *Cowboy Bebop* portrays a family of misfits, people who shouldn't really be able to get along with each other, people who drive each other crazy at times, who do stupid things, who complain about each other, yet who also care for each other. Undoubtedly, the family theme is one of the chief ingredients in the continuing popularity of the 1998 TV series.

For all the obvious reasons.

Using a familial set-up has been a staple of television since its inception. And families have been central to all storytelling since forever (at least 50-100,000 years, probably longer). The writers of *Cowboy Bebop* employ the family scenario in many of the conventional ways, and it works, because it always works. Though no mention is made of the parents of the principal characters (or brothers, sisters, aunts, uncles, grandparents, etc) – apart from Radical Edward Wong Hau Pepelu Tivruski the IV's father (in session 24, *Hard Luck Woman*) – each character also acts as a mother and father to the other characters.

Jet Black is the senior member of the *Bebop* team (the spaceship also belongs to him),[6] and he is often portrayed as both the father and the mother (right down to the sit-com stereotype of being mom and cooking for the misfits in his apron). Spike Spiegel is the older brother figure, occasionally vain, arrogant,

---

6 The *Bebop* spaceship is also a pirate galleon, wandering the Solar System – and when it lands on planets, it lands in water; and for much of the series, it is docked in the harbour of the Mars capital.

whingeing, and irritating, but also dependable, smart, fierce, brave, and eternally *cool*. Faye Valentine refuses to be typed as a mother figure (although she does act that way), but wilfully maintains her status as an independent woman, answerable to no one (she will come and go as she likes, without asking anyone's permission). An older sister figure to Radical Ed, she is also the wayward daughter to Jet, and the unpredictable, unfathomable and sarcastic sister to Spike.

MONEY AND FOOD.

I love that the characters in *Cowboy Bebop* laze about in the den, dozing on the couch, or not really doing anything[7] – it's the polar opposite of the starchy, hierarchical teams in the *Star Trek* series or *Babylon 5*. There's no captain, no authority, no leader in *Cowboy Bebop*, which automatically gives it a different dynamic (altho' Jet Black does assert his authority from time to time). The weariness and yeah-whateverness of the *Cowboy Bebop* team is infectious. They sit about, they yawn, and they talk (but not really about anything – they never have deep discussions; actually, they bitch and bicker more than talk).

The *Cowboy Bebop* team aren't really workers – though they *do* work (Spike Spiegel and Jet Black, fr'instance, are depicted fixing or cleaning their spacecraft). Their objectives are simple: money and food (money to buy food)[8] What grabs their attention most, what galvanizes them into action more than

7 In *Ballad of Fallen Angels*, Jet is shown pruning a bonsai tree, and Faye sits on the stairs doing her nails.
8 Food drives the first episode: Spike 'n' Jet're shown eating noodles without meat. So they launch into the plot partly to obtain some dough to buy some meat.

anything, is the promise of millions of Woolongs.[9]

It's difficult in these so-cynical, seen-it-all-b4 days to use food as a primary motive in a TV drama – it usually has to be summat Big 'n' Epic 'n' Important (saving the world, political rebellion, freeing slaves, that kinda thing). But *Cowboy Bebop* makes the simple but vital pursuit of food convincing (in that first episode, *Asteroid Blues*, you can believe that Spike an' Jet haven't had a good meal in ages. It's partly due to the way they sit about in an apathetic mood, listless, emotionless; they're not happy but they're also not dead yet).

SCRIPT AND DIALOGUE

Cowboy Bebop sure is clever with the way it introduces each member of the gang. Again and again, its the quality of the *writing* that really impresses with *Cowboy Bebop*. The screenwriting and the music. And the visuals. And the action. And the humour. Oh, well, *everything* about this 1998 show is impressive.

The scriptwriting is taut, inventive and compressed: the *Cowboy Bebop* show never loses its way, never meanders, and never indulges in lengthy talky scenes or long, philosophical discussions (which do appear in series such as *Ghost In the Shell: Stand Alone Complex*, unfortunately, and're the only thing that weakens the show).

Yes, *Cowboy Bebop does* slow down from time to time and has some longer conversations (such as between Jet Black and his ex-girlfriend in Alisa). But

9 A Woolong is equivalent to the Japanese Yen (there are 100 or just over 100 Yen to the U.S. dollar).

the scenes're always compelling. The editing and pacing is simply exquisite in *Cowboy Bebop* – such an important part of filmmaking, and very seldom remarked upon (but you sure notice it when it isn't working).

The filmmakers of *Cowboy Bebop* have opted to use the laconic style of using dialogue and convers-ation, which's in keeping with the 1940s, hard-boiled detective genre. Thus, Jet Black and Spike Spiegel speak in short, clipped sentences, with pauses and silences being employed everywhere, along with meaningful looks and super-cool gestures (like flicking a cigarette into the mouth – everybody in *Cowboy Bebop* smokes, a'course).

The less-is-more pattern of dialogue also means that the characters aren't revealed all at once: instead, their backgrounds're uncovered gradually, as the 26 episodes progress (but you also don't need a ton of exposition and back-story in an action show with action-based characters if you've established one or two overriding motives or goals in the first episodes: such as GET MONEY, or GET FOOD). And although *Cowboy Bebop* becomes more complicated as it goes along thru series, it still uses those simple objectives as the principal goals:

find food ♪ make money.

However, the motives change: Spike's motive in his over-arching storyline, about dealing with his criminal past, is more than self-preservation. For Antonia Levi, writing in *Samurai From Outer Space*, it's motivation that defines the Japanese hero, and the determination to go all the way, to see the job done. It's not about personal gain, and even the cause itself isn't important. It's about giving it your all. So a loser can also be a kind of hero.

Another element of *Cowboy Bebop*'s success is its integration of a *manga* æsthetic into an animated show. There are many shots and scenes which look just like panels from a comicbook, but they still work as animation. Many people have tried that (in live-action too), but *Cowboy Bebop* really does come over as an animation which can celebrate *manga* and the static-but-dynamic comicbook form while also being fundamentally animation and filmmaking.

THE OVER-ARCHING STORY.

Futuristic science fiction in Japanese animation often has a catastrophe in the past of some sort which affects the present – two world wars in the *Ghost In the Shell* series, for instance, the explosions of the Akira phenomenon in *Akira,* and the Elric brothers trying and failing to bring their mother back to life in *Fullmetal Alchemist.*

Many times these disasters and conflicts are oblique references to WWII and the Pacific War, and to the two atomic bombs dropped by the U.S.A. and the Allies on Japan. Futuristic sci-fi is often replaying the Pacific War, but in outer space, with fleets of spaceships replacing Japan's Navy: *Gunbuster, Star Blazers,* and *Nausicaä of the Valley of the Wind.*

In *Cowboy Bebop*, however, flashbacks peppered throughout the series depict Earth's climate being damaged due to an accident at a hyperspace gateway (which also blew a hole in the moon, so chunks of rock fall to Earth in showers). It's not an atomic bomb, then, or an alien invasion, but it is once again humanity's uneasy relationship with sophisticated technology that leads to the disaster.

THE WORLD OF *COWBOY BEBOP*

It's a Western combined with a space opera, but *Cowboy Bebop* avoids numerous clichés of the science fiction and Western genre, as if it's *reacting* to expectations. For instance, there are no aliens here: it's still just us gorgeous humans alone in the Solar System.[10] There are no robots or mobile power suits, mandatory in any Japanese sci-fi *animé* show (Sunrise, well-known for its robot shows (such as *Gundam* and *Escaflowne*), designed *Cowboy Bebop* as a show which would avoid robots). No time travel (but there is one form of sci-fi time travel: Faye Valentine's awakening after being frozen for 50 years. And, a'course, the series is very much about travelling into one's own past to find out what one is).[11]

Cowboy Bebop is set in 2071, in a Solar System which has a number of out-posts from Earth. Much of the action takes place on Mars, or on Venus, or the moons of Jupiter, or open space, or asteroids – but, of course, it's really Earth, and it's usually the giant metropolis of Japanese *animé* which, as usual, combines elements of Tokyo and New York City, plus pieces of Hong Kong and Los Angeles.

One of the striking aspects about *Cowboy Bebop* is its depiction of a multi-cultural, multi-racial, pluralistic or diaspora society (or whatever the PC term is at the moment). This is still very rare in *animé*, which seems to look back to the Edo period when Japan was an island which cut itself off from foreign influences. Even in the 1990s and 2000s, *animé* was

10 With humans as eccentric and unusual as those depicted in *Cowboy Bebop*, who needs aliens? (However, some of the people are portrayed in a stylized manner echoing the super-deformity of *animé*, such as the Elders of the Red Dragon clan).
11 The time dilation of hyperspace travel is ignored.

still predominantly (though understandably) about Japanese people in Japan (and if the shows were set in other countries or times or planets, it was still fundamentally Japan).

But *Cowboy Bebop* aggressively goes way beyond that; in the first couple episodes, it brings in Native Americans, African Americans, Mexicans, Arabs and Hindus, as well as a variety of Asian cultures (like the *Ghost In the Shell* franchise, *Cowboy Bebop* is very fond of Chinese culture, for instance). There are more African American and black characters in *Cowboy Bebop* than any comparable *animé*, including Udai Taxim, Abdul Hakim, Punch, Donnelly, Domino Walker, Shaft, Coffee and Miles.

Cowboy Bebop is specially good with creating fascinating and compelling secondary and minor characters, and extras who're only seen once. Young kids (often black) who become embroiled in petty crime are another motif in *Cowboy Bebop* (if there was going to be a new addition to the *Bebop* crew, it would probably be a kid like Rocco Bonnaro in the episode *Waltz For Venus*).

Cynics could point out that introducing so many international cultures, with North American cultures one of the most prominent among them, stems from the producers and backers wanting to appeal to the international and American market with the *animé* show. Yes, that is often the case, but not here: *Cowboy Bebop* is multi-cultural/ multi-racial/ pluralistic/ diasporic for many other reasons, not least that this is how the writers and filmmakers see the future.

Much of the culture of the future depicted in *Cowboy Bebop* is Chinese, which adds further cultural complexities to the mix: a Japanese *animé* set in a largely Chinese-oriented future which's in love with Americana and the Old West (it's the American West in reality, yes, but much more the Old West as it appears in popular culture, in particular movies and television). Yet it remains entirely Japanese.

China is regarded as a place of the unknown and the exotic in *manga* and *animé*, a completely different country, a place of foreigners: in short, China is just as foreign to Japanese as it is to Westerners. When Japanese go abroad (tho' most don't), they tend to visit Europe or the U.S.A., not other Asian countries.

So the Middle East, like Europe and the U.S.A., and India and other Asian countries, are subject in *animé* and *manga* to stereotyping and demonization (with the Arabic countries coming off worst – such as in *GoShogun, The Crystal Triangle, Area 88, Fullmetal Alchemist* and *Spriggan*). As Antonia Levi puts it, the Middle East is a 'place of sand, religious fanaticism, and terrorists' in *animé* (60). And it is too in many North American movies and TV shows (even more so following 9/11).

Cowboy Bebop has all the usual techie and *mecha* stuff of a Japanese *animé* show – the spaceships, the cars, the gadgets, the computers, and the amazing hardware. It has guns and fights. It has chases by car, boat, train, spaceship, plane, bike, and on foot. And it also has moments when the characters are sitting about in the lounge of their spaceship, bored or lazy, unable to do anything.

The cities in *Cowboy Bebop* draw on numerous cinematic forerunners, from the inevitable *Metropolis* and *Blade Runner* to *Akira*. Of real cities, the usual suspects are to the fore: New York, Los Angeles, Las Vegas, Hong Kong, and a'course, Tokyo. That the

designers *love* New York City goes without saying
(but who doesn't?): many parts of *Cowboy Bebop* are
adoring celebrations of the City That Never Sleeps,
from yellow taxi cabs, 'DON'T WALK' signs, delis,
skyscrapers, dingy bars (called 'Losers Bar'), and
those beautiful bridges over the River Hudson. When
Cowboy Bebop shifts into black-and-white stylization,
it comes over as a pæan to Raymond Chandler and
Dashiell Hammett, a 1940s *film noir* city of world
weary detectives, *femme fatale* blondes (like Julia), car
chases, mob feuds, shoot-outs and betrayals of blood.
There are *hommages* to the Chrysler Building, the
Flatiron Building, and the Brooklyn Bridge.

Another appealing factor in *Cowboy Bebop* is that
it doesn't feel the need to explain everything to the
audience. Apparently the decision to leave out the
exposition which would set up the world of the story
was director Shinichiro Watanabe's; so, no pedantic
and long-winded explanations about the world, *à la
Star Trek.*

There ain't usually time or money for research
trips in the Japanese animation industry – most
research is probably done with books and the web at
the animation house. Some big productions do have
the budget for a trip. But someone on the Sunrise/
Bandai team has definitely spent a day or two in the
American West, in amongst the motels, bars, casinos,
strip joints, and endless stretches of highway across
the beautiful Mojave Desert.

VILLAINS.

Unlike many TV shows, *Cowboy Bebop* eschews a
regular antagonist or villain for the heroes to go up
against. *Lupin III* has Inspector Zenigata, *Gunbuster*

has nasty aliens, *Escaflowne* has the Zaibach people, *Mushishi* has bugs, and *Fullmetal Alchemist* has the homunculi, but *Cowboy Bebop* prefers to create new villains for each episode (although there are some recurring characters).

Creating villains is one of the elements of *animé* in which *Cowboy Bebop* really excels. In fact, *animé* as a whole produces some really fascinating and convincing villains: this is one of the reasons why *animé* is so satisfying from a story and character point-of-view, why *animé* storytelling is so much more sophisticated than Western forms of story-telling in film. Compared to Western cinema, and American and Hollywood cinema, *animé* villains are far more complex, more attractive, much more convincing, and, crucially, *ambiguous*.

The *Cowboy Bebop* writers have fashioned a collection of memorable villains who are not only eccentric, complex and multi-layered, they are also very nasty, often bordering on psychotic (such as brutal mob hitman Udai Taxim in *Black Dog Serenade* or Vincent in the 2001 movie or Asimov in the opening episode), or they're outright insane – Pierrot the Fool in episode 20.

CIGARETTES.

Like the films of Jean-Luc Godard, and the *film noirs* of the 1940s in La-La Land, *Cowboy Bebop* shows are very much what I call cancer films – shows which feature a lot of smoking. These days smoking in movies means a bad guy, and smoking's been banned everywhere on Earth (except for casinos in Nevada).

Of course everybody in *Cowboy Bebop* smokes:

it's not only part of the detective and crime fiction genre, it's also the filmmakers delighting in being un-PC. They smoke! So sue me! Spike has a cigarette (usually bent) permanently glued to his lower lip, like Ginko in *Mushishi*;[12] cigarettes are always lit with a Zippo lighter (of course!); Jet Black stubs out a cig in a plant in the office of the Gate Corporation which turns out to be a microphone; characters often smoke in no smoking areas; if Spike and Jet found themselves in the contemporary Western world, where smoking is banned in all public areas except for nuclear bomb test sites (also in Nevada), they would go nuts!

In *Boogie Woogie Feng Shui*, Jet Black orders that the living quarters be a no smoking zone, so Faye and Spike're reduced to standing outside with a soda can to catch the ash. That's the way the PC culture has gone – now it's everywhere in the West, with the determined cancer addicts trekking outside in all weathers.

COMPUTERS.

Another inspired ingredient in the *Cowboy Bebop* universe is the use of the computer. The gang don't have giant TVs, and screens everywhere, they have a single computer terminal in their den, which is

---

12 Spike is always flipping cigs into his mouth; first thing he does after coming round after being shot n *Jupiter Jazz* is feel for a cigarette. For me it's a gesture that evokes one of the coolest actors in movies, Jean-Pierre Léaud. While for some the image of the Beatles or the Rolling Stones may embody the Sixties, for me the young Jean-Pierre Léaud encapsulates much of that era. The Léaud of the films of Jean-Luc Godard and François Truffaut, dressed in a jacket and sweater (or sometimes a tie), constantly flicking cigarettes into his mouth, slouching against walls, riding the Metro, sitting around in cafés, spraying anti-Vietnam slogans on walls, looking longingly at girls, earnestly discussing Existential philosophy, and spouting polemical views. Léaud, the alter ego of Truffaut and Godard, in many films, embodies a certain aspect of the Sixties: youth, intensity, high-blown idealism, lust, political activism, Existential angst, melancholy and lassitude. As well as a certain Gallic cool.

employed for all the usual functions in a TV show (exposition, plot points, TV broadcasts). But it's kinda low-tech. Low-tech, but also inventive: the gang do a lot of research on the computer (with wavy-armed techie-girl Ed heading up the rapid pounding of the computer keyboard: every *animé* character can type faster than any regular human).

Every hi-tech *animé* show has to create futuristic computer interfaces (echoing too how animation teams slave away for 100s of hours a year on computers): the ones employed in the *Cowboy Bebop* are more convincing and entertaining than most. They have a scruffy feel, and a child-like approach to the graphics, shapes and colours (Edo has custom-ized the computer, and has colourful fish and animals floating around in her hyperspace).

The floating approach to the symbols and images in the digital realm in the gang's computer (echoing the 'floating world' of Japanese art) is taken out into the real world: thus, as their spaceship *Bebop* approaches a city, advertizing hoardings hover about, so they're flying through a maze of billboards, just like Times Square or downtown Hong Kong (*animé* filmmakers just *love* signage, and freight their shows with tons and tons of it. Quite a bit of time is spent in making up fake businesses and services, and also in ageing up the signs, to give them that beat-up, lived-in texture. And there's graffiti everywhere).

MECHA.

Cowboy Bebop is *animé*, and science fiction *animé*, so there is *mecha* by the ton on display: the three adult crew of the *Bebop* each have their own spaceship, which suits their personalities. They are retro-styled spacecraft which the pilots fly crouched over, as if they're riding motorcycles. Jet Black's *Hammerhead* has a giant claw/ crane, while Faye's ship *Red Tail* is femininely spherical but bristles with guns and devices, and Spike's *Swordfish* is a sleek, red machine, beat-up but very fast (and fitted with a plasma canon, and guns, a'course).

The Sunrise/ Bandai filmmakers, like many *animé* filmmakers, fetishize weaponry. You can see guns in *Bebop* such as a Walther P99, IMI Jericho 941, Glock 30, and the futuristic guns attached to the spacecraft that Spike Spiegel and Faye Valentine fly.

And gadgets: like *James Bond* or *Thunderbirds* or *Star Wars*, the *Cowboy Bebop* universe is stuffed with gadgets: Faye has a communicator hidden in her lipstick (as well as an electronic hairpin for slipping out of handcuffs).

The writers of *Cowboy Bebop* keep the spaceship a social place, with most of the action occurring in the den. Some areas are rarely seen – such as the bedrooms (Faye Valentine's bedroom appears in *Hard Luck Woman*). And even the kitchen[13] and bathroom are hardly glimpsed (though the john is).

MIXING

Incredible action, spectacular visuals, wry and light-hearted humour, and a very contemporary, urban street style influenced by North American comics and movies (and retro 1970s fashion), *kung fu* movies, a bit of *Blade Runner* and *Akira,* samurai movies, and

---

13 The kitchen makes a rare appearance for a Faye-Spike chat in one of the later episodes.

two of *animé*'s sexiest action heroes, gangly, super-cool dude Spike, and Faye (in *animé*, breasts never sag, even when the heroine's performing high kicks or beating up a bad guy). There are many, more more influences and allusions in *Cowboy Bebop* (detailed below).

It's no surprise that *Cowboy Bebop* is a favourite *animé* show in the West, regularly appearing on top ten lists of animated shows. The elements mix skilfully, cleverly, humorously and eccentrically.[14] Its unpredictability is part of its charm: the shows are not all in the same vein, and you don't always know where the story's going to go. (There's nothing like *Cowboy Bebop*, but there are some TV shows with affinities: for instance, in Britain the BBC shows *Red Dwarf* and *The Hitchhiker's Guide To the Galaxy*, and in the U.S.A. *Futurama* and *Firefly*.)

When you put all of the cultural elements and genres and cinematic allusions that *Cowboy Bebop* employs together, you can see how it could so easily go very wrong. *Cowboy Bebop* could so easily be a total mess.

The *balance* or *mix* of the elements in *Cowboy Bebop* is simply spot-on: within 23 minutes, each show does everything, and then some. It's remarkable to watch how the filmmakers deliver formulas and clichés, but then spin them around. And how *fast* is this show? Where similar Western TV shows labour plot points for too long, or take, like, *forever*, to set up narratives and sub-plots, *Cowboy Bebop* hammers along at a breakneck pace. (This's one aspect of

14 'The episodes vary wildly in theme, setting, and style from one to the next. The mood can change from farce to film noir to space combat to mushroom-induced hallucinations to painful flashbacks that reveal a character's past', noted Brian Camp in *Zettai: Anime Classics* (81).

Japanese animation that is *very* appealing to me: when you've seen literally thousands of shows and thousands of hours of TV and cinema, a show that zips by is to be treasured. Where Western TV shows are still edging out of the first half of the first act, ladling out exposition with the clunkiness and creakiness of old men on their death-bed, *Cowboy Bebop* and similar shows (*Ghost In the Shell, Escaflowne, Dominion*) are slamming along happily, breezily and snappily).

WHATEVER YOU ARE, YOU GOTTA BE COOL

COOL, MAAAN. There's no doubt about it: *Cowboy Bebop* is the *coolest animé* TV show, OAV, video or movie. Yeah, there are many contenders for sheer coolness (*Ghost In the Shell: Stand Alone Complex, Akira, Metropolis, Gundam, Evangelion, Ninja Scroll, Patlabor, Tokyo Godfathers, Samurai X, Porco Rosso*, etc), but *Cowboy Bebop* is def the coolest (cooler than *Akira*?! Than *Porco Rosso*?! Well, yes).

The overriding tone of *Cowboy Bebop* is *cool*: it's as if the filmmakers decided, guys, whatever we do, it has *got* to be *COOL*. To look *cool*. To sound *cool*. To be *cool*. And it is. *Cowboy Bebop* is supremely cool: coolness sums up its overriding philosophy perfectly: it's like every French, Left Bank, Existential story; plus every American, hard-boiled, 'tec story; plus every *film noir* (A or B) picture you've ever seen; plus every Beat Generation, hip dude story; plus every hi-tech thriller you've consumed; plus every N.Y.C/ L.A., hiphop, street punk flick, all rolled into one. Forget

Quentin Tarantino, Robert Rodriguez, Guy Ritchie, David Fincher, and Christopher Nolan, and all those Western film directors trying to ape Jean-Luc Godard and Sam Peckinpah and Howard Hawks and Sam Fuller (but failing), *Cowboy Bebop* achieves it.

What's original or new in *Cowboy Bebop* is its witty, ironic and smart mix of cultural and cinematic elements. But no single element in *Cowboy Bebop* is new or original. As to the characters, Spike Spiegel, the main character, has been seen many times before. But Faye Valentine and Radical Ed are original inventions (again, from existing elements). As Simon Richmond noted in *The Rough Guide to Anime*, *Cowboy Bebop* is 'a dish made from leftovers that, on paper, ought not to work' (45). But it does work! (Forerunners in *animé* of *Cowboy Bebop* would include *Riding Bean* (1989), a cars 'n' guns American-style caper OAV (though *Cowboy Bebop* is far superior), *Gunsmith Cats*, *Dominion Tank Police* and *Detective Story*. Other forerunners are: *Space Adventure Cobra* (TMS, 1982), and the works of Haruka Takachiho – the *Dirty Pair* novels (1979) and *Crusher Joe* (1977)).

As Helen McCarthy and Jonathan Clements put it, *Cowboy Bebop* is

> little more than *Route 66* in space, with plots ripped off from generic U.S. crime shows. Space truckers, space mafia, and space hippies would be hack conventions in another series, but they seem to work here because the world seems so believable. (70)

It's also because *Cowboy Bebop* is presented with

such style and wit,[15] I think, and because the characters're appealing and easy to identify with, and because the show has plenty of genuine humour.

FORMAT

The format of each *Cowboy Bebop* show is established early on: the first half (ten or so minutes up to the commercial break), will contain: (1) a watering-hole scene (typically set in a diner, a bar, a café, a restaurant), where Spike and/or Jet Black are staking out a potential target; (2) an exposition scene (provided by TV news, the *Big Shot* bounty hunters show, or Jet at the computer);[16] (3) some jokey conversations in the living room of the *Bebop* spaceship; and (4) an introduction to the villain or guest star.

The second half typically includes: (1) set-backs and complications in the plot for the heroes; (2) a fight or duel or a short action scene; (3) an unexpected twist or reversal in the plot; and (4) the big action finale, typically set in open space or the sky above a futuristic city, and typically involving Spike, Jet or Faye in their spacecraft.

Although *Cowboy Bebop* employs every trick available to animation, and every possible camera angle, it also loves to be dead simple. Fr'instance, there are numerous scenes which're played in a

---

15 'It presses the pedal of improvization, while maintaining an essential coherence and freshness unequalled in the anime world, adding a dash of sober irony', as Stefano Gariglio put it in *Manga Impact!* (C. Chatrian, 219).

16 A recurring motif of the *Cowboy Bebop* shows is the use of many former colleagues of Jet Black to provide exposition. These grizzled old cops and cohorts pop up in many shows: Bob, Fatty, Fad, Donnelly, etc.

single, fixed, tripod master shot, with two or three characters composed in the frame in different sizes (often it's a group scene in the den, and they're looking at the computer screen). The camera lingers and lingers and doesn't move, one of cinema's classic techniques for focussing the audience's attention on the dialogue and the characters. It's almost like watching an Orson Welles movie in animation (and it's a rule of comedy cinema *not* to be too tricksy and complex, because it distracts from the jokes. Simple medium shots from fixed cameras work fine).

TITLES, CREDITS, CAPTIONS, BUMPERS, STYLES

Each episode ends with the salutation: 'SEE YOU SPACE COWBOY!'. Each bumper or 'eye-catch' in and out of the commercial breaks is different. Each title card[17] is different (the filmmakers are *major* font fetishists): *Cowboy Bebop* is a show that's been worked over and over, and then worked over some more, to ram it with details and incidents that are perfect for viewing on video and DVD, to catch every ingredient. (Jamming shows with *moe*-obsessive detail is a recent trend – the *Star Wars* prequels or *Avengers* are good examples; but *Cowboy Bebop* succeeds because the detail is so wittily and jauntily applied, whereas in *Star Wars* and *Avengers* it threatens to overwhelm the viewer with enormous but ultimately pointless material).

The graphic style of *Cowboy Bebop* is incredibly sophisticated, and wide-ranging: it adds up to a

---

17 Each title card has layered, semi-transparent text.

handbook of contemporary visual style, really, a summary of popular graphics from the 1940s to the present day. Handwritten on crumpled paper, 19th century Western fonts, COMIC FONTS, typewriter fonts, newspaper cut-out lettering (*à la* punk rock and the Sex Pistols/ Jamie Reid),[18] *Cowboy Bebop* has got it all. I can't think of another *animé* show with quite such a passion for graphic design and typography. (Some of the commercial caption cards include the phrase (in English): 'the work which becomes a new genre in itself will be called COWBOY BEBOP').

TV shows in *animé* typically spend a lot of time and money on the opening credits sequence, which acts as a commercial, a trailer, and a summary of the show. There's often a tie-in song (which is often a pop song) over the credits. Filmmakers know that the opening credits will be seen many times, so they have to be good. Some have become classics – like *Cowboy Bebop* and *Samurai Champloo*.

Each episode starts with the phrase: *I think it's time to blow this thing and get everybody and the stuff together. OK, three, two, one: let's jam!* In English. The opening credits sequence[19] for *Cowboy Bebop* can be watched again and again, for its incredible graphic beauty, its blend of music and cool, the way the animation matches up with the jazz, and its timing and pacing. It's a credits sequence worthy of any of the celebrated main titles in TV or cinema (including the ones created by Saul Bass or Maurice Binder). The

---

18 Jamie Reid is central to punk rock style: Reid didn't just oversee the design and image of punk's toppermost icons, the Sex Pistols, Reid's cut-up imagery became the embodiment of punk rock music itself. Reid's innovative cut-and-paste designs have become the core of punk iconography.
19 It recalls the credits for the *Lupin III* show.

credits close with the title *Cowboy Bebop*. After the credits, the episode proper begins, usually a short scene, which culminates with the title card of the episode (in English and Japanese), superimposed over layered texts.

EDITING.

Again and again, it's the editing of *Cowboy Bebop* that's so impressive, and keeps the show speeding along like a bullet. The filmmakers understand the importance of timing and editing in comedy, and *Cowboy Bebop* is cut for comedy with a veteran's assurance. There's no waste here, no precious seconds in a 20-some minute show that go astray.

The editing in *Cowboy Bebop* (by Tomoaki Tsurubuchi) is really punchy, driving along the show at a cracking, visceral pace. Especially impressive is the alternations between slow (talky) scenes and action scenes. Pacing is often one of the most important ingredients in Japanese animation, how it can move from reflective scenes when almost nothing appears to be happening, to bursts into action and noise. Thus, *Cowboy Bebop* will flip from a small gesture in close-up (such as Spike putting a cigarette into his mouth) to an explosive surge into action in wide shot (Spike's Swordfish taking off at high speed from the deck of the *Bebop* spaceship).

The *Cowboy Bebop* series makes terrific use of flashbacks; often in black-and-white (actually, it's restricted/ selective colour), they explore the main characters' pasts. The flashbacks're inserted via rapid editing as flashcuts (in the superb pre-main titles sequence of *Asteroid Blues,* the first episode, for instance). Sometimes voiceover is added (as in the Jet

Black episodes), but because the visual storytelling is so deft, it's not needed.

ALLUSIONS AND INFLUENCES

Among the influences on *Cowboy Bebop* are the clutch of sci-fi movies that influence every Japanese sci-fi *animé* outing: *2001: A Space Odyssey, The Terminator, Alien/s, Blade Runner, RoboCop*[20] and *Star Wars.* Indeed, there are references to *2001: A Space Odyssey* in every single episode of *Cowboy Bebop* – including the centrifuge corridor, the airlock and vacuum gag, wheel-shaped space stations, the design of the *Discovery* spaceship, floating objects, HAL, HAL's eye/ camera, classical music played over spaceships, and on and on.

The 'New Hollywood' movies of the late 1960s to the late 1970s are distinct influences on *Cowboy Bebop*: the cities, the view of the future, the characters, the action and staging, the attitudes, and even the visuals of *Cowboy Bebop* all draw heavily on classic movies such as *The French Connection, Bonnie & Clyde, Easy Rider, Taxi Driver, Mean Streets, Convoy, Badlands, Smokey and the Bandit, Vanishing Point, The Sugarland Express* and *Thieves Like Us,* to name some of the obvious references.

The *film noirs* and crime movies of the 1940s that influenced quite a bit of *Cowboy Bebop* include *Double Indemnity, Build My Gallows High, The Big Sleep, To Have and Have Not* and *The Maltese Falcon,* each

---

20 *RoboCop* was another important influence on Japanese animation: you can see *RoboCop*'s influence in *Ghost In the Shell, AD Police Files, Overfiend, Dominion Tank Police* and *Appelseed.*

movie a much-revered classic. And *Cowboy Bebop* also draws on the gangster classics of the Thirties: *Scarface, Angels With Dirty Faces,* and *Dead End*.

Here are some of the specific influences or allusions in *Cowboy Bebop*: there are many allusions to the Rolling Stones[21] (and not only in show titles such as *Sympathy For the Devil* and *Jamming With Edward*); to 1960s music (including Bob Dylan); to heavy rock (including Led Zeppelin); to Humphrey Bogart; to Woody Allen; to *Alice's Adventures In Wonderland*; to blaxploitation cinema; to *James Bond;* to *Star Trek;* to *Flash Gordon;* to Spaghetti Westerns and Sergio Leone; to *Thelma and Louise* (1991); to *Twelve Monkeys* (1995); to Sam Peckinpah (*The Wild Bunch*, 1969); to John Woo; to Howard Hawks; to Stanley Kubrick (*A Clockwork Orange, The Killing, 2001: A Space Odyssey*); to Orson Welles (*Touch of Evil*, 1958); to *kung fu* movies; to Hong Kong action movies and martial arts movies; to *Enter the Dragon* (1973); to Bruce Lee; to hard-boiled detective fiction *à la* Raymond Chandler and Dashiell Hammett; to *Berlin Alexanderplatz* (the name of a rail station in the 2001 movie); to *Stairway To Heaven* (a.k.a. *A Matter of Life and Death*, 1946); and to *Desperado* (1995).

Porn is also referenced in *Cowboy Bebop* a number of times: a coupla kids snitch some skin mags from a store (only to be foiled by Spike, inevitably); the truckers in *Heavy Metal Queen* have pin-ups plastered all over their cabs; and in *Gateway Shuffle,* Jet Black's former cop buddy is reading porn.

The North American TV series, *Firefly* (2002-03), a favourite with sci-fi and fantasy fans, which led to a movie, *Serenity* (2005), seems to have quite a bit in

21 One can imagine the filmmakers enjoying an alternative soundtrack comprised entirely of Rolling Stones songs.

common with *Cowboy Bebop*. Generous fans reckoned that *Cowboy Bebop* and *Firefly* were simply drawing on the same popular culture pool; less generous fans thought that *Firefly* had ripped off *Cowboy Bebop*. Some of the similarities are incredibly close (the *Firefly* spaceship, for instance, is amazingly similar in numerous details to the *Bebop* spacecraft, including the general layout).

And yet, despite drawing on all of those influences, and often referencing them in very visible ways, *Cowboy Bebop* managed to create something new and satisfying, the opposite of a fragmented, awkward, postmodern hodge-podge. And *Cowboy Bebop* has undoubtedly influenced subsequent shows and artists (with all of those allusions and references, *Cowboy Bebop* is bound to be a favourite with film-makers), including *Getbackers* (2002), *Space Travelers* (2000), *Coyote Ragtime Show* (2007), *Cinderella Boy* (2003), and *Gad Guard* (2003), which has a jazzy score by *Gunbuster*'s Kohei Tanaka.

THEMES

So, anyway, what are the themes in *Cowboy Bebop*? Or is it too hi-falutin', too ponderous/ pompous to talk about grandiose topics such as themes in this Pop Art, pop culture TV series that seems designed by the filmmakers purely as entertainment? Isn't *Cowboy Bebop* all about going along for the ride, and having a good time?

Oh yeah. Sure! An' it's a very fine ride, too!
But there are quite definitely themes in *Cowboy*

Bebop. One of the most obvious, which the filmmakers and the writers build whole episodes out of, is the past, how the present relates to the past, how people are formed by their past, and how they can escape (the negative aspects of) their past.

Are you what you *were*, or are you what you *are* now? Are you the sum of your experiences, or can you just *be*, just *be* in the present moment? If you did bad things in the past (as Spike Spiegel and Faye Valentine have done), does that mean you will always be a bad person? Does the past define your personality forever?

These are some of the questions that the *Cowboy Bebop* series raises. The theme of the past and time is raised most particularly in the sessions which feature the Red Dragon crime syndicate and Vicious, which relate to Spike Spiegel's past, and in the sessions which explore Faye Valentine's past. Faye, after all, is a time traveller, someone who was frozen and brought back to life decades later (like Woody Allen in 1973's *Sleeper*). Faye is an ultimate kind of displaced person, someone literally out of her time, an outsider desperately trying to fit in (that she's a woman, and on her own, makes it even more poignant).

Both Spike Spiegel and Faye Valentine are haunted by their pasts, to the point where they can't move forward much anymore, unless they face the past. For Spike, it means dealing with an unresolved love affair (with blonde *femme fatale* Julia), with a former partner-in-crime who's turned against him (Vicious), and with the crime syndicate (Red Dragon), his former employers, who won't let sleeping dogs lie. For Faye, it means trying to make

sense of being alive decades in the future (as well as
amnesia). [22]

ACTION

There's no doubt that a key feature of the success of
Cowboy Bebop is its fantastic action. Like the
filmmakers of *Akira* or the *Legend of the Overfiend*
movies or *Ghost In the Shell* or other classic exponents
of Japanese *animé*, the Sunrise team are geniuses when
it comes to staging chases, or battles between flying
machines, or gun fights in enclosed spaces. It's not a
question of being 'free' in animation to draw anything, or being able to do things you can't do in live-
action, it's a question of imagination (and staging,
and timing, and research, etc).

The hand-to-hand fights in *Cowboy Bebop*
typically involve fists – of course – but only as one
ingredient in fights which draw mainly on martial
arts and *kung fu* (with plenty of kickboxing, too). The
filmmaking team have clearly seen every single
martial arts movie to come out of Hong Kong: Jet Li,
Jackie Chan, Yuen Woo-ping, Donnie Yuen, Bruce Lee,
Tsui Hark, etc, they're all in there.

For the gun fights, the team at Sunrise/ Bandai
draw on all the usual suspects: Sam Peckinpah, Sam
Fuller, John Woo, Takeshi Kitano, and *yazuka* genre
movies, etc. The Mexican stand-off, popularized most
memorably by Woo, is used a few times (*animé* shows
are very fond of Mexican stand-offs in which the

22 There are two love triangles in *Cowboy Bebop*: Spike-Faye-Julia
and Spike-Julia-Vicious, though the second one pales into
insignificance besides Spike and the two women.

guns're pointed right at the heads, face-to-face, another Woo motif).

It's Spike Spiegel who's the primary fighter in the *Bebop* crew – if anybody's going to go up against the villains physically, it's usually Spike. And often he's out-matched, and often he gets beaten up (scenes where Spike's recovering on the couch in the *Bebop* spaceship all bandaged-up are recurring gags).

For the fight scenes (and all of the action scenes, really), the Sunrise/ Bandai team are quite happy to use many clichés; they can do that partly because *Cowboy Bebop* is so off-the-wall anyway, despite every single element being very, very familiar. The *zing* of *Cowboy Bebop*'s success is its *mix*, the way it *combines* all of those familiar elements.

HUMOUR

Cowboy Bebop is a show where comedy is not only a vital ingredient, but often *the most important*. Gilles Poitras uses the term 'Shakespearean quality' to refer to the way that Japanese animation (and *manga*) will include broad comedy in the midst of serious drama. It seems to jar with Western audiences, who expect the serious tone to be maintained throughout. Poitras refers to William Shakespeare's tragedies which had light-hearted moments (2001, 55).

An example is the Tachikoma robots in the TV series of *Ghost In the Shell* (and in Masamune Shirow's *manga*): they horse around like children, introducing some silly and lighter moments in what is usually regarded as a 'serious' or 'intense' cyber-thriller. In *Cowboy Bebop*, some broad comedy with Radical Ed will be introduced into an otherwise serious or straight scene.

One aspect of *Cowboy Bebop* is very Western or American, and that's the parody, the spoof, the satire ingredients: *Cowboy Bebop* is self-conscious and post-modern, cleverly allusive of other movies and TV shows and 1,000s of elements in popular culture.[23] Dressing up is a recurring motif in the *Cowboy Bebop* TV show: Jet Black dressed as a hippy, or a gambling high roller, or, during a mushroom trip, smearing his faced with lipstick. There's often no explanation given – instead, the writers simply introduce the characters in disguise.

Weightlessness provides a number of gags in *Cowboy Bebop* – there are many, many scenes where characters and detritus are floating slowly about. Sometimes characters (Spike Spiegel) dive into space without spacesuits. Ed likes to float along the connect-ing corridors on the *Bebop* spaceship holding onto Jet. Ein the dog tries to run in zero gravity.

In one hilarious scene (in the episode *Bohemian Rhapsody*), Spike Spiegel and Faye Valentine encounter all manner of floating things in a space-craft: it's a running gag: first plants (and vegetables), then pets (dogs and cats), then cannabis plants, then sleeping space pirates and rednecks, and finally stoned hippies smoking pot in a giant spaced-out version of San Francisco or the Middle-earth or UFO clubs in London *circa* 1968. *Cool, maaan!*

---

23 Contemporary animated movies are stuffed with those allusions and pop culture references: *Finding Nemo, Chicken Little, Cars, Ice Age,* and, most notoriously, the *Shrek* series.

COWBOY BEBOP: FILMMAKING AS PURE BLISS

The impression you immediately get with *Cowboy Bebop* is that the filmmaking team understand completely the genres, motifs and clichés they are employing, and that they *love* those genres and clichés, and they really know how to use them in new and imaginative ways. There's a flash of recognition – 'oh, they're going to do *that*' – then absolute delight as you see the filmmakers spinning the cliché around, mixing it with new ingredients, and re-presenting it in a new way.

You can only do that if you understand the many forms of cinema and animation, and know how to twist and mould the existing material into something new. You need not only a lot of skill and imagination (and hard work), you need loads of confidence. Or put it like this: a TV show like *Cowboy Bebop* could not have been produced by amateurs or fans or first-time filmmakers (even though the filmmakers are also clearly major *otaku*). At the same time, *Cowboy Bebop* is not the work of jaded, weary veterans who're churning out pages or cels like robots, clocking on, doing their shift, then sloping off to the bar.

Or put it like this: the *joy* of filmmaking, and the *delight* in what cinema is and what it can do, is instantly apparent in *Cowboy Bebop*. The filmmakers seem to be enjoying themselves (the characters are – usually!), and that exhilaration rubs off on the audience. It's an aspect of cinema that film critics don't often comment upon, but I think that taking pleasure in the craft and art of movie-making can be an important ingredient in cinema (or in any art). In animation, you can certainly see Jan Svankmajer,

Hayao Miyazaki, Katsuhiro Otomo and Walerian Borowczyk enjoying themselves. In live-action, Orson Welles and the Marx Brothers are having a ball: *Citizen Kane* and *The Magnificent Ambersons*, despite their serious drama leanings, are the product of a young film director inspiring his team to come up with extraordinary cinema (there's no question that the bunch of filmmakers and actors Welles gathered around himself in 1940-1942 was dead keen on going all the way, on doing whatever it took to deliver amazing cinema).

SEXUAL POLITICS

Cowboy Bebop includes more references to homo-sexuality and more gay characters than probably any comparable *animé* series or TV show. Altho' the four characters in the *Bebop* crew aren't gay, many secondary and minor characters are (including Gren, V.T., V.T.'s husband, male prostitutes, and many extras). Undoubtedly homoerotic undercurrents flow in the uneasy relationship Spike has with former buddy now rival mobster Vicious; and the *yakuzas* and brotherhoods in *Cowboy Bebop* also have homoerotic undertones (as they do in the crime and gangster genres in general). Although admittedly there are many clichés and stereotypes involved in the representations of gay culture and characters, *Cowboy Bebop* doesn't stoop to cheap jokes or crudity (the crudity and gags are saved for other targets).

Asian cinema has a more relaxed attitude to alternative gender roles – transvestism, for instance, has a long tradition in Japan, as Helen McCarthy pointed out (1993, 49). *Animé* shows which feature transvestites, apart from *Cowboy Bebop*, include *Mospeada, Tokyo Godfathers, 3 x 3 Eyes, Ghost In the Shell* and *Joker Marginal City*. In Hong Kong cinema, as in *animé*, female voices are sometimes employed for the villains, and gender-bending is quite common in characters (and women often voice male heroes, such as Romi Pak and Rie Kugimiya who produce the remarkable voices of the Elric brothers in *Fullmetal Alchemist*).

In Japanese animation and *manga*, there are elements of *yaoi/ shonen ai* in the Gren-Vicious and Vicious-Spike relationships (*yaoi* are emotional stories between men with women as onlookers), and also *shonen ai* (love between boys, usually aimed at a female audience).[24] Gren in particular, and Vicious to a degree, is given a *bishonen* look (the beautiful, young boy of *animé*).

The sexual politics of *Cowboy Bebop* is still patriarchal, though, reflecting Japanese society as a whole. Japan is still a patriarchal society: women earn 66% of what men earn (compared to 76% in the U.S.A., and 83% in Britain), and only 9% of seats in the government (in the Diet).

And in the world of the *yakuza* (which *Cowboy Beblop* explores), patriarchy rules OK – the regimes are based on feudal models from Japan's past. In *yakuza* cinema, women tend to be hookers, porn stars, housewives, mistresses and occasionally a card

24 *Yaoi animé* and *manga* is about boys in love (also known as *ju-ne mono*); the romantic female equivalent is *yuri*. (*Yaoi* comes from the *yama-nashi, ochi-nashi, imi-nashi*, which means 'no climax, no punch-line, no meaning'). Gay *manga* aimed at women is called *shonen ai* or *yaoi*. It typically involves pretty boys (*bishonen*). The unspoken love embodied in the soldierly brotherhood of Gren and Vicious in the war scenario is a classic *yaoi/ shonen ai* set-up.

dealer.

Talking about sex, it's totally typical of the eccentricity of the writers and filmmakers at Sunrise/ Bandai that the only kiss f significance in *Cowboy Bebop* should be between Faye Valentine and Radical Ed, two women! Not, as one might expect, between the potential couple of *Cowboy Bebop*, Faye and Spike Spiegel. And it's not a typical ♥ scene, either: in *Hard Luck Woman*, Faye grabs Edo's cheeks and plants a kiss on her mouth – partly out of frustration, because she's been trying to find out where the home video of her childhood was filmed (she's on a quest to find her childhood self, to revisit the past, and to remember it all).[25]

25 The kiss was maybe debated at length in the production offices at Sunrise/ Bandai. But if you have to ask why, you'll never get it!

Illustrations

Images of some inspirations and influences on the show.

Hard-Boiled with Chow Yun-Fat (above).
Once Upon a Time In China 2 with Jet Li (below).

Alien

Robocop

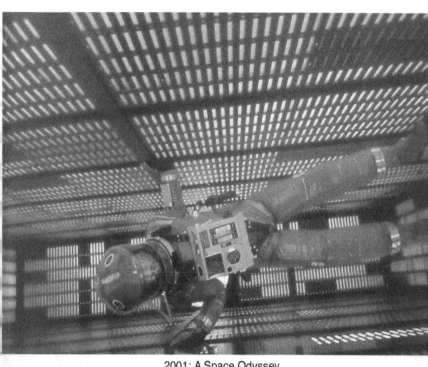
2001: A Space Odyssey

Blade Runner

James Bond movies
of the 1960s

Star Wars

A Clockwork Orange (1971)

The Big Sleep (above). Touch of Evil (below).

Alice's Adventures In Wonderland

Disney movies and Disneyland are more inspirations on Cowboy Bebop (and are of course enormous influences on Japanese pop culture).

The Rolling Stones in Hyde Park, 1969 (above).
And still going strong: on the 50 years tour (below).

The great city of animé: Tokyo, where nearly all animé is made, and much of it is set.

Cowboy Bebop draws heavily on Gotham (Photos: author)

Another inspiration for Cowboy Bebop – the American West.
California (above). Near the San Antonio Mountains, New Mexico (below)
(Photos: author)

Costume play at Anime Expo, 2011 (above)
At Anime Expo, 2009 (below. Photo: Eurobeat King).

COWBOYBEBOP

05

'SEE YOU SPACE COWBOY!'
THE 26 EPISODES OF
COWBOY BEBOP

COWBOY BEBOP EPISODES

Episode 1. *Asteroid Blues*
Episode 2. *Stray Dog Strut*
Episode 3. *Honky Tonk Women*
Episode 4. *Gateway Shuffle*
Episode 5. *Ballad of Fallen Angels*
Episode 6. *Sympathy For the Devil*
Episode 7. *Heavy Metal Queen*
Episode 8. *Waltz For Venus*
Episode 9. *Jamming With Edward*
Episode 10. *Ganymede Elegy*
Episode 11. *Toys In the Attic*
Episodes 12 and 13. *Jupiter Jazz*
Episode 14. *Bohemian Rhapsody*

Episode 15. *My Funny Valentine*

Episode 16. *Black Dog Serenade*

Episode 17. *Mushroom Samba*

Episode 18. *Speak Like a Child*

Episode 19. *Wild Horses*

Episode 20. *Pierrot le Fou*

Episode 21. *Boogie Woogie Feng Shui*

Episode 22. *Cowboy Funk*

Episode 23. *Brain Scratch*

Episode 24. *Hard Luck Woman*

Episodes 25 and 26. *The Real Folk Blues*

The Spike Spiegel episodes run from crazy (*Cowboy Funk*) to serious (*Jupiter Jazz*). The Jet Black episodes tend to be sober and delve into the past (*Ganymede Elegy* and *Black Dog Serenade*). The Faye Valentine episodes are quests for identity and the past (such as *Honky Tonk Women* and *My Funny Valentine*).

Some *Cowboy Bebop* episodes are purely comedy, such as *Toys In the Attic*, *Speak Like a Child* (most of it), and *Mushroom Samba*. *Pierrot le Fou*, meanwhile, is half and half insane and sombre.

Some of the episodes in *Cowboy Bebop* centre on one of the main four characters. Often these episodes explore the characters' pasts. For example:

SPIKE SPIEGEL

Episode 5. *Ballad of Fallen Angels*

Episodes 12 and 13. *Jupiter Jazz*

Episodes 25 and 26. *The Real Folk Blues*

JET BLACK

Episode 10. *Ganymede Elegy*

Episode 16. *Black Dog Serenade*

Episode 21. *Boogie Woogie Feng Shui*

FAYE VALENTINE

Episode 3. *Honky Tonk Women*

Episode 15. *My Funny Valentine*

Episode 18. *Speak Like a Child*

Episode 24. *Hard Luck Woman*

RADICAL ED

Episode 9. *Jamming With Edward*

Episode 17. *Mushroom Samba*

Episode 24. *Hard Luck Woman*

However, in most episodes all four main characters appear, and some episodes that centre on one character – such as *Mushroom Samba*, where Radical Ed gets to have an adventure on her own – also feature the others. And Spike Spiegel, being the central character in *Cowboy Bebop*, appears most often. You could watch the Faye Valentine episodes or the Jet Black episodes one after another, and they would work as a continuous story. However, the five Spike Spiegel episodes portraying his rivalry with Vicious and his time in the crime syndicate were crafted consciously as an on-going narrative: episode 5, *Ballad of Fallen Angels,* episodes 12 and 13, *Jupiter Jazz* and episodes 25 and 26, *The Real Folk Blues*.

Episode 1. *Asteroid Blues*

> *I think it's time to blow this thing and get
> everybody and the stuff together. OK, three –
> two – one – let's jam!*

Episode one of the *Cowboy Bebop* series (written by
chief writer on the show, Keiko Nobumoto), opens
with an enigmatic pre-titles sequence[1] involving Spike
Spiegel's nefarious past and his involvement in
organized crime.[2] Then comes the famous credits
sequence, a *tour-de-force* of animation, design and
music by Yoko Kanno and the Seatbelts. And then the
episode starts with introductions of Jet Black
(Unshou Ishizuka) and Spike (Kôichi Yamadera) over
dinner.

There is a very lengthy shot that tilts upwards,
up and up, revealing the deep space setting of *Cowboy
Bebop*: spaceships fly through hyperspace gateways
(the equivalent of air travel on Earth), there are
asteroids, stars, distant planets (with Mars
prominent), huge space stations, all the usual
attributes of a space opera show (and with conscious
nods to *2001: A Space Odyssey* – the first of many in
Cowboy Bebop – an influence of pretty every *animé* set
in space).

The shot is reprised a number of times – at the
opening and close of the *Jupiter Jazz* sessions, for
instance. It replays a point-of-view shot of someone
craning their head back and back, up and up. There
are many scenes where characters look up at the sky,
or lie on their backs looking up (as Spike Spiegel does
in this show). When Spike's shot by Lin in the middle

---

1 Staged in near black-and-white.
2 Some of the plot and characterizations in *Asteroid Blues* cropped up
in the *Cowboy Bebop* movie.

episodes, there's a p.o.v. shot tilting up, as Spike falls backwards.

But when *Cowboy Bebop* travels down with Spike Spiegel to the surface of the asteroid New Tijuana, it ain't futuristic at all: it's a city 🏙 instantly familiar from anywhere in the real, developed world. It's scuzzy, it's stuffed with cars, roads, apartments, signs and graffiti; it's place of gas stations (where you fill up your spaceship[3] just like a car),[4] of seedy bars, of old coots playing poker, of dodgy drug deals, and of petty criminals.[5]

Asteroid Blues is not set on Mars, which is the centre of the *Cowboy Bebop* universe (*Cowboy Bebop* goes to Mars most often, with the devastated Earth second), but on an asteroid, called New Tijuana, a reference to the famous border town between California and Mexico, for some folk a fun day trip from the U.S.A., for others a sleazy town to be avoided (Tijuana was the setting for perhaps the finest *film noir*, and one of the last of the classic *film noirs*, *Touch of Evil*).[6]

The world of *Cowboy Bebop* is utterly convincing: down-at-heel, lived-in, grungey, graffitied, and dirty. It has glamour and luxury (there're casinos, fr'instance, and sleek spaceships, and hyperspace travel via gateways), but most of the time the settings're instantly recognizable slices of the real world, cut and pasted, mixed together by a team of

---

3 Spike pumps his own gas – he would! – 'cos it would save the tip!
4 It's also amusing how the filmmakers make spaceships as regular and everyday as cars – the car lots feature large parking spots for spacecraft, including the car lots that stack spaceships on risers.
5 One of the early establishing shots of New Tijuana depicts a guy chasing a thief on the street.
6 However, *Touch of Evil* was shot mainly in California, in Venice, South of Santa Monica. As Charlton Heston put it, Venice 'looked marvelous, better than anything we could have found on the border, and logistically, far easier' (1995, 155).

virtuoso designers (led by Toshihiro Kawamoto and Kimitoshi Yamano). *Cowboy Bebop* definitely has one of the most appealing and finely crafted alternative worlds in Japanese *animé* (the cinema of Hayao Miyazaki I would put at the top of a list of world-builders, in any cinema anywhere).

Asteroid Blues introduces many motifs which recur throughout the 1998 TV series: hunger and food; money; crime; computers and cyberspace; big cities; the past; dressing up; sex; death; multi-culturalism; movie references; and popular culture allusions.

The filmmakers have given themselves a single credo: to be *cool*: anything wot ain't cool is jettisoned. The stories're cool, the characters're cool, the action is cool, the gadgets're cool, the *mecha* is cool, the costumes are cool, the hair is cool, the dialogue is cool, the music is cool, the vfx are cool, the camera-work is cool, the editing is cool, the sound design is cool, the voice cast is cool, the performances are cool, and the themes are cool.

Our first introduction to Spike Spiegel is in the pre-credits sequence, a classy show in black-and-white (and blue-and-white) featuring Spike strolling super-cool thru an Old World city like Prague or Vienna, carrying a bunch of flowers (is he meeting a girl? visiting a cemetery? – in *Cowboy Bebop*, love and death are intimately intertwined).[7] Only in later episodes is this mysterious prologue explained. As a fallen rose in the rain turns from black-and-white to colour (perhaps an allusion to *The Wizard of Oz* [1939], or to *Stairway To Heaven* a.k.a. *A Matter of Life*

---

7 In Japanese culture, there is a beauty in death – the *mono no aware* tradition in literature and drama (beauty in death and impermanence). *Cowboy Bebop* certainly draws on that tradition.

and Death [1945]),[8] there are flash cuts of gun battles and *film noir* images (relating to Spike's time in the Red Dragon crime syndicate, we later learn. Notice that Vicious, a principal participant in the crime syndicate flashbacks, is absent, as is Julia. The church setting is also explained later, in ep five).

On the *Bebop* spaceship, Spike Spiegel is introduced with an extended *hommage* to Bruce Lee and *Enter the Dragon* (there are plenty of other references to the king of *kung fu* in later episodes, including billboards of the 1973 Hong Kong movie[9] – one of which is prominent above the spaceship on Mars), as Spike practises some *kung fu* and kick boxing moves, in deep blue colours.

In the first episode, *Asteroid Blues*, as Spike Spiegel and Jet Black trail the drug pusher Asimov Solenson (Rintarou Nishi) and his wife/ lover Katrina (Yurika Hino), hoping to collect the 2.5m Woolong (= $250,000) bounty on his head, the evocation of the city, the bars, the gas stations, the grubby streets and the chases all pay tribute to classic North American movies of the 1970s. The chase at the end, for instance, when Asimov and Katrina end up hurtling into space only to be confronted by a road block posse of police spaceships, might be the ending of *The Sugarland Express, Convoy* or a Burt Reynolds picture. In the finale, the bad guys expire in a hail of bullets, right? Which's what happens to the Bonnie and Clyde characters in *Asteroid Blues*. (The animation of the chase draws heavily on the work of

---

8 *Stairway To Heaven* dissolves between colour and black-and-white on a close-up of a flower. Maurice Goring's angelic messenger, for example, in an aside to camera when he visits Earth, which's in colour (while heaven's in b/w), says, 'One is starved for Technicolor up there'.
9 And a reference to *Gamer of Death* in the next episode.

Hayao Miyazaki, as well as *Macross Plus*, which some of th*Cowbow Bebop* team worked on).

Asteroid Blues introduces Spike Spiegel as an all-round, cool hero: a terrific fighter (with fists, martial arts and guns), an amazing pilot, a wily thief, a smooth talker, a master of disguises, a bounty hunter with a nefarious past (glimpsed in the prologue), and with an eye for women. Notice, for instance, as Spike's being strangled by Asimov Solenson at the gas station and nearly expiring, he manages to lift the Bloody Eye capsule from Asimov's jacket (a recurring Spike gag – in the midst of danger, Spike is still thinking ahead). We also see of some Spike's other attributes: he can juggle cigarettes (and capsules), has nimble fingers, is a crackshot (he can shoot a tiny capulse with a gun when it's hurled into the air), loves his food, and he's very independent. Spike's guiding philosophy is simple: 'whatever happens, happens'.

♫

Asteroid Blues opens with one of the key themes of the *Cowboy Bebop* series: hunger and food. Part-cyborg (well, he's augmented with *mecha*), ex-cop Jet Black is the resident chef on the spaceship, but here he cooks up a dinner that's supposed to have beef in it but doesn't, much to Spike Spiegel's disappointment. It's this, perhaps, that persuades Spike to go after the drug pusher bounty in New Tijuana, because, as Jet tells him, you can get good beef noodles on the asteroid. The episode closes with a mirror of the opening scene, as Jet cooks the same grub, but now with beef, and Spike is again doing some martial arts exercises (tho' now also looking out of the window and musing upon the events on the asteroid, including the tragic death of Katrina, a woman that Spike might've teamed up with).

Asteroid Blues also introduces a recurring motif in the series: dressing up: Spike Spiegel appears in a giant sombrero and poncho[10] when he meets Asimov Solenson on a bench at a café (like a dumb tourist who's visited the real Tijuana for the first time). Yet another motif is the Native American shaman, Bull (a.k.a Laughing Bull, played by Takehiro Koyama), whom Spike visits as part of the crime genre convention of the detective scouting for information (introducing a Native American does seem kinda out-there, but this is a show called *Cowboy Bebop*).[11] The shaman offers mysterious but also doomy prognostications (it can't be anything else, can it, if you're a grizzled, old witch doctor?).

The Native American guy Bull is one of a number of recurring characters – the three old coots and gamblers were others: Antonio (Jinsho Hirao), Carlos (Toshihiko Nakajima) and Jobim (Hiroshi Naka), who spend the show bragging about things they haven't really done. Bull was revived for the 2001 *Cowboy Bebop* movie (and the theme of death, and coming back from the dead, is central to both scenes: in the movie, the shaman helps to bring Spike back to life following his run-in with the villain, Vincent; in *Asteroid Blues*, the shaman tells Spike that death lies ahead. Spike's retort is classic Spike: 'oh, again'. Again? wonders the shaman. Yes – because Spike has already died once (one of the indications of Spike's murky past which will be examined in later episodes;

---

10 The filmmakers seem to think that all Mexicans wear ponchos and sombreros! And that they all act like extras in a TV show from the 60s or 70s. *Si, amigo!*
11 Katrina says to Spike, 'adios, Cowboy'.

a woman was involved).

Pop culture allusions: the sheer number of cinematic references in the first 23 minute episode of *Cowboy Bebop* is striking: *Enter the Dragon, Natural Born Killers, Stairway To Heaven, Taxi Driver, The Killing, 2001: A Space Odyssey, Touch of Evil, Desperado*,[12] and numerous American movies of the 1970s (and probably many more).

Sex: *Cowboy Bebop* introduces a very sexy gangster's moll, Katrina, to Asimov Solenson's drug pusher (this's before the introduction of Faye Valentine in episode three, *Honky Tonk Women*). There's an (inevitable) unspoken flirtation between Katrina and Spike Spiegel. A dark, sultry woman, Katrina is eroticized in the customary *animé* manner: she has big boobs (there's a giant close-up of Katrina's bazongas in the bar looking like giant asteroids while the three old coots in the background ogle them). There's also a grotesque parody of pregnancy and motherhood, with Katrina keeping the little phials of drugs in a pouch on her belly (which, true to form in the crime genre, falls open, and the drugs go everywhere, like the scene in *The Killing* (1956), when the heist loot's blown all over the airfield).

Katrina just wants to settle down on Mars – *Asteroid Blues* is set on an asteroid, New Tijuana (Katrina idealizes Mars, like someone in the sticks in Iowa dreaming of New York City or Paris as a potential paradise).[13] Unfortunately, she's fallen in ♥

12 As well as 100s of American movies of the 1970s, *Desperado* (1995) is a reference in *Asteroid Blues*, with the two criminals alluding to the mariachi (Antonio Banderas) and Carolina (Salma Hayek). However, despite its starry cast of Quentin Tarantino-era actors, desperate-to-be-cool *Desperado* ain't a patch on *Cowboy Bebop*.
13 Mars must be great, Katrina wonders to Spike (he says he was born there).

with the Wrong Guy. Inevitably, Katrina spends some of the episode trying to persuade Asimov to go straight, to give up the life of crime (you can bet she's tried this argument many times!).

♪

The stand-out sequence in *Asteroid Blues* is the shoot-out that climaxes the first half. It's long, intricate and very violent, and includes plenty of blood.[14] The drug that Asimov Solenson is peddling is called Red Eye or Bloody Eye: it's a slither of red liquid in a capsule filled with purple liquid which's placed over the naked eyeball and squirted into it.[15] It turns Asimov into a crazed killer (with giant, bloodshot eyes): the *animé* makes much of handheld, point-of-view shots with a red filter over the lens[16] (subjective images of this kind crop up many times in the *Cowboy Bebop* series, and were also used in the 2001 movie). There are also bullet-view shots, and images which directly reference *Natural Born Killers* (1994), in particular the OTT, roadside diner shoot-out. (One of the curious effects of the Bloody Eye drug is that people can shoot repeatedly at the user, but the user – Asimov here – is able to dodge them, as if they're in another world).[17] Meanwhile, the action scene in the street nearby, where Spike trounces a bunch of hoods, is a wild *Lupin III* parody.

Asteroid Blues has a grisly ending: the wanted felons are speeding away in a hijacked spaceship, trying to elude Spike Spiegel, who's hot on their tail

---

14 The bloodshed and graphic violence in Japanese *manga* are part of a cultural tradition (such as in kabuki theatre) which goes back 100s of years.
15 Inserting a drug into an eyeball offers postmodern theorists, college students and psychoanalysts plenty to discuss in terms of voyeurism, the gaze, scopophilia, and eye violence.
16 This might be a reference to *Taxi Driver.*
17 The concept was reprised in the *Pierrot le Fou* episode.

(it's a long chase, one of the staples of the crime genre, and a staple of *Cowboy Bebop*). Asimov Solenson is taking more of the Bloody Eye drug, to the point where he's barely able to pilot the vehicle, and is degenerating into a snarling monster. Katrina is trying to make him stop, to turn themselves in. Of course Asimov doesn't. The cops are waiting ahead, lights flashing on their spaceships: there's no escape. We don't see it but we know what happens: Katrina shoots Asimov and kills him – it's the only way to stop him. As Spike flies past the spaceship in a high drama moment, we see Katrina cradling her dead lover in her arms, seconds before the cockpit is shot to pieces by the cops (good job the cops're great shots – Spike is flying right next to the hoods!).

Yes – here is a scene where a woman kills a man, her lover – it's pretty extreme. And it's also a kinda suicide, as if Katrina would rather end it herself than turn herself in. Or maybe there isn't time between shooting Asimov and stopping the spaceship to surrender themselves over to the authorities.

The wastefulness of the twin deaths at the end of *Asteroid Blues* is striking – Katrina, at least, deserved better than this. The image of Katrina's dress spilling open and releasing the capsules of drugs as she floats in space, dead, is heavily ironic, a cruel parody of the children she might've enjoyed had Asimov relented and given up.

Cowboy Bebop thus announces its intention to mix comedy with violence, laughs and guns, a mix which makes broadcasters (and all of the media watchdogs that broadcasters liaise with) very uneasy. It's no wonder, then, seeing this first episode, that this and other parts of *Cowboy Bebop* were not broadcast. The aim is to be hard-hitting (to open with a bang, so to speak), to deliver what is basically a crime show, which also means including some brutal violence, but also with a mix of elements you've never seen before.

There has been never a TV show like *Cowboy Bebop* before – or since.

Episode 2. *Stray Dog Strut*

In the second episode of 1998's *Cowboy Bebop* (*Stray Dog Strut*),[18] written by Michiko Yokote (the series' 2nd chief writer – actually three writers), set on Mars, the bad guy is a tall (*very* tall!), gangly black guy with an Afro who's stepped right out of 1970s blaxploitation movies.[19] Abdul Hakim (Ryûzaburô Ôtomo) has snitched a super-dog (yes, a dog!)[20] from a dodgy, experimental scientific group (who are desperately seeking it),[21] and the episode revisits numerous old chestnuts of thrillers and cop shows, including switches, betrayals and reversals, mistaken identity, cool cars, gadgets, and of course chases and gun fights.

Stray Dog Strut is set on Mars, where much of the episodes in the *Cowboy Bebop* series take place (long shots cover the *Bebop*'s arrival on Mars, including its ability to land on water like a pirate galleon. These images will recur throughout the TV series, and some shots will be re-cycled as they are in the usual manner of cutting corners in TV animation, while others will be re-cycled with different backgrounds added).

The filmmakers exploit the Amsterdam-ish canal

18 The title *Stray Dog Strut* might allude to the Stray Cats' song 'Stray Cat Strut', though *Stray Dog* is a concept found in Japanese culture (it's related to the *ronin*, for instance, the wandering, loner samurai).
19 NBA player Kareem Abdul-Jabbar (one of the pilots in *Airplane*) was an inspiration for Abdul Hakim's look – in particular Abdul-Jabbar's appearance in *Game of Death* (1978). Black guys with Afro haircuts have cropped up elsewhere in *animé*, including the 2006 show *Afro Samurai*, with its hip-hop soundtrack. Needles to say, another character drawing on the same pop cultural pool in a sci-fi movie released a year later, *Star Wars: The Phantom Menace*, became one of the most hated charas in recent cinema.
20 Why is a dog a super-computer? It's not entirely made clear – tho' it's a classic concept in Japanese animation.
21 They drive around in a hi-tech RV kitted out with gadgets and weaponry, right out of a Sixties caper movie.

region of Mars in *Stray Dog Strut* with a chase reminiscent of *The French Connection,* along both sides of the canal (and both Spike[22] and bad guy Abdul fall into the water, of course, after fighting on a bridge – yet another refernece to *Game of Death,* Bruce Lee's last movie). That is, to counter the shoot-'em-ups and tragic ending of the first episode, *Asteroid Blues*, the action in *Stray Dog Strut* is played entirely for comedy (appropriate when the MacGuffin is a cute dawg). No one gets killed, and no one is even seriously injured: after the car crash of the criminals, where they land right in front of the police HQ from a *very* high freeway over-pass, they all survive.

Dogs! – cartoon dogs! – yep, *Stray Dog Strut* is a Cartoon Dog Episode of *Cowboy Bebop*, with, in the climax, a pack of dogs chasing a truck right out of Hanna & Barbera or *101 Dalmatians* (animators absolutely love dogs – even more than mice or cats). Yeah, and there's even a pet store (*Animal Treasures*), run by a kooky old dame (who wears a turtle on her head – apparently that was director Shinichiro Watanabe's idea!).

♫

The second episode of *Cowboy Bebop* introduces the TV show-within-a-show, *Big Shot* (broadcast for the 300,000 bounty hunters in the Solar System – that's a *lot* of bounty hunters!), as a way of rapidly delivering exposition and information about the villains of each episode. *Big Shot* is hilarious: it's an OTT American-style info show decked out in sparkly, Las Vegas costumes of the Old American West (a

---

22 Spike Spiegel is most prominent in this episode, with Jet Black remaining on the *Bebop* ship.

black cowboy dude, Punch[23] (Tsutomu Tareki) – hints of *Blazing Saddles*, the Mel Brooks masterpiece – and a bubbly, blonde woman, Judy (Miki Nagasawa), in a cowboy vest that allows for plenty-a cleavage). *Big Shot* seems to be the only TV show the crew of *Cowboy Bebop* watch (apart from the news).[24]

Big Shot's so on-the-nail, it delivers exposition in such a crushingly obvious manner – yet, somehow, the writers of *Cowboy Bebop* (Keiko Nobumoto, Michiko Yokote *et al*) get away it. Perhaps because the show is so out-there and camp, and in-your-face, too (and, in later episodes, the presenters of *Big Shot* become part of the stories themselves – when their show, inevitably, is axed due to low viewing figures, one of many wry commentaries on television in *Cowboy Bebop*).

---

23 The characters are named after Punch and Judy, the British puppets, and also perhaps *ponchi-e*, the 'punch pictures' Japanese cartoons named after Punch and Judy, and Britain's *Punch* magazine.
24 The writers even squeeze in a scene towards the end of the 26 sessions when Punch, the black TV presenter of *Big Shot* (his real name is Alfredo) meets his mom at an airport (a minor subplot has *Big Shot* being cancelled due to poor ratings – a comment on TV, of course, and also on *Cowboy Bebop*, perhaps).

Episode 3. *Honky Tonk Women*

> I met a gin soaked, bar-room queen in
>   Memphis,
> She tried to take me upstairs for a ride.
> She had to heave me right across her shoulder
> 'Cause I just can't seem to drink you off my
>   mind.
>
> It's the honky tonk women,
> Gimme, gimme, gimme the honky tonk blues.
>
> The Rolling Stones, 'Honky Tonk Women'

FAYE VALENTINE IN THE CASINO.

Faye Valentine is introduced in *Cowboy Bebop* series in a casino – where else?! – and of course she's heavily in debt (just the fact of Faye appearing first in a casino – on her own, and in debt – tells us all we need to know about this good time girl). In episode 3, *Honky Tonk Women* (the title of a Rolling Stones' song, with our Mick at his sleaziest and funkiest), the world of gambling, mob bosses, petty criminals, and fugitives on the run is wittily and seemingly effort-lessly evoked. I say 'effortlessly' – but the effort that shows like *Cowboy Bebop* take is enormous. Each *Cowboy Bebop* show zips by as if animation isn't a labour-intensive, 16-hour-day, sleeping-under-the-desk job. But it is.

The world of casinos and gambling is brilliantly observed in *Honky Tonk Women* (which was written by Keiko Nobumoto and Ryota Yamaguchi): the *Cowboy Bebop* series is one of the great Las Vegas shows (*One From the Heart, Mars Attacks!* and *Showgirls*, among movies, would be others – yes, *Showgirls*!), even tho' it's not set in Vegas, but millions of miles away (actually the casino wheel-shaped spacecraft is floating above Mars). I especially like the atmosphere of the border town and the frontier zone in *Cowboy Bebop* (in this case, it's a casino complex shaped like a roulette wheel near one of the hyperspace gateways, where spaceships enter hyperspace thru giant hoops). Thus, *Honky Tonk Women* is not set in somewhere like Las Vegas, but in one of the cities on the border of Nevada (if you've driven from California into Nevada, you'll know what I mean: it's like the two halves of Lake Tahoe: the Californian side is modest, small-town America, but the Nevada goes nuts with casinos and signage).

Why is there so much gambling in *Cowboy Bebop*? Well, casinos and gambling fit the hard-boiled/ gangster world, of course, and gambling, tho' illegal, is huge in Japan. The *pachinko* industry (the ball-game arcades in every town) is bigger than the *manga* industry ($300 billion was spent on *pachinko* in 1994). There're also links to organized crime.

Jet Black dresses up in a white linen suit and hat to visit the casino: you might expect him to join a select group of high rollers at a private poker table in a select, roped-off corner of the casino. But no, he's on the main concourse with the other gamblers working the slot machines – just as people are doing *right now*, as you read this, and 24 hours a day, in Las Vegas.

In *Honky Tonk Women*, our first sight of Faye Valentine focusses erotically on her body, as she enters an old-fashioned (Chinese) herbal store: there're close-ups of her l-o-n-g legs, her cute ass, her neck an' hair, and her eyes. From the outset, she is depicted as a super-babe, *animé*-style: fab body, fab voice, fab quips, fab face, fab moves; she's ultra-cool. 'Course, within 20 seconds, she's yanked out a gun and is shooting out the front of the store at the guys come up pick her up (and of course she smokes, and times her cool action hero quips with spitting out the cigarette butt. In fact, quips are one of Faye's key characteristics: the writers love to give Faye the closing gag line in a scene).

Faye Valentine's been captured and taken to crime boss Gordon (Shinji Ogawa) in *Honky Tonk Women*, because of her debts (it takes a *lot* of hoods to bring her in, too: a whole group show up at the store to capture her, demonstrating how fearsome she is). With Faye handcuffed in the mob boss Gordon's office (note the open fire burning away in the background – in space!), the sexual undercurrent is bubbling away, but actually the most significant ingredient occurs in the dialogue. On first viewing you might miss it, but it involves the possibility that Faye is actually someone who's been frozen for many years who's come back to life, and is actually a famous gambler (Alice), from way back, who never lost. Only in later episodes of *Cowboy Bebop* is this explored in depth.

THE STORY.

The plot of *Honky Tonk Women* is pretty bonkers, but many of the plots of *Cowboy Bebop* are (tho' it never matters, because the storytelling is so ecstatically delivered). It centres around a classic Hitchcockian MacGuffin – a piece of super-software that can decode anything (or something like that), which's been smuggled out of some research facility (S.I.T., not M.I.T.), and hidden in a casino chip (oh, but whoever cares about the MacGuffin?!). The scheme of the fence guy slipping the chip to Faye at a blackjack table (where Faye is the slick dealer),[25] is very silly (but it's a staple of the crime genre that the villains' plans have to be dumb).

Forget the crime syndicate's kooky plans – because the mix-up between Spike Spiegel and the fence guy (who's also in a blue suit and tie, and does look a bit like him, tho' more dishevelled, and nowhere near as cool as Spike!), means that Spike can meet and flirt with Faye Valentine. Of course the plan goes wrong (Spike hangs onto the casino chip – after winning handsomely, then losing it on a last hand – Spike often scuppers the villains' plans without realizing it in *Cowboy Bebop*), and of course there's a big fight (with Spike taking on every security heavy in the casino. Jet Black, fresh from winning big time at the slots, sighs heavily when he sees Spike in yet another brawl).

All of this is fun, but much more unexpected is Faye Valentine's amazing escape: this is a girl who thinks ahead! – she activates her *Red Tail*[26] spaceship remotely ('show time!'), using her bracelet (with a voice print mechanism, of course!), and it zooms into the casino. The action is brilliantly executed, with the filmmakers making it look effortless as well as exciting and comic. And how the writers (Keiko Nobumoto, Michiko Yokote *et al*) find ways in which one character trumps or bests another in *Cowboy Bebop* is just marvellous – here they have Faye escaping, firing two missiles to blow an escape hole, and thinking she's got away clean, but then she looks up to find Spike and Jet hanging onto the outside of her vehicle (the writers cleverly elide just how Jet and Spike got Faye back to their spaceship after this:

25 Women in the *yakuza* genre are sometimes card dealers.
26 Of course Faye Valentine would have a spaceship called *Red Tail*!

instead, they cut straight to Faye handcuffed in the bathroom!).[27]

The writers of *Honky Tonk Women* – Keiko Nobumoto and Ryota Yamaguchi – enjoy themselves immensely with taking routine cop and crime show clichés and spinning them around, and adding their own twists and humour. Thus, the scene where the heroes and the villains meet to exchange the gold/ money/ diamonds/ drugs/ software is staged on the outer shell of the crime lord's spacecraft, between Spike Spiegel and a heavy, both in spacesuits (with the hull of a spaceship standing in now for the empty stretch of a dusty street in a cowboy movie). The customary betrayal and gunfight occurs, as expected, but with all sorts of twists (of course, Jet Black and Spike know Gordon's gonna double-cross 'em). For instance, Spike wins the deal, sending the henchman spinning away into the deep blackness, while Mr Big in the control room splutters 'kill them!' But Faye Valentine comes of nowhere, to coolly lift the suitcase o' money (with a remote arm).[28] In the midst of a hail of gunfire and missile trails, she flees (while Spike wisely speeds back to the *Bebop* ship). The timing, staging (and rapidity) of the space battle is just gorgeous, as is the poetic justice: because it's clever Faye, evading the missiles and sending out a cluster of decoys, who forces the rockets to turn around and explode upon the crime lord's ship (so she gets her revenge).

Among the many movie allusions in *Honky Tonk*

27 And there's a brief scene with the heavies, where boss Gordon shoots the hapless fence (partly to show how nasty the crooks are, and to justify their come-uppance in the finale).
28 Note how in a later episode (7: *Heavy Metal Queen*), Faye is uncomfortable using the remote claws pick up some explosives. But when it comes to a suitcase of money, she's fine!

Women is a very prominent one: on a giant screen in the casino an old black-and-white samurai flick plays, with our Spike silhouetted against it in the foreground. Oh, we know that Spike is a samurai figure (and a *ronin*), but just as significant is this evocation of a classic Japanese genre, and a slice of Japanese cinema history.[29]

FAYE VALENTINE.

Faye Valentine is introduced as a mass of contradictions: sexy and sassy but without a steady relationship (she can't find the right guy), she's cynical yet naïve and wistful, and she's always broke and always in debt (so on that score she fits in perfectly with the crew of the *Bebop*, who never seem to have any money, or if they do, not for long). Faye's what used to be called in old Hollywood movies of the 1930s and 1940s a 'good time girl': she's a survivor, she's been around, and she can handle herself.[30] She can punch out a guy, she's amazing with a gun, she can programme a spacecraft to perform very complex manœuvres, she has a video communicator built inside lipstick (so 1960s!), she can fly a spaceship in combat, and she can escape from handcuffs (all very useful skills!).

The filmmakers never lose an opportunity to eroticize Faye Valentine, with a large number of 'fan service' shower, bath and sun-bathing scenes. The *My Funny Valentine* episode unashamedly sexualizes Faye when the storyboard artist plumps for a close-up point-of-view shot of Faye lying down on an

---

29 I'm not sure which show or movie it is – there are thousands of possible candidates.
30 Guys who hit on Faye Valentine don't realize what they're getting into. When Spike goes to the shower to tell Faye she's gotta leave, all we hear is a gunshot.

operating table which emphasizes her bazongas, barely covered by a towel.

Faye Valentine is the equal of Spike Spiegel, and is of course the perfect mate for him: she's got the moves, the sassy talk, the genius with guns, fights and spaceships, the criminal background, the seen-it-all-before weariness, and the hunger to make good past mistakes. But the *Cowboy Bebop* series, though heavily romantic and lyrical, eschews ❤ lovey-dovey romance,[31] and uses the familiar old trope of two people who'd be great together but somehow don't get together.[32] Instead, they argue, or they're indifferent, or they're competitive. It's the romantic relationship out of 1930s screwball comedies, where couples – such as those played by actors like Cary Grant with Katy Hepburn (in *Bringing Up Baby*, 1938), or Clark Gable with Claudette Colbert (in *It Happened One Night*, 1934) – bicker throughout the movie, only to fall into each other's arms in the final reel. (Fr'instance, it would've be a cinch to put Spike and Faye together on their own, but the writers constantly avoid that, and have Spike and Jet Black meeting Faye together, and deciding what to do with her in a long conversation outside the john, and Faye tries out her spiel about being a gypsy).

By the end of episode three, *Honky Tonk Women*, Faye Valentine has been depicted shooting up the bad guys, delivering sassy quips, being handcuffed – twice! (and escaping),[33] being admired by guys (and

31 If you want to see Spike and Faye get freaky, there are *hentai anime* versions around, as well as erotic *manga*.
32 Helen McCarthy compares the Faye-Spike relationship to that of Fujiko and Lupin in one of *Cowboy Bebop*'s forerunners, *Lupin III* (2006, 135).
33 Faye Valentine is a girl who can escape from handcuffs – in a twist on the usual set-up, in *Gateway Shuffle*, she's left alone with Ein the dog, and the mutt ends up handcuffed to the railing.

groped),[34] playing the dealer at a blackjack table in a casino (of course, Faye's the kinda girl who'd be nifty with a deck o' cards!), and flying her spaceship thru a casino (!).

Faye Valentine takes a very jaded view of men and romantic relationships; she has the air of someone who's been unlucky in love, perhaps let down or jilted,[35] so has resolved not to get involved again. For instance, when she's at her most pin-up gorgeous, sunning her near-naked, oiled body, Faye declares: 'men are such romantic fools' (as Jet Black speeds away to look up a former girlfriend).

Faye Valentine knows her effect on men all too well. But she also can't help herself. It's kinda fun to see men acting like dorks when they're around her. But Faye also pities them: who'd want to be a man?! Not Faye! No $$$$ing way!

Faye Valentine's the most mature member of the *Bebop* crew, along with Jet Black. You feel she's been there, done that. She's just trying to survive (and outrun her creditors). And she takes a certain pride in her outlaw status: in *Honky Tonk Women*, she's pissed that the bounty on her is only 6 million Woolongs (= $600,000). It should be a lot more (her gambling debt is certainly more than that!).

But there's also a sweetness and naïveté to Faye Valentine which the *Cowboy Bebop* TV show explores in the flashbacks to her past life. We see the teenage girl doing cheers, for instance, in her cheerleader outfit, or appearing young and bashful with her mates in an amateur video recording. Truth is, Faye is also,

34 The crime lord feels up Faye's thigh, and pulls out a card (the ace o' hearts, a'course) from her underwear.
35 We find out one of the reasons why in the episode with the shyster lawyer, *My Funny Valentine*.

like Spike Spiegel, a drifter, not quite sure what she wants, or what she wants to do with her life (but food and money are uppermost on her list – notice how she cleans out the fridge before escaping from the *Bebop* ship – the boys are gonna love her for that! If anyone wolfs down food in secret, it's usually Faye! But how does she stay so slim?!).

Faye Valentine is also a gambler: there are memorable images of Faye at the races, betting on horses or dogs. So Faye's always in debt, and always on the run from somebody or other (usually people who can get quite nasty). In some respects, Faye is the familiar tomboy persona of *animé*, and also the girl next door persona (in the flashbacks), as well as the super-babe and action hero.

Most of all, Faye Valentine is an *appealing* character, with a skilful mix of characteristics. Interesting characteristics, in an intriguing mix. The *Cowboy Bebop animé* series is not meant to be 'deep' and 'meaningful' like Sophoclean or Shakespearean tragedy, but it does present characters who have more sides to them, and more depth, than your usual TV characters. Faye is far more satisfying, convincing and appealing than recent attempts at putting sassy, strong women into the action cinema genre, such as Karen Allen in the *Indiana Jones* series. North American movies tend to tick 7 out 10 boxes in creating powerful, independent female charas, but not all of them. Faye ticks every box – and some that weren't even on the list!

The appeal of Faye Valentine is very much in the way that the writers (Keiko Nobumoto, Michiko Yokote and all the others) have combined her character traits. While a typical character in a comedy-drama TV show might have two or three sides to their personality (at most), the *Bebop* team are richer than that.

For instance, the babe/ bimbo/ beauty aspects of Faye Valentine, which the *animé* introduced first (with close-ups on her cute body), are actually the least interesting. When you consider that Faye is an independent woman, with no relations (or relationships), making her way in the universe, her sex appeal is the last aspect to consider (altho' that super-babe body sure is easy on the eye!).

We should also mention the marvellous voice work of Megumi Hayashibara as Faye Valentine: the lines which're sometimes croaked or barked are great (reminiscent of the way Lauren Bacall spoke in her *film noir* appearances). The sudden eruptions of frustration or despair. And of course the so-weary, can't-be-bothered lines. Look at the dialogue – some of it's so simple, so straight, and listen to way that Hayashibara delivers the lines (aided by the amazing sound director, Katsuyoshi Kobayashi). Hayashibara adds a whole, new level to Faye Valentine and *Cowboy Bebop*.

Episode 4. *Gateway Shuffle*

Techno-thrillers such as *Twelve Monkeys* (1995) and *Outbreak* (1995), and religious cults such as the Sublime Truth cult, and ecological activists like Greenpeace are perhaps some of the inspirations for episode 4, *Gateway Shuffle* (written by Sadayuki Murai), in which our beloved misfit heroes get involved with a band of eco-terrorists called the Space Warriors. A gang of mother's boys,[36] led by their domineering, S/M-loving[37] Cruella de Vil of a smothering mother,[38] Twinkling Maria Murdoch (Maria Arita), the Space Warriors (who wear silly big fish masks – not the fish's face, but the whole body!) – plan to wreak havoc with a deadly virus[39] (the Space Warriors are fighting to preserve the Ganymedean sea-rat – there's a wonderful montage of news clips and news photos detailing their acts of protest, which directly evoke political groups such as Greenpeace, including familiar scenes of Greenpeace boats spooking whaling vessels). The Space Wariors have the self-righteousness, the 'holier-than thou' attitude of rights activists.

As well as techno-thrillers and eco-thrillers, among movies, there's also parts of *Planet of the Apes*

36 They also recall the pirate gang of boys led by the forbidding Dola in *Laputa: Castle In the Sky* (1986), an outstanding Hayao Miyazaki adventure. Space pirates crop up in *Coyote Ragtime Show* (2006).
37 Momma tortures her boys who disappoint her – by putting them in a cubicle beside other apes and feeding them the virus which makes them more ape-like. Bonkers, and *very* sick.
38 The design of the mother recalls Disney's Cruella de Vil (by Marc Davis), as well as other cartoon villains.
39 The effects of the virus are designed to reduce humans to the state of apes. It's quite mad, but also grotesque, when we see the effects of the virus on the hapless Harrison, one of momma's boys (named for Harrison Ford, perhaps?! Or sci-fi author Harry Harrison? (d. 2012).)

in *Gateway Shuffle* (if you're using apes in science fiction, you're always gonna refer to *Planet of the Apes*),[40] as well as (yet again), *2001: A Space Odyssey* (and the 1984 MGM sequel, *2010*, which also used Jupiter prominently).

Altho' the Space Warriors are partly played for laffs, they are also vicious, murderous terrorists: *Gateway Shuffle* opens with Spike Spiegel and Jet Black staking out a possible target in a restaurant (quite a bit of time is spent over Spike and Jet deciding what to eat – food yet again in *Cowboy Bebop*!). But things turn very ugly when the Space Warriors open fire and kill most of the diners, including many women (Jet and Spike take refuge under their table; their bounty, yet again, is slain (a guy surroudned by groupies) – presumably simply for the crime of eating sea-rat!).

Gateway Shuffle takes place in the space around Jupiter, this time in the vicinity of one of its many satellite moons, Ganymede (Ganymede turns up later in the series – it's Jet Black's home). The show opens with Faye Valentine out of gas, adrift in space (and snacking big time on anything containing chocolate, salt or sugar). Nobody stops to help the damsel in distress, even when she pours on the honey over the radio. Typically, it's the *Bebop* spaceship that picks up Faye in the end (and the first thing the guys do is to handcuff Faye! Yeah, but it doesn't work – Faye escapes, and handcuffs the dog Ein). At this point, Faye plays the classic teenager – when they've spent all their money, they come back home, hungry, wanting somewhere to crash.

40 The original *Planet of the Apes* movie of 1968 was directed by Franklin J. Schaffner and scripted by Rod Serling and Michael Wilson from Pierre Boulle's 1963 novel *Les planète des singes*.

There's also time in *Gateway Shuffle* for some political shenanigans, as Twinkling Maria Murdoch and the Space Warriors put pressure on the Ganymede government to stop fishing for sea-rats (Japan was of course well-known for its whaling industry).[41] *Gateway Shuffle* also introduces a minor character, Bob the cop, a former I.S.S.P. buddy of Jet Black's, who crops up from time with info (he's basically an exposition character, tho' even with such a minor character the writer (Sadayuki Murai) includes a little characterization. No, not the porn mag that Bob's looking at when he talks to Jet, but the fact that Jet can blackmail him into coughing up the info).

As in *Honky Tonk Women* (and in quite a few subsequent episodes), it's Faye Valentine and Spike Spiegel who're involved in the climax out in space in their spacecraft, as they race to demolish the missiles containing the virus that the Space Warriors have unleashed. As usual, the filmmakers pile on the obstacles, one after another (such as having the missiles split up), so it looks as if our heroes can't nobble all of the missiles in time, and can't escape the hyperspace tunnel closing (by the Ganymede government), before everything blows up. And in the midst of the hi-octane finale, Faye and Spike are arguing about percentages (Faye wants a bigger slice than 10%, of course! she demands 80%! but of course Spike won't agree to that!), when they have only moments to escape the closure of the hyperspace freeway.

Once again, it's Spike Spiegel's quick fingers that cause the villains their comeuppance, when Spike

41 It also sends up activism over dolphins, tuna, turtles, etc. On the side of a can of tuna it'll say: 'no dolphins were harmed in the creation of this product!

slips the little phial containing a deadly virus into
Momma Murdoch's jacket (it flies out of her pocket
when the villain's ship brakes sharply in space, and
cracks when it hits the windshield).[42]

---

42 Despite Spike spending quite a bit of time trying to break the
container around the phial. But let's not carp about details – the
poetic justice is perfect.

Episode 5. *Ballad of Fallen Angels*

With *Ballad of Fallen Angels* (written by Michiko Yokote), *Cowboy Bebop* ventures into an older mode of the crime genre, couched in a grand opera style, reminiscent of *The Godfather, film noirs* of the 1940s, and *Le Samourai* (1967).[43] Hong Kong thrillers and *yakuza* movies are also touchstones here. Shady crime syndicates, feuds with rival mobs, betrayals, and the inevitable assassinations and reprisals, form the background of this much more serious episode.

When 27 year-old Vicious (voiced by Norio Wakamoto) appears in episode 5, *Ballad of Fallen Angels*, he's the very familiar villain of Japanese *animé*: tall, thin, angular, white, blond hair, narrow eyes, evil grin, wielding a samurai sword,[44] a stylized big, black crow as a pet/ spirit familiar, utterly heartless, a nasty piece of work all round. Vicious is an old style villain, – he might've stepped out of *Hellsing, Vampire Hunter D,* or *Escaflowne.* Vicious is too good to waste on one episode, so he crops up again in the two *Jupiter Jazz* episodes, and in the final coupla episodes. The evocations of the Red Dragon mob (Spike Spiegel's old crew), of the drugs, of the three aged, monk-like coots who run the mob (who appear later), is familiar Hong Kong action cinema, John Woo and Takeshi Kitano territory

43 The celebration of 1940s, 1950s, 1960s and 1970s popular culture (much of it American) is wonderful, especially when it's skewed through the eclectic lens of high class Japanese *animé*, and delivered by a team of simply marvellous filmmakers.
44 There is an element of Platonic friendship which merges into unexpressed homoeroticism in samurai culture (typically between an older samurai and his ward). This relates to both Vicious and Gren. The effeminate, beautiful samurai is a common figure in samurai stories (and also in *animé* and *manga*), who has his origin in the 12th century warrior Yoshitsune Minamoto. Instead of heroes, however, the brilliant, feminized warriors are often villains, the *bishonen* type.

(Vicious and Spike are the fallen angels of the title. Vicious makes a reference to fallen angels when he first meets Spike in the Cathedral).

Jet Black warns Spike Spiegel repeatedly (and sternly) about getting involved with his old job, about going to meet Vicious and his crew (Jet doesn't know everything about Spike's shady past, but he knows that getting involved with the mobs again won't be good for Spike. And of course, as a former cop with the I.S.S.P., Jet knows enough about Spike's old gang). This is the first episode of *Cowboy Bebop* where the past returns with a vengeance to grab our heroes by the balls, to drag them back. Spike has unfinished business which he can't ignore anymore (like much else in the *Cowboy Bebop* universe, it happened three years ago). He mutters summat about it being the duty of his kind of life to go (which doesn't wholly convince – but something compels him to go, even tho' he knows it might be a trap).

In an episode jammed with incidents and drama (like a two-hour movie in 22 minutes!), *Ballad of Fallen Angels* also has time for Spike to do some detecting, when he visits an old acquaintance, the shop owner Annie (Miyuki Ichijou; Annie's introduction – a formidable mamma grabbing two under-age punks who whip some porn mags – is terrific. As is the detail that Spike lifts the skin mag from the kid, and continues to study it in the store as he talks to Annie, while she throws back alcohol! *Cowboy Bebop* is full of such humorous details). Indeed, the extra elements the filmmakers add to the mix are more entertaining than the dialogue or the meat of the scene, which explains (some of) the back-story of Spike, and also his relation to Mao Yenrai

(Kazuaki Ito), a parental figure.[45]

While the *yakuza* / gangster clichés are enjoyable enough, by far the most impressive aspect of *Ballad of Fallen Angels* is the fantastically staged duel between Spike Spiegel and Vicious in a meticulously designed (and researched) Gothic Cathedral.[46] There are numerous still images of the Cathedral which enhance the moody atmosphere: stained glass windows, rows of statues, giant crosses…

Here the Olde Worlde imagery of the pre-credits sequence of episode one of *Cowboy Bebop* (the grey-on-grey city recalling Paris or Prague), is explained and expanded (we see Spike wandering thru the old town in grey and violet hues[47] to the rendezvous, and Vicious waiting for him in the dark Cathedral, while composer Yoko Kanno delivers a suitably moody orchestral cue called 'Rain', with vocals from Mai Yamane). The action is spellbinding, ramped-up and each edit of the celluloid is made with a blink-and-you-miss-it slice from a glass splinter falling from a broken stained glass window. (The action begins with Faye being held hostage (still in that slinky dress!), with Spike, of course, taking the shot, and killing the heavy, spattering Faye with blood: this inaugurates the intense firefight where Spike is a one-man army, battling his way up to the tower. The scenario will be repeated in the final show).

The filmmakers surpass themselves with the fight

45 Annie and Mao Yenrai thus act as parental surrogates for Spike: the show repeatedly cuts to a close-up of a photo of the three of 'em.
46 *Animé* shows love buildings like churches and Cathedrals (there're giant, Gothic Cathedrals in the 2004 *Ghost In the Shell* sequel, the 2007 *Appleseed* sequel and *Fullmetal Alchemist*). Japan was never Christianized, but filmmakers love the exotic imagery.
47 Some of the colours in *animé* are simply not found in Western filmmaking, or are used in the same manner. *Cowboy Bebop* exploits the purple end of the spectrum, in lilacs, violets and mauves in a striking manner.

between Spike Spiegel and Vicious in *Ballad of Fallen Angels*, using that old staple, the gun vs. the samurai sword (it's reprised in the climax of the whole 1998 series).[48] The Mexican stand-off between the two weapons is pure John Woo, a brilliantly staged climax to the fight, with the sword and the gun pointing at each other. Vicious hurls Spike out of the rose window (after strangling him), but our Spike shoots Spike and cleverly throws back a grenade at the last second.

The filmmakers then indulge in one of the longest montage sequences of its kind in Japanese animation: as Spike Spiegel falls out of the window of the Cathedral tower, under the rose window (you gotta fight in the tower in an action movie, right? – for the high fall, right?), *Cowboy Bebop* flashes back to numerous moments in Spike's life, as well as more recent events (the screenwriters enjoy killing off their main protagonist in *Cowboy Bebop*, then bringing him back to life – it's a recurring theme for Spike).

It's a *tour-de-force* of editing (by Tomoaki Tsurubuchi), as Spike Spiegel falls to the ground backwards in endless slow motion, while shards of glass spin slowly around him (the rose window on the West front of the Cathedral is colossal, dwarfing the famous ones at Chartres, which the filmmakers probably looked at). Sam Peckinpah would've loved it (the Peck was very fond not only of slo-mo montages, but *very long* slo-mo montages): the montage in *Cowboy Bebop* goes on and on, fore-grounding cinema's greatest special effect, the

48 Swordplay is not only part of the samurai genre in cinema and television (and *manga* and *animê*), it is also part of gangster stories set in the 1890-1930 period. So Vicious wielding a sword is very part of a Japanese genre, and not an anachronism or a piece of nostalgia on the part of the filmmakers.

invisible dynamo which powers everything: *editing*.

In the dense, poetic and dramatic montage in *Ballad of Fallen Angels*, the back-story of Spike Spiegel is told in splinters, but you can put it together easily: every image might've come out of a 1940s *film noir* like *Double Indemnity* or *The Maltese Falcon:* there's Julia, the luscious, blonde *femme fatale* and ex-girlfriend, there's Spike fighting back-to-back with his one-time buddy Vicious, there are sepia-toned flashbacks to Spike's earlier life in an American-style tenement, and snatches of his career working for the mob.

We also see Spike Spiegel nearly dying (in a blurry point-of-view shot of a city street at night), and being tended afterwards by Julia (Gara Takashima), who finds him collapsed on the street: this precipitates the shift, over two elegiac fades to black, back to the present day, as Spike gains consciousness back on the *Bebop* ship (entirely bandaged up like a mummy, on the couch), with Faye Valentine watching over him and singing (the past thus repeats itself, and Spike doesn't seem to have learnt much, or changed much).

Thus, Faye Valentine replaces Julia as his inamorata, not only visually, as Spike Spiegel regains consciousness and the camera takes his point-of-view, but also aurally (the women sing the same song), and emotionally. As if to protect himself from possibly becoming too involved with Faye, Spike beckons her closer and whispers that he's tone-deaf. Faye's angry outburst (off-screen), offers a humorous close to this marvellous episode (leaving Spike lost in a cloud of feathers, presumably from a burst cushion or couch that Faye whacked Spike with).

As each new member joins the team of bounty hunters on the spaceship, the writers of *Cowboy Bebop* (Keiko Nobumoto, Michiko Yokote *et al*) have to find something for them to do. In *Ballad of Fallen Angels*, they give newcomer Faye Valentine plenty to do (while Jet Black stays back at the *Bebop* spaceship). This being a crime syndicate genre piece, it's inevitable that Faye will get captured by the bad guys and be used as bait (for Spike Spiegel – and that automatically links together Spike and Faye, with Spike as the prince rescuing the damsel in distress). Thus, there's yet another scene where Faye is tied up (the filmmakers seem to have a fetish for this!); yet it's also clever that Spike tells Faye over the video phone that he's not coming to save her as the princess in jeopardy, no, he has a score to settle! (Their spiky relationship is a key ingredient from the outset of their meeting in *Cowboy Bebop*. Yet these two people were made for each other!).

Faye Valentine's weary delivery of the hostage's message, instead of the expected desperate, weepy one, is wonderful. Faye has clearly been handcuffed to a pole before! She doesn't want to be seen begging – especially begging Jet and Spike! But also witness her surprise and delight when Spike, who hasn't been very warm to Faye thus far, says, yes, he will be coming (but not to rescue her!). Folks, this is *great* screenwriting!

There's a terrific opera scene in *Ballad of Fallen Angels:* Italian opera suits this particular form of the crime genre perfectly (opera-plus-gangsters reached its apogee in cinema with the *Godfather* movies,[49] favourites with anybody who loves the crime genre, and for many fans the *Godfather* movies are still *the* gangster epics to beat all others).[50] Thus, Faye becomes the *donna* at an opera performance in a grand theatre[51] (featuring gorgeous backgrounds), and gets to wear a slinky, red dress (plenty of *décolletage* and slit to the hip, of course! And the animators make sure Faye's bouncy boobs jiggle. The designers – Toshihiro Kawamoto and Kimitoshi Yamano – love to put Faye in new costumes. Well, if ever there was a gift to designers who like to dress up super-babes in outrageous clothes, Faye Valentine is that girl!).

Faye, thinking she's getting ahead of the game by trailing Mao Yenrai to the opera, visits the big shots in their box, only to find herself in hot water, yet again (that Vicious has brought the corpse of the head of the mob to sit in the theatre box seems odd and doesn't make sense, if you think about it, unless it's Vicious's idea of a sick joke. Or maybe it's Vicious's way of baiting Spike. Anyway, it means that Faye is snagged by the bad guys). There are powerful close-ups of Faye in the opera box as she sits between the corpse on one side and Vicious on the other: she knows that Vicious is a very malevolent guy.

---

49 The third *Godfather* movie embraced the (Italian) operatic aspects of the gangster genre wholeheartedly. Francis Coppola envisaged *The Godfather* 3 having the elements of opera, backstage murder, family business, the Vatican, old/ new morality, Las Vegas, death of the empire, Roman Empire rituals, big money, Shakespearean scale, authenticity, redemption and rebirth.
50 And also more recent operatic gangster flicks – Abel Ferrara, Sergio Leone, Tsui Hark, etc.
51 In typical style, Faye simply screams up to the theatre in her spacecraft, ahead of everyone else, handing her key to a lackey.

Episode 6. *Sympathy For the Devil*

Sympathy For the Devil (written by head writer Keiko Nobumoto) is a weird episode featuring a child who's really an 80 year-old man in a child's body (due to the uncanny survival of an explosion). The strangeness is of the *Akira* order, with its psychic, prematurely-aged children,[52] and it's Spike Spiegel who's primarily involved with the main story. This guy keeps a man (Zebra) who's dead or nearly dead in a wheelchair to act as a guardian, so he can continue to go about as a boy without arousing suspicion (it has a Hitchcockian sickness about it, a kinda Norman Bates-ish feel).

The writer of *Sympathy For the Devil*, Keiko Nobumoto, stuck for a way to deliver some exposition, resorts to a really crude narrative device out of a 1950s science fiction B-movie, but somehow it hobbles past the viewer, gasping for breath: a memory reader (dubbed the 'Alfa Catch'), which is strapped onto the head of Wen's dying companion so they can replay what happened on a screen (and, a'course, of all the things Zebra could be remembering, as he nears death, it's the all-important hotel scene, when Giraffe (Ryuji Nakagi) demanded payback).

And while the story of *Sympathy For the Devil* doesn't wholly make sense, it doesn't matter, because there is so much wit and style on display. For a start, the filmmakers at Sunrise/ Bandai are once again presenting a passionately evoked futuristic city, which once again draws heavily on New York City

52 And the design of Wen recalls the psychic kids in *Akira,* and also the psionic children in the *Urotsukidoji* series.

(there's a long shot of Wen playing his mouth organ against a crimson sunset with the Chrysler Building prominent). And they deliver another version of the crime genre's visit to a deserted warehouse at night, with an exciting shoot-out between Wen and Spike.

Also, episode 6 *Sympathy For the Devil* does deliver some explanations about the back-story of the *Cowboy Bebop* series, and what happened to the Earth: there was an explosion at a hyperspace gateway near the Earth, which caused part of the moon to break up (reminiscent of the *Akira manga,* when psycho anti-hero Tetsuo ravages the moon). The population of Earth retreated underground, as the surface became unliveable, with constant rock falls, while others fled to distant parts of the Solar System (episode 9 explains more of this. This event also causes Faye Valentine's accident).

We see this in a flashback depicting Wen's childhood – happy families on a sunny day when Wen's playing the harmonica for his mom and dad turn into a post-apocalyptic nightmare. The explosion near the moon is colossal, carving a huge chunk out of it, and filling the screen with white light. Thus, Wen's fate mirrors that of Faye Valentine – they were both injured during the gate explosion, and both lived on Earth b4 the catastrophe.

The explanations of the future world of *Cowboy Bebop* are integrated into the plot of episode 6, as it details Wen's fate. Many another TV show would've put this set-up into the opening episode/s. The filmmakers at Sunrise/ Bandai assumed that all you need to know is that Something Bad happened on Earth, and humans have gone to other planets.

♫

It's Spike Spiegel who gets to put Wen out of his misery in the finale shoot-out, a marvellous scene – of course it's on waste ground in an industrial zone outside of the Gothamite city, lit with lurid, red sunset glows (the whole episode is colour designed (by Shihiko Nakayama) around deep, saturated reds). Spike stands stock still while Wen shoots at him barely missing (luckily it's dark and Wen has just shakily emerged from a giant explosion (yet another *Akira*-like image) – his commandeered taxi handily crashes into a gas station!). Spike has one bullet – a magic bullet, a'course[53] (and it uses the episode's MacGuffin, a ring that contains the only substance that might nobble Wen), which he waits to fire, right into Wen's forehead (an amazing shot at that distance! – which causes Wen to age-up (with the aid of CGI morphing), to a shrivelled prune, and finally expire.

I didn't realize until after seeing the episode a few times that Jet Black and Faye Valentine simply allow Spike Spiegel to go off on his own to face Wen! We've already seen how the team works together (in the *Gateway Shuffle* episode, for instance), but here it's all down to Spike to deal with Wen. True, Jet does help Spike with some background research, and he does fashion the magic bullet that will nail the freak, but he and Faye just let Spike walk out. Hell, Faye even hangs around to say *sayonara* to Spike – because she doesn't think he'll be coming back (yeah, but she could go with him to help out! However, you could also say that the scene shows that Faye is developing some feelings for Spike. The scene is reprised in the finale *Cowboy Bebop* episode – and by that time Faye

53 Built into a special gun by Jet Black.

has defintely grown very fond of Spike, and it's their most intense love scene).

♫

Sympathy For the Devil also foregrounded music again, with Yoko Kanno and the Seatbelts delivering some marvellous American-style blues music, with the mouth harp prominent (Spike Spiegel goes to see Wen playing the harmonica at a blues club).[54] Yet Kanno and co. also composed some amazing percussion pieces with pounding Turkish drums to accompany the action scenes.

No prizes for guessing where the episode title *Sympathy For the Devil* comes from:

> Pleased to meet you
> Hope you guessed my name, oh yeah
> But what's confusing you
> Is just the nature of my game
> Just as every cop is a criminal
> And all the sinners saints
> As heads is tails
> Just call me Lucifer
> 'Cause I'm in need of some restraint
> So if you meet me
> Have some courtesy
> Have some sympathy, and some taste
> Use all your well-learned politesse
> Or I'll lay your soul to waste, oh yeah

'Sympathy For the Devil' comes from the era at the end of the 1960s when the Rolling Stones fooled around with supposedly 'Satanic' material (during the *Their Satanic Majesties* album and 'Sympathy For

---

54 There's a montage of flashbacks during the blues club scene, which at first might appear to be those of the new character, Wen, and detailing the scientific/ medical treatment he underwent following the catastrophe. But no, as the montage ends, we see we've been looking at fragments of Spike's past, as he wakes up from his dream (eyes – Spike's new eye – are prominent in the dream).

the Devil' days).[55] 'Sympathy For the Devil' has become somewhat notorious: rock critics always seem to cite the fact that Meredith Hunter was murdered at the famous Altamont Speedway concert during the Stones' song 'Sympathy For the Devil', as if this is a terribly poignant, ironic event.[56] Like *wow*, the youth died while Mick Jagger sang about having 'sympathy for the Devil'. So someone's death becomes food for a journalist's story, as if the stabbing and the murder wasn't enough. (The Altamont concert is often referred to as 'the day the Sixties died'. 'America at Altamont could only muster one common response. Everybody grooved on fear. One communal terror of fascist repression.'[57] Altamont is seen by critics as the end of the era of free love and hippy-dippy ideals.)

55 Actually, Mick Jagger's dalliance with Satanic/ occult material was fairly superficial (and was soon dropped). Rock stars such as Jimmy Page (of Led Zeppelin) were much more into it. Page was a well-known Aleister Crowley fanatic.
56 Actually, as the movie *Gimme Shelter* shows, it was during 'Under Your Thumb'.
57 George Paul Csicsery, "Altamont, California", *The New York Daily News*, December 8, 1969.

Episode 7. *Heavy Metal Queen*

Heavy Metal Queen (penned by Michiko Yokote) is (among other things) an extended *hommage* to 1970s American trucker culture, with many quotes from *Convoy* (Sam Peckinpah, 1978 – yep, the Peck directed *Convoy*!).[58] Spaceships long and triangular (again, inspired partly by the *Discovery* vessel in the *2001: A Space Odyssey* movie)[59] trundle thru open space and between giant docking craft, driven by truckers who deck out their cabins with exuberant, colourful individuality (we're talking more than nudie pin-ups, Vietnam War veteran, and soccer regalia – there are plants in glass jars, pendants, medals, guns in holsters, etc).[60] And when they cruise thru the asteroid belt, of course they play heavy rock music at ear-splitting levels (and of course they communicate via CB radio – remember CB, ten four good buddy? Sooo 1978!).

Most intriguing in *Heavy Metal Queen* is the evocation of gay culture – V.T. (Victoria Terpsichore, played with an appealing weariness and sass by Tomie Kataoka),[61] the principal new character, is a transvestite (blond hair, cap, trucker jacket, pet cat, low voice), mourning his/ her dead lover (we find out why V.T. hates bounty hunters at the end of the running gag of people betting money (including the three old dudes from the café) to guess what the

---

58 Director Watanabe enjoyed *Convoy* and also the show *Trucker Yaro* as a youth.
59 The shot of the lengthy pass by the camera of the *Discovery* ship in *2001* has led to numerous rip-offs in sci-fi cinema.
60 Art director Junichi Higashi does an terrific job of conjuring up memorable, individualized settings for each trucker.
61 The name Victoria might refer to the wonderful gender-bending comedy *Victor/ Victoria* (Blake Edwards, 1982). And V.T.'s appearance does recall Robert Preston in that great movie.

initials V.T. stands for: turns out her dead husband was a famous bounty hunter (whom Spike Spiegel says everybody has heard of). Reading between the lines, his death probably resulted from bounty hunting, hence V.T.'s detestation of them).

Meanwhile, the true villain of *Heavy Metal Queen*, shifty trucker/ bounty hunter turned killer Decker,[62] is visually modelled on Woody Allen in his 1970s *schlemiel* persona (when he took to wearing green combat jackets, around the time of *Annie Hall*). So edgy and scared is Decker, he doesn't have any lines, but issues nervy whimpers (*animé* is especially adept at capturing how people communicate with noises rather than words). Decker is a nasty weasel of a criminal, however, sneaking about in his combat jacket and thick-rimmed glasses, and dropping tubes of explosives; he winds up dead following the chase in the asteroid tunnel (much to Faye Valentine's disappointment – there goes her 12 million Woolongs bounty (and she *needs* that money!) – so often in *Cowboy Bebop* the quarry of the bounty hunters ends as toast).

♬

The first half of episode 7 *Heavy Metal Queen* has two parallel scenes set in North American-style diners: the dingy bar full of bounty hunters where V.T. goes for a drink after clocking off work (and where Spike Spiegel is recovering in the john from a hangover, later mixing a prairie oyster at the bar); and the amusing satire of McDonald's restaurants and North American fast food joints, where Faye Valentine is staking out another bounty, and looking as miserable as sin as she sits in amongst the happy-

62 The name's probably another reference to Rick Deckard in *Blade Runner*.

happy diners and chattering kiddies, with her elaborate ice cream sundae (when Faye is on the prowl for criminals, she is at her best: in the restaurant she teasingly comes on to a burly rough-neck, b4 holding him at gunpoint, only to discover that he's the wrong guy, and that snake tattoo on his chest is really a silly, cartoony eel. Luckily, she glances up to see the real Decker exiting the diner, and spots his tattoo. Thus ensues another chase, but Decker manages to elude the determined Faye, making her more pissed than ever!).

Meanwhile, there is a classic barroom brawl involving V.T., who chivalrously beats up some ugly Mexicans with bad teeth (wearing sombreros and ponchos!, and drawn in a Miyazakian style), when they lecherously harass the waitress (another carica-ture, this time blue-eyed, blonde, bimbo-ness). The rough-and-tumble ruckus might be a scene from any American horse opera from 1930-1970 (inevitably, Spike Spiegel gets involved in the fight, but he tries to ignore it for a while, as all true heroes tend to do – Spike is fundamentally a lazy guy, and there's no need getting involved in someone else's dispute (especially when you have a murderous hangover!). The Mexicans get their own back when they vandalize Spike's *Swordfish* spaceship outside the diner. So that's how both Spike and Faye get to hitch a ride with V.T. It's a little convoluted, script-wise – why doesn't Jet Black simply fly the *Bebop* ship over and pick them up while they wait? But it's necessary, to set up the finale).

7: *Heavy Metal Queen* contains a terrific action finale inside an asteroid that's being mined: the writer (Michiko Yokote) gives Faye Valentine, Spike

Spiegel and V.T. each things to do, as they fight their way out of the asteroid that's crumbling around them due to errant reactor explosions[63] (Faye trying to be delicate and careful with the controls of her spaceship's pincer arms in order to extract some explosives from the tanker is the funniest moment). Once again, the filmmakers use the motif of leaping into space without a spacesuit (it's Spike who does that here – he's crazy enough – and at one point he uses his gun to alter his trajectory when he's zooming away from V.T.'s spaceship during the thrilling last-second climax. So cool! Would it work? Doesn't matter: it looks great!).[64]

[63] Talk about explosions! – *Heavy Metal Queen* is probably the loudest and bangiest of the series. As Hayao Miyazaki commented, you might have to know how to draw explosions to be an animator, but being interested in people was more important. However, on a show like *Cowboy Bebop*, it sure helps!
[64] In the *dénouement* scene, Spike guesses V.T.'s real name, but declines taking the huge wad of cash he's won (but Faye Valentine would!).

YOUTH LED ASTRAY.

Waltz For Venus, written by Michiko Yokote, was another episode mainly featuring Spike Spiegel (and his relationship with a young criminal). The theme of a young guy who gets involved in crime recurs in the *Cowboy Bebop* universe (and also crops up in *Samurai Champloo*). It's about being young and idealistic and out of your depth and uncertain about the adult world. Notice, for instance, how much time the filmmakers spend on the scene at the airport where the wannabe criminal, Rocco Bonnaro (Ryusei Nakao), is desperate to learn from Spike (they even have an impromptu martial arts lesson right on the ground outside the terminal building! That scene allows for some martial arts staples, including the *sensei/ sifu* and pupil scene, with Spike offering his philosophy of martial arts, the familiar *wushu* or Taoist approach, using the opponents' force, made famous recently by Jet Li in movies such as the completely wonderful *Tai Chi Master*, 1993). One of the main reasons for the martial arts scene, however, is the bonding between Rocco and Spike, to give the finale of *Waltz For Venus* more dramatic juice, when Rocco expires, wondering if they could've been friends.

Rocco Bonnaro is a good kid; part of the reason that he gets involved in rackets is because he has a sister Stella (Maya Sakamoto)[65] who's gone blind, that he cares for (the sweet, brotherly relationship, more than anything that Rocco says, tells us all we need to know). Spike Spiegel finds out this with a bit of footwork, when he goes to visit Stella in her home (which, in a wonderfully designed sequence, is set in a crashed, abandoned spaceship that's now over-grown with bushes and trees – another recurring motif in *Cowboy Bebop*).

Waltz For Venus opens with some hijackers taking a spaceship hostage at gunpoint as it comes in to land on Venus. After 9/11, the scene takes on even more sinister connotations (for that reason it was not shown in the U.S.A.).[66] Luckily, Faye Valentine and Spike Spiegel are posing as passengers, and the villains are more Most Wanteds on the bounty hunters' list. (Spike deals with the hijackers in his usual nonchalant, sorta accidental manner, making the rounding up of felons looks amazingly easy (which impresses Rocco). And Faye, exiting the bathroom, is on hand to help with a li'l squirt from her gadget lipstick-turned-immobilizing-spray – for the female hijacker).

This is one of the few times when the *Bebop* crew get their quarry without killing them! So they have some dough for the first time in ages.[67] And we see

---

65 Maaya Sakamoto (b. 1980) was Hitomi in *Escaflowne,* Julia Crichton in the second *Fullmetal Alchemist* movie, Makuri in *Naruto,* Deunan Knute in the *Appleseed* remakes, and the young Motoko in *The Laughing Man*, the *Ghost In the Shell* TV series and movie. Sakamoto's other credits include: *Clover, Black Butler, Death Note, Evangelion, Hellsing Ultimate, Kanon, Macross Frontier, Mushishi, Gundam, Record of Lodoss War, Saint Seiya, xxxHolic, Star Driver* and *Wolf's Rain*.
66 But security on space flights is terrible! The hijackers are allowed to carry on guns, and Rocco has a giant knife and a million dollar plant!
67 There's a great joke of an ATM sort of machine in the airport, where bounty hunters can collect their rewards.

Faye and Spike arguing about the money in the airport terminal (of course, as soon as Faye receives her credit, she's off to the casino! Where she no doubt gets into debt again – hence her desperation to hunt down mob boss Piccaro Calvino, to snaggle more bounty dough to pay it off!).

VENUS.

Venus: it looks quite nice in this episode (rather than the incredibly hot and inhospitable planet it really is). Yeah, but all of the planets and moons in *Cowboy Bebop*, as in science fiction in general, are reasonably pleasant (*Cowboy Bebop* draws the line at visiting the surface of the gas giants like Jupiter or Saturn, though. You gotta have a planet with some desert to stand on in sci-fi shows – deserts which always look like Arizona, Utah, Nevada and California).[68]

The Venus in *Waltz For Venus* has floating green islands out of *Laputa: Castle In the Sky* (and other fantasy stories), and a yellow-green palette. Yet the city where the action is set is modelled very closely on Istanbul: there's even the famous image of Santa Sophia with its minarets and towers at sunset from the other side of the Bosphorus.

There is a disease on Venus which disables some but not others (Rocco Bonnaro's sister Stella has it, and she's lost her sight). Handily, there's also a plant which can counteract the illness (thus, instead of drugs or money, it's the plant and the seeds that form the episode's MacGuffin).

---

68 The filmmakers admitted that it could be difficult sometimes to find places to set the stories in, which's partly why so many episodes go to Mars (or back to Earth).

THE SHOOT-OUT.

Meanwhile, Faye Valentine is on the trail of Mr Big, Piccaro Calvino (Yu Shimaka). And when Faye gets her teeth into her prey, she never lets go. Talk about persistent! One of the funniest scenes has Faye entering yet another dive bar, and single-handedly taking on the clientele (all male, a'course! – this is a distinctly Arabic *milieu*), in order to answer her burning question: where is Piccaro Calvino? Faye effortlessly shoots out all of the weapons from the clintele's hands. (Homosexuality is again foregrounded when Faye bursts in on two guys making out in bed. I bet broadcasters hate that scene! To ram home the gay-oriented theme, Faye thrusts her gun into the mouth of one of the guys so he can't breathe. It's not often you see a *woman* doing that – to a man!).

Piccaro Calvino is a nasty piece of work, a cigar-chomping mob boss of the old school[69] (and modelled visually after the rapper Notorious B.I.G.). As his boys beat up Rocco, he simply grins broadly.

The big shoot-out that climaxes *Waltz For Venus* brings the two story strands together, with Spike Spiegel meeting Rocco Bonnaro at the rendezvous at the Cathedral at night, and Faye Valentine appearing not long afterwards, in the midst of the fire-fight, in her spaceship (Jet Black also turns up). The joke of killing the bounty is used yet again.

There is a genuine pathos in the moment where Rocco Bonnaro is shot and killed, and in Spike Spiegel's horror at seeing the boy near death (though he leaves to find help and misses when Rocco finally

---

69 He stubs his cigar out on Rocco's forehead. This is Rocco's first encounter with gangster violence.

expires).[70] It's quite right to play the death scene seriously – this waste of a life is not the time for jokes.

But there is also lighter sweetness in *Waltz For Venus*: there's a music box, for instance, a favourite totem in so many *animé* shows (so of course we get to hear the musical box music – in the *Jupiter Jazz* episodes, a music box does a lot of narrative work). In *Waltz For Venus*, a seed's hidden in the box, which'll help Stella. The episode closes with some 'pillow moments', as spores fall from the sky like snow; Spike Spiegel, wandering the Istanbul-like streets, looks up to see the pretty sight (snow, like butterflies, is a favourite motif of transience and impermanence in Japanese culture – *mono no aware*).

---

70 The jazzy music cue for the firefight stops abruptly when Rocco is shot, and the glass jar containing the plant falls and smashes.

Episode 9. *Jamming With Edward*

THE STORY.

Jamming With Edward, episode 9, written by Dai Sato (the title is an allusion to the 1972 Rolling Stones album), is the *Bebop* episode which introduces the wonderful girl hacker Radical Edward Wong Hau Pepelu Tivruski the IV (as Ed insists, when onlookers quiz her, she is, despite her name, a *girl*!). Apparently, a boy[71] had been considered: a young hacker/ geek/ *otaku* character might typically be a teenage boy in a sci-fi/ Western/ comedy show of this type. But making Radical Ed (Edo) a girl is so much more interesting (and her age, 13 or 14, is also significant). It's common in *animé* and *manga* to have teen charas playing around with gender.

Among the ingredients in *Jamming With Edward* are: the lines of Nazca in Peru (animals and symbols carved in the desert), super-computers (played by Jouji Nakata) getting Existential and metaphysical *à la* HAL in *2001: A Space Odyssey*,[72] a search for the mystery hacker behind it all (with a big bounty on their head), and hacker culture. However, all of those ingredients, while entertaining, pale beside the new character, Radical Ed: and when Ed's on screen, even colourful characters like Spike Spiegel and Faye Valentine have trouble staying the focus of attention!

Jamming With Edward has the *Bebop* crew visiting the Earth for the first time (in the present tense, that is – earlier episodes had shown Earth, but in the

---

71 Apparently this would've been based on the black kid who snaffles some skin mags in episode 5. There's also a black kid that Jet Black meets on Earth, who sells him some delicacies.
72 Ed dubs the satellite computer 'MPU', and Jouji Nakata provided the solemn voice.

past). We see Jet Black quizzing a bunch of eccentric people on Earth about Radical Ed – another example of the filmmakers stuffing each amusing vignette with a host of details packed in around the to-camera vox pops (they look like the kinda weirdos you find on the boardwalk at Venice Beach). Spike Spiegel meanwhile opts to stay on the ship, snoozing on the couch.

We also find out more about what happened when the hyperspace gate blew up near Earth, and everyone retreated underground (and also why the planet is still being bombarded with debris – one large piece lands near Ed in the opening scenes and sends her flying).

The weather forecast for Earth is thus how heavy the rock showers are going to be today (there are several television spots in *Jamming With Edward*, including a discussion about aliens and the mysterious hacker, and satellites, and weather. Just how much the filmmakers cram into a single episode of *Bebop* is amazing).

The thrilling finale of *Jamming With Edward* has the *Cowboy Bebop* team up against a bunch of satellites orbiting the Earth which're attacking them with lasers,[73] defending the satellite that's gone AWOL (jeez, who gave the satellites giant lasers which can burn up the surface of the Earth 100s of miles below?… Oh yeah, humans).

RADICAL ED.

Radical Ed sure isn't your typical animated character (though in Japanese animation, maybe Ed isn't so unusual). A scrawny, happy-go-lucky kid who bends with every breeze, a genius computer

[73] Satellites with lasers are a common trope in sci-fi, appearing in *James Bond*, of course, and in *Akira*.

hacker, Ed sprouts wild, orange hair, lycra shorts, a white Tee shirt, and very large *anime* eyes. Actress Aoi Tada contributes immensely to the success of Ed as a character (composer Yoko Kanno was rumoured to have been one o' the inspirations for Ed).

Radical Ed is all sinuous, unpredictable movement: she possesses long, skinny, floppy arms which she waves, she goes barefoot, often walks on her arms and operates her computer with her toes, does backflips when excited, often wears VR goggles (when using the computer), and speaks in a high, girlie voice that's often naught but babyish noises.

You can't help being won over by Radical Ed, because she's so much fun. She embodies play, idealism, and innocence (despite their world-weary cynicism, all of the crew of the *Bebop* possess an appealing naïveté). From mythology, Ed is Puck, she is Ariel, she is an elf, a fairy, a spirit – and she is the future.

The satellite computer who gets so lonely (and bored) in *Jamming With Edward* that it starts to draw its own version of the Nazca Lines in the deserts of what was once South America is of course a parallel with Radical Ed (lonely in space... lonely on Earth). Because when Ed is introduced, she is living on her own, in a cluttered, abandoned building, where she spends most of her time surfing the net on her trusty laptop, wearing virtual reality goggles (she customizes the web interface so it appears as a colourful, child-like underwater world with fish and octopuses – everything in cyberspace connotes playtime. Her hacker logo pops up with a big, yellow smiley face and a cheeky giggle). But she is alone, and lonesome.

Radical Ed celebrates hacker culture and the

hyperspace of the digital realm with the same gusto as many other *animé* shows (*Ghost In the Shell* being probably the most sophisticated). That is, computers are everywhere in *Cowboy Bebop*, as they are in so many *animé* shows (and not only the hi-tech thrillers and science fiction outings).

It's odd, though, that some elements of the plot of *Jamming With Edward* ain't explained: we know that Radical Ed is lonely and craves for a family, but there is no explanation of her present predicament as a kid of 13 or 14 who's living on her own (presumably in South America).[74] No mention of parents, or siblings (what would a brother to Radical Ed be like?!). And it isn't explained, either, just why Radical Ed settles on the *Bebop* (and its crew of adults) as the place she wants to live; they are adults, not kids her own age, and she doesn't really know much about them,[75] and hasn't met them! The way that Ed gets to join the *Bebop* crew is very odd, if you think about it afterwards (and the sceptical attitudes of all three adults towards Ed don't mask the oddities).

Instead, the filmmakers rather smugly rely on the sheer strangeness of Radical Ed to win over the audience. Ed's a character they clearly love having created, and they hope that the feelings of good will the audience will develop towards the character will carry them over any peculiarities. And Ed does prevail – because the second thoughts only come after the episode is over, and you think about it (if you were simply enjoying *Cowboy Bebop*, and not studying

74 There's a great touch in the final scene, depicting the *Bebop* ship orbiting the Earth, while all across South America is a big Radical Ed smile (each line of the smile and the eyes would be wider than Sao Paolo!).
75 Tho' Ed does demonstrate her research about the *Bebop* and what the crew have been doing (including their failures to secure bounties).

it afterwards, it wouldn't matter).

So by the end of *Jamming With Edward*, the *Bebop* crew have found another member. Jet and Spike commiserate in the closing minutes: Spike says he dislikes kids (cut to a shot of Ed waving her arms madly), animals (Ein), and tomboys (Faye).

Episode 10. *Ganymede Elegy*

In episode 10, *Ganymede Elegy* (written by Akihiko Inari), Jet Black returns to Ganymede,[76] where he was a cop, to look up an old flame, Alisa (Seon Lee). Yep – *Ganymede Elegy* really does have a scene where a guy ambles into a bar and his former (still beautiful) lover is behind the bar to offer him a glass of the usual (and the bar's called 'La Fin'!). The subtext (time passing) is delightfully, playfully and self-consciously shoved into the foreground with the pocket watch symbol employed as boldly as possible (at the end of the show, Jet simply hurls it into the sea – he isn't clinging onto the past anymore, one of the key themes of *Cowboy Bebop*).[77]

Jet Black's quest to achieve some kind of 'closure', as psycho-speak has it, is the subtext in *Ganymede Elegy*. Of course, his meeting with Alisa doesn't go quite as he expected (though he's also not sure what he expected – an explanation as to why Alisa walked out on him[78] all those years ago, perhaps). Jet gives his longest and most personal speech in the 1998 TV series,while sitting at the bar. But Alisa has 'moved on' (another irritating phrase in New Age-ology), and her relationship with Jet is now just another story, she tells him, and she's not interested in raking over the ashes o' the past. (The physical blocking of the characters says more'n the

---

76 Ganymede's portrayed as a seaport which's seen better days: seagulls, boats, water, blue seas, docks, etc. Jupiter looms above, in the sky.
77 This being sci-fi, the pocket watch has 15 hours on it, not 12.
78 Yes, the filmmakers really do include a shot of Alisa walking away from the camera, right out of the cheesiest chart pop promo. And, yes, it *is* raining. And, yes, the lighting is low and slanting. You could put all sorts Western and Japanese pop over these images.

speech, anyway: Alisa sits with her back to Jet, and Jet sits at the bar, not looking at her at his side).

Rhint Celonias (Kappei Yamaguchi)[79] is Alisa's new boyfriend, a rather hopeless and hapless (though attractive-lookin') youth who breaks down rather pathetically like a cry-baby in the bar when he discovers that there's a bounty on him (Rhint's another of the many younger, would-be criminals in the world of *Cowboy Bebop* who fall in with a bad crowd).

In *Ganymede Elegy*, Faye Valentine and Radical Ed provide the comic relief: Ed appears in a short sequence at the top o' the show, when she terrorizes a captured criminal by biting his ears and legs (!), after he had kicked a can at Ein the dog (the animation of Ed is highly exaggerated). Later, Faye catches some rays on a lounger on the deck of the *Bebop* spaceship, while Ed fishes nearby. It's a pure *otaku*, fan service moment, serving no purpose other than the sight of the *animé* super-babe Faye stripping down to a skimpy bikini which barely contains her boobs and crotch, and oiling up her pneumatic body (Ed looks on wonderingly as Faye applies sun tan lotion).

Ganymede Elegy is rather predictably plotted,[80] but that doesn't matter, because it's about moods and emotions and characters more than stories. Are you gonna hang on to the past 'til the day you die? Or are

<hr>

79 Kappei Yamaguchi (b. May 23, 1965) has appeared in just about every modern *animé*, it seems.Among his famous roles are 'L' in the incredible *Death Note,* Tombo in *Kiki's Delivery Service*, Inuyasha in *Inuyasha,* Ranma Saotome in *Ranma 1/2,* Tanda in *Moribito: Guardian of the Spirit,* Low in *Shadow Skill,* Shinichi Kudo (and Kaito Kid) in *Detective Conan*, Usopp in *One Piece,* Feitan in *Hunter x Hunter*, Shesta in *Escaflowne*, Hikozaru in *Pokémon,* and Nin-nin in *La Blue Girl* (!).

80 There's yet another grizzled, old (black) cop who knows Jet (Donnelly, played by Fumio Matsuoka), who turns up to provide the basic exposition.

you gonna set yourself free, and start living *wholly* in the present? It's challenge fired at Jet Black in this episode, but it is also asked of Spike Spiegel and Faye Valentine, too (indeed, both Faye and Spike are mired in the past far more than Jet, or Ed).

Ganymede Elegy climaxes with yet another chase, with Jet Black taking over from Spike Spiegel, and nailing the fugitives (it's a very lengthy chase, which shifts into an elegiac mode – the local sound dips out, and music prevails. The chase goes thru a number of phases – from Spike's shoot-em-up tactics, to Jet's dogged, patient holding in there until they tire).

At the end, Alisa stands by her injured boyfriend Rhint at the side of the bay, and shakily holds up a gun to shoot repeatedly at Jet Black, who simply keeps walking towards her without flinching. A woman with a gun firing at close range at a man who was her former lover: it's a typically extreme version of a *film noir* staple, painting Alisa as the wronged *femme fatale* and Jet as the cool, implacable hero who doesn't even flinch when a gun's shot at him from a few feet away (the scenario's reprised a few times in *Cowboy Bebop,* including the scene where Spike Spiegel faced Wen in ep 6).

So Jet Black walks away, perhaps a little smug in the knowledge that Alisa's new guy Rhint is a cowardly loser who's out of his depth. Or maybe he realizes that she (or their romance) has no hold on him anymore. What is the past, but memories, dreams, thoughts, feelings (or the memory of feelings?). In *Cowboy Bebop,* the people who hang onto the past too strongly endanger their own lives in the present.

What's great about *Cowboy Bebop* is that

although the old-flames-meeting-again motif was already a cliché in cinema by the time it achieved its most famous incarnation – in, of course, *Casablanca* (1942) – it can still be employed to great effect. When it's done with this amount of style, humour, and knowingness. Oh, the filmmakers *know* exactly what they're doing in *Cowboy Bebop* – the team at Sunrise and Bandai who created the show come over as very clever veterans of entertainment. And they're slick and stylish and witty enough to carry off every cliché, every formulaic motif, and every familiar routine.

It's as if the filmmakers of *Cowboy Bebop* have acknowledged Jean-Luc Godard's view that everything has already been done in cinema (this view was expressed in the 1960s), and said, fuck it, we're *still* going to do this show!

Episode 11. *Toys In the Attic*

The episode *Toys In the Attic*[81] (written by Michiko
Yokote), like most of *Speak Like a Child* and *Mushroom
Samba,* is pure silliness. *Toys In the Attic* is a hilarious
spoof on *Alien (*and *Aliens*) and monsters-in-a-
spaceship scenarios (*2001: A Space Odyssey* is sent up
too). Instead of the blob of 1950s sci-fi flicks, it's a
lobster that's festered in a fridge in the cargo hold for
months, to become a piece of purple goop picking off
the crew one by one. Michiko Yokote and the
filmmakers gleefully trot out every cliché of monster
movies, from the monster's red-eye point-of-view as
it crawls along the ducts (why is it always ducts?,
complains Sigourney Weaver in *Galaxy Quest*), to the
mandatory scene where a cute babe is bathing nude
and the monster appears (the filmmakers at Sunrise/
Bandai put the lovely, crazy Faye Valentine into the
shower and the bath quite a few times, and they
always include a 'fan service' shot of her nude body).

The whole of the *Toys In the Attic* episode is
played for laffs (although Spike Spiegel narrates the
episode in voiceover in mock solemnity. In fact, each
of the four characters gets to narrate their section of
Toys In the Attic, which're given chapter headers –
'lessons').[82]

The episode opens with the *Bebop* crew very
bored – Faye Valentine is using dice to scam Jet Black
into losing everything he owns, including his clothes

---

81 Aerosmith have a song 'Toys In the Attic'.
82 The design of the 'lesson' captions – in red and blue lettering on
white – evokes Jean-Luc Godard's movies of the Sixties.

(and his underwear),[83] Spike Spiegel is cooking vegetables with a home-made flame-thrower, and Radical Ed is asleep.

One of the funniest scenes in *Toys In the Attic* also involves Faye Valentine – when she breaks down diva-style at the prospect of dying young from being bitten by the mysterious critter (while Spike Spiegel looks on in disbelief. 'I've never committed any crime!' Faye wails, 'I'm still young and lively!' That Faye would switch so rapidly from her tough broad persona to totally losing it is wonderful! And to tell so many lies in what appears to be a sincere rant against the injustices of life!).

The finale of 11: *Toys In the Attic* has Spike Spiegel surviving to the end like the 'final girl' of horror cinema, the only person left who can vanquish the beast. By this time, *Toys In the Attic* has explored every inch of the *Bebop* ship so that the vessel becomes, as in a haunted house movie, a character in itself (*The Shining* being a good example).

Spike Spiegel uses the device in *Alien* of expelling the monster by evacuating all of the air from the spaceship – and *Alien* in turn drew on the famous air lock sequence in *2001: A Space Odyssey*, as well as the whole haunted house scenario from the horror genre.[84] The quotes from *2001: A Space Odyssey* are numerous in *Toys In the Attic*, right down to the spinning fridge, the framing, the blocking of the action and the use of classical music – from the

83 Of course Faye is using loaded dice. What, you expected Faye to play fair? Well, Spike warned Jet Black, and Jet shoulda known better. It's great that Faye wins everything from Jet – not only his guns but also his bonsai trees!
84 Director Ridley Scott admitted that *Alien* was essentially a haunted house story set in space. It's just a monster and a bunch of people. The audience had seen it all before – but they love to see the same stories told in a slightly new manner, and *Alien* was very successful for 20th Century Fox.

Nutcracker Ballet by Peter Tchaikovsky – in the final sequence as the crew members, all asleep, float in zero gravity).[85]

The *Toys In the Attic* episode also explores the total boredom of travelling for months on end. Only then would Jet Black agree to playing dice with a confidence trickster like Faye Valentine. And the plot – about a piece of food left in the fridge that turns into a monster – might come out of a silly, drunk (or stoned) late night conversation. Or the kind of story a room full of desperate writers might cook up when the deadline is three hours' away. (That a horror genre scenario would be employed for the *Bebop* spaceship seems inevitable, as is the production team playing it entirely for comedy. In *Cowboy Bebop*, the comedy comes first, but the horror genre offers so many possibilities for humour, it's a gift to a writing team).

As filmmaking, *Toys In the Attic* is a masterful parody of every horror movie cliché you can think of. Especially wonderful are the fancy camera angles and subjective shots, the pacing, and the evocation of mood and attitude. Once again, *Cowboy Bebop* inds the perfect balance between storytelling and comedy. But it's the sound effects editing[86] that really impresses on a technical level – just listen to the enormous battery of sounds that the sound team have collated and edited and mixed into the soundtrack of *Toys In the Attic*.

85 Except that using a vacuum has already been used in *Cowboy Bebop*.
86 Shizuo Kurahashi did the sound effects; Sound Box and Audio Planning U were the companies producing the soundtrack.

Episodes 12 and 13. *Jupiter Jazz*

The two-part *Jupiter Jazz* episodes (12 and 13), written by chief writer Keiko Nobumoto, are especially wonderful, very dense with narrative material, perfectly formed script-wise, meticulously and imaginatively staged, and thoroughly enjoyable on every level: in short, these two episodes are one of the chief reasons why *Cowboy Bebop* is such a stellar TV series. The big, contextual story involves Spike Spiegel vs. Vicious, and the Red Dragon gang; subplots include Spike's quest to find his lost love, Julia; Faye Valentine hooking up with ex-con, ex-soldier, androgynous, gay sax player Grencia Mars Elijah Guo Eckener; Jet Black and Spike falling out; and Jet pursuing the bounty on Gren (altho' the characters go their separate ways, they end up, as usual in *Cowboy Bebop*, in the same place, chasing down the same quarry). It is set mainly on Callisto, a moon of Jupiter.

The two *Jupiter Jazz* episodes are spell-binding television. They seem to take in everything, including a few kitchen sinks. There's even time in *Jupiter Jazz* for a framing scene of Native Americans at the beginning and the end sitting round a fire outside their teepee! (It was reprised in the 2001 *Cowboy Bebop* movie). It's pretty remarkable that a TV show can begin and end with a mystical scene of sunset and night skies[87] and shooting stars and open fires and teepees and Bull the Native American shaman[88]

---

87 The imagery of the sunset in the mountains and the teepee is especially reminiscent of the Hudson River School of painters – Albert Bierstadt, Frederic Edwin Church, Thomas Cole *et al.*
88 And both scenes with the shaman are very similar, and recycle the same animation. But this time, it really works.

(Takehiro Koyama), who chants, and then shift into a variety of forms and genres: 1940s *film noir* settings and *femme fatales*; Hong Kong action cinema gangster fight dynamics and John Woo-ian brotherhood themes; 1960s, Beat generation, saxophone jazz in smoky bars; soap opera-style arguments; an intimate, erotic two-hander in an apartment at night; and an aerial dogfight! And more!

And altho' so much is crammed into the two *Jupiter Jazz* sessions in terms of story and action, it's actually a character-driven piece, and it's what's revealed about the characters that's at the centre of the episodes.

The first *Jupiter Jazz* episode opens with the introduction of the Red Dragon's Elders, a bunch of Buddhist monk-like old coots who recall the council in Masamune Shirow's *Appleseed*. They represent tradition, heredity, deference, power – very 'old school'. The scene is staged like a meeting of a wayward prince with the gods in a palace. Of course, we know that the ever-resentful Vicious is gonna deal with the mob's leaders at some point, especially when they order him around like a kid (altho' they ominously warn him that a snake can't swallow a dragon). Of course, the Red Dragon crime syndicate cruises around the Solar System in a giant, scary-lookin' spaceship (which's red and very Chinese, a'course). So it is a while before we shift to the *Bebop* spaceship, after the scenes with the Red Dragon, and Vicious, and Bull the shaman.

(Buddhism has a somewhat sinister atmosphere in many *manga* and *animé* – like Shinto (and Christianity), it is regarded with suspicion and cynicism as well as indulgence. It's common for

Buddhist monks in Japanese popular culture to be corrupt/ ugly/ sinister, as the Elders do in *Cowboy Bebop*. In Japan, Buddhism is linked to death and funerals – Buddhist priests oversee burials, for instance).[89]

♩

The event that sets the two *Jupiter Jazz* shows in motion comes from Radical Ed: she is looking for Faye Valentine on the computer (tho' it seems as if she's playing a video game of coloured, girlie blobs in the shape of strawberries and hearts!). When she finds some information about Julia, Spike – lazing on the couch (as usual – his default position!) – is suddenly and violently galvanized into action. His agitation tells us more than any dialogue could about the significance for him of the word *Julia*. Because as soon as he hears that Julia may be in Blue Crow, Spike is snatching up his jacket, a bag, and is on his way.

Then follows an argument between Spike Spiegel and Jet Black which's more like two lovers than two friends and colleagues. It seems to be a major dis-agreement (Jet is once again warning Spike about rushing heedlessly into danger, as he has done before), but of course, by the end of the two *Jupiter Jazz* episodes, Jet is welcoming Spike back aboard his spaceship (the animation in this scene is especially fine – animators love to stage intimate, emotional scenes, where humans get to act and express them-selves, without competing with action, explosions, sound effects, music, etc).

The setting of *Jupiter Jazz* is yet another city that's seen better times (it's reminiscent of Detroit or

---

89 As Antonia Levi notes, 'most Japanese tend to turn to Buddhism only in times of need', usually when a funeral is required (51).

Toronto for me),[90] and also mining colonies and the snowbound industrial towns of Alaska or Northern Russia (Russian signage is prominent, and some of the characters recall Russians, such as the leader of the street hustlers that waylays Spike and Faye. If we're in Russia, we're in a country with numerous historical rivalries with Japan).

The quality of the world building in *Cowboy Bebop* is so high – in terms of creating atmospheres and architecture, the filmmakers at Bandai's Sunrise (and the associated companies) are geniuses. The two *Jupiter Jazz* episodes magically capture chilly Northern climes, where it seems to have been Winter for years, where women haven't been seen for months, where it's only guys.[91] It snows, and everyone (but Faye)[92] is muffled up (even Spike dons a puffy jacket), and the colour palette is dirty blues and greys. (The end of the scene with the Native American shaman features one of the incredible shots in the *Cowboy Bebop* series: a tilt up and up, from the mountains and the sunset skies and the sparks from the fire, into the stars, and continuing up to space, to the hyperspace gateway, and finally ending on the gas giant planet Jupiter).

♫

Faye Valentine goes off on her own (again): this time scuppering the spaceship *Bebop* (and its air conditioning),[93] and snaffling the dough from the safe

90 The long shot of the frozen river or lake and the city beyond lit up at night is yet again New York City seen from Central Park, though.
91 Movies such as the 1981 *The Thing* remake, or *Ice Station Zebra*, form intertexts here.
92 Even when it's freezing outside, Faye continues to wear her sexy-as-fuck yellow shorts 'n' croptop combo (But she does sneeze!). And even when she finds out that women are not just scarce, but there *aren't any* (!), and that the men are leching over her, she doesn't alter her behaviour one iota, let alone her clothes. What a girl!
93 Thus the charas travel from very hot to very cold.

(though she later claims it was only 20,000 Woolongs = 200 bucks). You gotta ♥ Faye – this is a girl who can really handle herself; a girl who goes into a bar and doesn't realize she's not only the only woman there (she's drinking heavily all night, alone), but the only woman in the whole city! She's simply not concerned with how men look at her at all. (A city where there are no women – *at all* – is very unusual, because it's a regular city, not sci-fi staples like a mining colony or a prison (*Alien 3* combined the two).)

I love the gag where Faye Valentine, faced with a posse of no-goods and thieves armed with metal pipes (very *Akira*!) in an alley (a recurring gag – Spike had already encountered them), takes time to put on her gloves (because, she says, she doesn't want to break a finger nail). Yet she doesn't have time to beat them up, because Grencia Mars Elijah Guo Eckener (Kenyu Horiuchi), thinking she needs help, rescues her (also, because we've already seen one Spike vs. thugs fight, we don't need to watch another).[94] Look at Faye's face as they flee, how she's thinking: wow, why do guys just wanna look after me, and rescue me, when I can take care of myself just fine? And why does this sax-playing pretty boy turn out to be gay?! (That Gren is gay is introduced as soon as Faye and Gren meet, thus nixing the pick-up scenario).

In *Jupiter Jazz* the flashbacks and journeys into the past of the characters pay off big time – especially with Spike Spiegel's troubled past. There's always a woman involved, in this kinda hard-boiled thriller genre: Spike's old flame Julia (Gara Takashima)

---

94 And that fight was especially violent. Partly due to Spike's fury at being mistaken for Vicious (even tho' they have many similarities, of course – a theme which's taken up later, in the *Cowboy Funk* episode, with 'Cowboy Andy').

haunts the two episodes. Glimpsed in the flashback montages, which we'd already seen in episode 5, *Ballad of Fallen Angels*[95] (though she doesn't speak in them – but she does speak in voiceover), the filmmakers play with fusing the past and the present in numerous ways (such as having Spike come round after being badly beaten up to find Julia singing in episode 5, and in the present day coming round and finding Faye singing). Of course, the girl is never clearly defined and remains a mystery: she's not so important, but her effect on Spike is (the Red Dragon deal is about the Red Eye drug, introduce din episode one, which's given the code name 'Julia').

♫

Homosexuality and transvestism are once again introduced in the two *Jupiter Jazz* episodes of *Cowboy Bebop* – Faye Valentine discovers that Gren Eckener is not only gay, he's not exactly a guy, nor a woman: he's given the looks of a *bishonen*, the pretty boy type in *animé*. (Gren has breasts,[96] and later explains that his in-between gender status was a by-product of taking drugs, partly because of insomnia – after he was sold out by Vicious and went to jail).[97] The moment of discovery, with Faye approaching Gren in the shower with a gun, is brilliantly intercut (by editor Tomoaki Tsurubuchi) with the face-off in the snow between Spike Spiegel, Vicious and Vicious's colleague Lin (Hikaru Midorikawa) happening at the same time (they are both connected narratively, too). Spike encounters some male hookers on the street (but

95 Handily, flashbacks mean that filmmakers can recycle existing footage, which in animation helps considerably.
96 In the drugs<>money hand-over scene, Gren appears in drag.
97 Gren's a more richly textured character than the usual guest star in *Cowboy Bebop*, and not only because he is allotted more screen time due to the story running over two episodes. It's that Gren has inspired writer Keiko Nobumoto to produce some fascinating work.

of course, this being a somewhat mainstream show, he gets very embarrassed and declines their (repeated) offer of a good time).

♪

The scene in Gren Eckener's apartment is the most intriguing section in the *Jupiter Jazz* episodes – and one of the finest scenes in the whole *Cowboy Bebop* series (it is brilliantly written by Keiko Nobumoto). It is a small-scale and intimate scene, which really boils down to the most common scene in all drama and cinema, two people talking. But something about the story and themes and atmosphere of *Jupiter Jazz* really inspired the filmmakers, because the quality of the filmmaking ramps up even higher (and it was very high already!). The technical aspects of the filmmaking raise an apparently simple scene into something very special: the choice of angles, the storyboarding, the cutting, and the fusion of sound effects and slinky music. Dramatically, it's one of the finest scenes in the series. (The camerawork in the *Jupiter Jazz* episodes is astonishing – look at how the filmmakers manipulate subjective shots, and very big close-ups which track slowly over faces).

The scenario – of two people in an apartment while outside it's cold and night and snowing – is meticulously exploited by writer Keiko Nobumoto for all of its unspoken eroticism. It's a man and a woman in a room at night – anything could happen! They are both attractive, both are complex individuals, both have troubled pasts, both are intrigued by the other, and both are also wary (and both are potentially dangerous).

The talk of course covers relationships – Faye Valentine offers her familiar line of trying not to rely on anybody, on being alone but strong (she talks – in a superb monologue, one of the finest in the *Cowboy Bebop* series (and one of Faye's longest) – about her new 'family' in the *Bebop* spaceship). Gren Eckener responds with enigmatic smiles and soft words (in their first introduction, Gren has told Faye he's not interested in women; it's ironic, of course, that a guy Faye might like turns out to be gay!)

But even tho' Grencia Eckener is homosexual, and has professed his lack of interest in the voluptuous Faye Valentine earlier (a girl who has a whole bar ogling her every inch), the scene in the *aparto* drips with sexual energy. There's a shot of Faye on the couch, for instance, with the camera inches from her bare thigh and ass, when she lies down. And the animators have paid special attention to placing Faye in sultry poses (Faye is never more glamorous in *Cowboy Bebop* than here). There is also nudity – when Gren opts to take a shower.

The *aparto* scene in *Jupiter Jazz* reverses genre expectations: in the *yakuza* or *film noir* genre, it would be the man going back to the woman's place, and the woman taking a shower while the man snoops around. Having Gren Eckener take a shower allows Faye to discover more about his background – using the age-old device of a wall of photographs. The *sound* in this scene is unusual – it comprises just the shower, in the distance. The camera moves in ever closer on a photo of Gren and a shadowy figure, in military desert garb: it's Vicious. So when Vicious calls and the answering machine picks it up, Faye guesses the voice on the phone as Vicious (arranging a rendezvous – a piece of foreshadowing).

The music helps, of course! Yoko Kanno

composed a slice of 1960s-era jazz, the kind of music that might've been heard in the late night jazz clubs in Greenwich Village or Chicago (and can still be heard in some bars and taverns). It suits the themes and atmospheres of *Jupiter Jazz* perfectly (and of course the jazz music has to foreground the saxophone – played by Masato Honda).

And the voice acting – by Megumi Hayashibara and Kenyu Horiuchi as Gren Eckener – is very impressive. Particularly how Hayashibara delivers her monologue in a much quieter and more resigned tone than expected: when she's on her own, Faye is a different personality than how she is amongst the *Bebop* crew (where she puts on a confident front).

I've spent a coupla pages looking at the *aparto* scene in *Jupiter Jazz* to demonstrate some of the reasons why it is so impressive, and why *Cowboy Bebop* is so beautifully written. You know how some people talk about animation and say they forget they're watching a cartoon, and constantly compare it to live-action? So irritating! Well, you do that here – but not because animation is a lame cousin to live-action: animation this good goes *way* beyond live-action! It becomes simply terrific storytelling.

Why should animation be 'second' to live-action? Why should viewers still denigrate anim-ation compared to live-action? Is live-action is more 'realistic'? *Rubbish*. More 'powerful'? *Rubbish*. More 'entertaining'? *Junk*!

♫

There's time too in the *Jupiter Jazz* episodes for the back-story of both Gren Eckener and Vicious: of course, it's a macho, heroic back-story of fighting side by side in the Titan War of 2068 (Gren retains a soft spot for Titan, and asks Spike to send him back there as he's dying). Thus, the finale of the *Jupiter Jazz* episodes involves the three guys – Spike, Gren and Vicious.

The screenwriter Keiko Nobumoto includes every cliché of the melodrama and war genre, including photographs of the guys in the war as buddies, a montage of heroic poses of the soldiers fighting (some of the images are made to look like old newsreel footage, *circa* WW2), trench warfare reminiscent of WW1, and a hyper-situated object, a toy musical box (well, just the music mechanism). Vicious gives Gren the musical box. He also uses a huge dagger to stab a scorpion right next to Gren's head – unsubtle phallic symbolism in a homoerotic context (and foreshadowing Vicious' penchant for swords).

Same-sex friendships are sometimes depicted as intense and close to romantic/ erotic in Japanese culture. There's a homoerotic component in the relations between samurai in some stories. Intense friendships on the battlefield between young men is a common motif. *Cowboy Bebop* draws on that tradition here (the back-story of Gren and Vicious is a good example).

♪

The gangster genre hand-over scene of drugs an' money atop a skyscraper (involving the Red Eye drug, introduced in the first episode, *Asteroid Blues*), plays out some of the dramatic conflicts: both sides come along to double-cross the other (as expected!). Gren Eckener berates Vicious for letting him down, for his lack of ideals; Vicious retorts with total nihilism – there is nothing to believe in, nothing worth believing in. Gren's put a bomb inside the suitcase o' money, which explodes (handily, this alerts Spike to their whereabouts, a mile or two away – another reason for the hand-over taking place on the roof of a skyscraper). Lin is shot by Gren (as he dives in front of Vicious to protect him, which he did earlier in the scene with Spike), and Spike zooms in, guns blazing, which inaugurates the swift segue into an aerial battle between three spacecraft, which the Sunrise/ Bandai team are absolute masters of (some of the team had worked on *Gundam*, *Macross Plus* and *Escaflowne*, which contain outstanding aerial scenes).

It's an extended, hi-octane dogfight, a real marvel of staging and animation, which further dramatizes the relationships between the characters.[98] So poor Gren Eckener winds up fatally wounded, and Vicious survives (despite a bomb in his vehicle triggered by the MacGuffin, the musical box),[99] limping back to the Red Dragon vessel (that Vicious seems to be getting the better of Spike throughout the encounter is a staple of the genre – it's reprised in the final episodes).

The Spike <-> Vicious duel is thus put on hold again. And Spike proves what a good guy he is at heart by carrying out Gren Eckener's last wish: to visit Titan one last time (Spike tows Gren's spacecraft into orbit, then releases the cables, the space opera

98 In amongst permanently overcast skies, grey skyscrapers, and edge-of-town wastes.
99 The music box is a favourite MacGuffin in *animé* (musical box music plays a big role in the *Ghost In the Shell* movies, for instance). In *Jupiter Jazz* the musical box is a token of the friendship between Gren and Vicious (the fact that homoeroticism is part of their relationship hardly needs to be stated). Screenwriter Keiko Nobumoto milks that musical box!: there's also a transmitter hidden inside it, and Gren picks it up as he remembers his time with Vicious.

equivalent of a Viking burial at sea).[100]

Gren Eckener is kept alive also to deliver some information about Julia to Spike Spiegel – the scene in the cockpit of Gren's spacecraft is ironically more about Spike than Gren, who's rapidly dying. The camera holds and holds on a giant, steady, wide-eyed close-up of Spike, as Gren talks about Julia, and how she told him about Spike's different-coloured eyes.

♫

One of the bones of contention between Spike Spiegel and Vicious is of course a woman, Julia. And it's part of the ironic conventions of drama that the hero (Spike) should be so much more in love with Julia than Vicious.

The *Jupiter Jazz* sessions add plenty, then, to the back-story of Spike Spiegel (and Vicious and Julia), and the crime syndicate. They also recycle many scenes from episode 5, *Ballad of Fallen Angels* (but now, in a new context and with new voiceovers, the scenes take on new meanings).

♫

One aspect of the two *Jupiter Jazz* sessions is immediately apparent: the quality of the screen-writing, and how the storyboard artists (Shinichiro Watanabe and Tensai Okamura) and the editor (Tomoaki Tsurubuchi) have been inspired by the writing to create *animé* with beautiful pacing, with perfect camera angles and editing, so the whole thing flows like a dream. Every shot in *Jupiter Jazz* seems just right, completely logical, fitting in perfectly with the narrative, the characters, the themes and the emotions.

---

100 Don't ask how Spike managed to get Gren's vessel airborne when it had crashed!

♫

The running gag of Faye Valentine being handcuffed crops yet again in *Jupiter Jazz*. How does a girl get handcuffed so often?! (When Jet Black discovers her on the bed in Gren Eckener's *aparto* (he's hunting down Gren for the bounty), oh, he says, Gren's one of *those* guys. Faye is too tired, or pissed, or bored to argue. How Faye *doesn't* react in an angry or OTT manner is appealing – she is thus the female equivalent of Spike. Tho' in his case it's lethargy verging on coolness, but in Faye's case it's boredom or fatigue. Notice too Faye's air of defeat as she flies in Jet's hammerhead craft back to the *Bebop* ship: she seems to be resigned to the fact that she can't escape her misfit family (she ignores Jet's accusations of her scuppering the *Bebop*). But also notice Faye's question – a character's question in this context tells us a lot about what they're thinking: 'who's Julia?' Thus, Faye is contemplating the effect that the mysterious and now almost mythical Julia person has had on Spike, and also Gren, and also Vicious. Faye likely reckons Julia must be a super-babe in the Marilyn Monroe class. But no, Julia's not a patch on Faye! That's part of the point: all the beauty in the world (Faye) is staring Spike right in the face, but he keeps harping on the girl from the past. Get over Julia already, Spike!).

Talking about the two women of *Cowboy Bebop*: at the start of the *Jupiter Jazz* sessions, Spike Spiegel says he's going after his woman, and tells Jet Black to go after 'the other woman'. Except that Jet knows that Spike is chasing a ghost, his past. And that's how it plays out: Jet does rescue Faye Valentine (who's been handcuffed by Gren Eckener when he goes to the rendezvous with Vicious. We know by now that Faye can escape easily from handcuffs (!). This time she wisely opts to sleep, and to let the men be men, and do their macho facing-up-to-the-past thing on their own[101] (the selfishness of men is one of the subtexts of the two *Jupiter Jazz* sessions, culminating in Faye shooting at Gren).)

Faye Valentine in *Jupiter Jazz* thus offers a critique of men and their ways simply by interacting with them. For her, Gren Eckener is a good guy who's been led astray by a negative, nasty bully like Vicious (as well as having a terrible time with illness and drugs), and so has Spike (who has the added Achilles' heel of pining for Lost Love Julia). For Faye, Gren and Spike would be better off leaving the past behind (which Vicious symbolizes). Yet that is something that Faye is struggling to do herself.

Another running gag in *Jupiter Jazz* has Spike Spiegel 'dying' once more (he's on the ground[102] in the snow lying face-up, as he ended up at the gas station in episode one).[103] But the explanation – that the gangsters (Lin and Vicious) were using tranquillizers not bullets doesn't quite hold up (those *yakuza* guys would not bother with tranquillizers! Yes, Lin does seem like a regular guy, not a cold-hearted psycho like Vicious. So he stands in front of Vicious partly to stop Vicious attacking Spike with his samurai sword, and partly so he can shoot Spike with the tranquill-

101 Faye also suspects that her relationship with Gren as gone as far as it can, and that Gren is to e pitied rather than captured for the bounty.
102 Another recurring *Cowboy Bebop* motif has Spike lying on the ground – sometimes after being shot, or attacked, or just because he wants to. He also flops on the couch, and is also often bandaged up lying down, and recovering from another escapade that went wrong.
103 Of course, he lights up a cigarette first. Or rather, puts one in his mouth. The poetic touch of the crow (the location is called 'Blue Crow', after all), is another reminder of Vicious.

izer. Even so, when does a gangster in a John Woo, Takeshi Kitano or *yazuka* flick use tranquillizers?!).[104]

Before we return to Spike Spiegel lying in the snow, there is a dream sequence – which reprises material from the *Ballad of Fallen Angels* episode (five), of Spike's former life. The dream, which constitutes a flashback (from Spike's point-of-view), is re-ordered from episode five, and has new material added to it – such as the images of Spike's eyes (presumably repairing him following his near-fatal injuries during the *yakuza* incident). We also hear Julia speaking for the first time. And the erotic triangle between Spike-Julia-Vicious is further explored.

---

104 Unless Lin does it without Vicious knowing.

Episode 14. *Bohemian Rhapsody*

Bohemian Rhapsody (written by Dai Sato) is another *Cowboy Bebop* episode that doesn't quite make sense, but it's fun. It involves the somewhat shady Gate Corporation, who run the entertainment and casinos at the hyperspace gates, and an accident at a hyperspace gate 50 years ago, and the scientist involved in developing the gates (the Gate Corporation – think of the crime syndicates that may or may not still operate in Las Vegas combined with an airline company that doesn't have a 100% safety record – would prefer to keep any problems with the gates secret).

That's the broader narrative context of the 14th episode of *Cowboy Bebop*, and it isn't that interesting, but the other elements in *Bohemian Rhapsody* are very entertaining. Radical Ed comes into her own by playing the mysterious Chessmaster Hex (Takeshi Watabe) in a game of inter-galactic chess via the internet/ ethernet/ geeko-net (one of the ultimate geek or *otaku* activities). Ed inadvertently leads the *Bebop* crew (who're at a loose end in tracking down their bounty) to the location of Chessmaster Hex (partly because she's an ace at chess, of course), who turns out to be the scientist who led the way in developing the hyperspace gates, as part of the Hyperspace Gate Project (and who built in a flaw that would unravel 50 years later – a very Japanese concept. But in his doddering old age, he forgot what he'd done, and now he just wants to spend his last years playing chess).

The most amusing scene in *Bohemian Rhapsody* occurs when Spike Spiegel and Faye Valentine enter Chessmaster Hex's domain in spacesuits (in a giant, space junkyard in the middle of nowhere), only to find the place over-run with a clutch of hippies, stoners, hangers-on, dogs, cats, parrots, and the Chessmaster himself, a 98 year-old guy who's gone senile but still likes playing chess over the net (and he's connected to life support systems via pipes into body, a familiar sci-fi motif in *animé*).

That hippies would hang out in this space trash heap makes sense – you don't have to pay tax, there's no police, and it's rent-free! The three old coots also make an appearance (they seem to crop up every-where). As does an old bounty hunter buddy of Jet Black's, called Jonathan (Yukimasa Kishino), come to collect some dough from Chessmaster Hex, but finding a senile old man and no WW in sight (so he goes nuts and shoots up the place – until someone, Spike or Faye, punches him out). The *Bohemian Rhapsody* episode closes with Chessmaster Hex bliss-ing out into death (or maybe sleep) after check-mating a furious Radical Ed (who's been up playing chess for a week straight, without even sleeping, apparently, much to Faye's amazement – well, chess is not Faye's game!).

Another character-based episode, without too much action in it (it's difficult to follow the two previous, scorching episodes of *Jupiter Jazz*), *Bohemian Rhapsody* is enjoyable, with some great comic moments between the *Bebop* family o' mavericks, and it does contain some further references to the back-story of *Cowboy Bebop*, in which hyperspace travel is problematic (the accident at the hyperspace gate near Earth was the catastrophe that caused the migration out to the other planets, and for the inhabitants to live underground).

Illustrations

Images from the *Cowboy Bebop* series, starting with the four principal characters.

Episode 15. *My Funny Valentine*

> My funny valentine
> Sweet comic valentine
> You make me smile with my heart
> Your looks are laughable
> Unphotographable
> Yet you're my favourite work of art.

Richard Rodgers & Lorenz Hart[1]

My Funny Valentine[2] (written by Keiko Nobumoto) is a Faye Valentine episode, in which we discover plenty about Faye's seemingly murky background. Turns out she was in a very bad accident and was revived 54 years later from frozen with a colossal medical bill (of over 300 million Woolongs = $3m); well, that's what her lawyer, Whitney Hagas Matsumoto,[3] tells her (but it turns out that the lawyer – with whom Faye has a relationship – is in cahoots with the doctor, Baccus (Kousei Tomita), who turns out to be his uncle. The lawyer is played by the totally wonderful Akio Otsuka, who is Batou in all of the *Ghost In the Shell* movies and TV shows).

So Faye Valentine's been involved in yet another big money scam (which seems to be how her life plays out all too often). The *My Funny Valentine* episode is another take on playing someone for a sap, in the *film noir* manner, but Faye is the kinda girl who'll escape from a hospital half-naked at night (by shinning down a drainpipe and fleeing to a nearby freeway).

The characters are once again unusual and drawn from the crime genre: the African American

---

1 Lyrics © Sony/ATV Music Publishing LLC, Warner/Chappell Music, Inc., EMI Music Publishing, IMAGEM U.S. LLC.
2 Another musical reference, to the song by Richard Rodgers & Lorenz Hart.
3 The shyster lawyer was modelled on George Clooney, according to writer Keiko Nobumoto.

doctor, Baccus, and his secretary/ nurse, Miss Mandel (or Mandly/ Manley – Chiharu Suzuka), turn out to be a bizarre coupla shysters. It's crazy that they think a girl with no money can be scammed for 300+ million Woolongs! (The insanity of the scam is part of the comedy).

♫

Cowboy Bebop is a postmodern, Pop Art, retro-styled action comedy, yet by the end of the series, you can't deny the emotional impact the characters possess: the emotionalism kicks in around episodes 15 (*My Funny Valentine*) and episode 18 (*Speak Like a Child*), two Faye Valentine episodes. By this time, the emotional relationships in the *Bebop* crew have been explored in detail (and not forgetting the two Spike-led *Jupiter Jazz* episodes). The comedy and the action tends to overshadow the drama and the feelings, but they are there (indeed, without that grounding in drama and characterization, the comedy wouldn't work so well).

The scene where Faye Valentine recovers consciousness in a medical facility (the machinery is reminiscent of *Akira* and *Ghost In the Shell*), is played partly for laughs, but it's also sinister, and cheesily eroticized (there are point-of-view shots of Faye's breasts looming like planets in the foreground as she lies down in the cryogenic machine. So for this part of *My Funny Valentine*, the audience is invited to become Faye, peering at the world over the twin hillocks of her boobs).[4]

In episode 15 *My Funny Valentine*, Faye Valentine is depicted as being on the run yet again –

---

4 Of course, Faye should be nude, coming out of one of those elaborate sci-fi machines. The filmmakers tease the audience with Faye's nudity or partial nudity all the time in *Cowboy Bebop*.

and not only from the doctors and the massive debt, but also from herself. Her short-lived relationship with the lawyer Whitney Hagas Masumoto has the air of a fairy tale (Faye is portrayed in a beautiful evening gown dancing with the lawyer, and riding in his flashy, retro-styled car), and we know it can't last (everybody knows it can't last – as soon as Faye recovers her usual self!). That Masumoto is in on the hustle, which's revealed in the present day scenes, back on the *Bebop* ship, is particularly despicable. But this is a crime genre plot, and it is a staple of *film noir* narratives that the con artists have to be nasty.

♬

My Funny Valentine is an OTT explanation of Faye Valentine's forgetfulness and diztiness – as well as her Major Babe status, her bad luck with guys, her independence, her courage, her vulnerability, her distrust, and her sweetness. The vast medical bill is only one explanation of Faye's enormous debt, and her penchant for gambling. She's the kinda girl who'd gamble anyway.

My Funny Valentine is also about crappy boy-friends: we find out why Faye Valentine is jaded when it comes to men and romance: this guy Whitney Hagas Masumoto, who says he fell in love with her when she was in cryogenic sleep, turns out to be a crooked lawyer who's going to fleece her, along with his uncle Doctor Baccus. So the evening gowns, the dancing, the romancing, was all a lie.

We find out in *My Funny Valentine* that Faye is 20 – or was 20 when she was frozen, 54 years before 2068 – in 2014 (the episode is set, like so much in the *Cowboy Bebop* universe, three years later – in 2071. So Faye is effectively 23). Notice, tho', that the spiky, spunky, kooky side of Faye isn't employed when she finds out in the all-important scene in the hospital room with the lawyer Masumoto that she has been in cryogenic sleep for 54 years. Faye's response is muted, confused, and disbelieving. The later Faye, that we love, would've exploded in fury at being told that. But *Cowboy Bebop* has Faye go all meek and quiet and wistful when she's thinking about what it means to be 54 years out of your time.

Faye Valentine's quest is for her own identity: she doesn't know who she is, or who she was. The quest is thus psychological and thematic – it's not an action quest, or a symbolic one, or a religious one, or a political one. But the filmmakers always find ways in which this psychological quest can play out in drama and action. And they also exploit the comedy in the predicament.

♫

My Funny Valentine is a complex story structurally, with writer Keiko Nobumoto dipping into Faye Valentine's past at different points: Faye is relating her story to Ein, the dog, on the *Bebop* spaceship (with Spike Spiegel listening in, when he's in the bathroom), but the scene where she comes round in the medical centre (in 2068) is merely the beginning. The *My Funny Valentine* episode employs scenes in the past related in flashback as montages as well as regular narration. It also has voiceover (from Faye). The narrative complexity is heightened when the events from 3 years ago (when Faye was awoken in 2068) catch up with the present day scenes (2071), and the bounty that Jet Black has captured just happens to be the lawyer Whitney Hagas Masumoto (now ironically a crooked marriage law shyster, and his George Clooney looks have gone to seed with fat implants to act as a disguise, so he's ballooned to an ugly 200+ pounds. Masumoto's bloated body is also a joke on ex-boyfriends – how only three years later they've become fat slobs. And, jeez, what did you see in them in the first place?!).

Meanwhile, the doctor, Baccus, and his secretary, Miss Mandel, turn up in a purloined police spaceship, and Faye Valentine takes matters into her own hands by fleeing with Whitney Masumoto in her spacecraft. Not only that, Spike Spiegel decides that Faye needs to be taught a lesson, and indulges in a dogfight in space (yet another dogfight in *Cowboy Bebop*! Do you know how much those bullets cost, Spike?!).

Did you wanna see a love scene between Spike Spiegel and Faye Valentine, where they get freaky? Well, it's right here in *My Funny Valentine*, 'cept it's expressed as a fight (in the 1930s screwball comedy manner, where the hero and heroine squabble continuously), combined with a flying scene (both fights and flying are common synecdoches for sex in cinema. The sexual connotations of flying are numerous). So here's Spike and Faye swooping around each other like lovers in their spaceships (and Spike pilots a sleek, phallic, red craft!).[5] Not only that, they are shooting at each other!

The filmmakers could've had other characters listening in to Faye Valentine's hard luck tale told to the dog: that it's Spike Spiegel (and how he reacts to her story), highlights the erotic-romantic link between them (of all the *Bebop* crew, Faye probably wishes it

[5] It's reminiscent of the scene in *Porco Rosso* where the man-pig flies over Gina's Hotel Adriano in his big, shiny, red plane – it's typical of Hayao Miyazaki that a love scene should be played out in the air, and in a plane!

hadn't been Spike there in the john!). Only when Spike overhears (on the intercom) the confession from the lawyer Whitney Masumoto and the confirmation of Faye's situation from Dr Baccus, does he realize that she has been telling the truth (up to then, he thinks it may be a tall story. And it's too long, he quips).

That screenwriter Keiko Nobumoto manages to squeeze so much narrative material into the 20 or so minutes of episode 15: *My Funny Valentine*, as well as the twists and turns necessary in the crime genre, is really impressive. Like many of *Cowboy Bebop* 's episodes, it's a whole movie squashed into 20.5 minutes (it would win prizes at festivals and screen-play awards).

Episode 16. *Black Dog Serenade*

Episode sixteen, *Black Dog Serenade*6 (written by Michiko Yokote), is a Jet Black episode7 (it's gotta be, with a title like that – Black is known as the 'Black Dog', who hangs on and never lets go of his prey) – which means, as the trailer for the next episode at the end of episode 15 explains (with Unshou Ishizuka as Jet Black narrating it), a scant supply of pretty people, and a bunch of crusty, old guys instead. Yes: apart from Faye Valentine's appearance in her dressing gown (on her way to the shower),8 *Black Dog Serenade* is very much a Crusty Old Guys' Show: a police (Inter-Solar System Police) spaceship is taken over by the murderous prisoners it's carrying (to Pluto – a suitably distant place for a maximum security jail – *Cowboy Bebop*'s equivalent of Siberia or New Jersey). The score to settle in *Black Dog Serenade* is between Jet Black and the criminal who maimed his left arm so he lost it – Udai Taxim (Kousei Hirota), an icy-cool, black hit man for the mob (a nasty piece of work, Taxim is seen dispatching a fellow convict during an argument in the hijacked ship's cabin by slashing his neck with a knife – the spray of blood that results is probably a reference to the master of samurai movies,

---

6 The title may allude to Led Zeppelin's 'Black Dog', though a term like 'black dog', as with 'stray dog', is pretty commonplace.
7 Thus, Faye, Spike and Ed appear only briefly: Faye to complain about the cold water in the shower, Ed to douse Jet's bonsai trees with a hose, and Spike to be bemused by everything.
8 With the expected shots of Faye nude in the shower – but silhouetted in the shower curtain as she jumps about madly and complains yet again.

Akira Kurosawa).[9]

So it's very familiar hard-boiled, detective fiction combined with downbeat, sci-fi thriller material: prisoners on the loose, an assassin, an old score to settle, and a former cop buddy Fad (Masashi Hirose) who turns out to be not quite as loyal as he seemed in the old days (so it was Fad, Jet's old buddy, who took out Jet's arm. In *Cowboy Bebop*, the police're corrupt, too, and in league with the crime syndicates, which in the world of *Bebop* are all-powerful).

Flashbacks in *Black Dog Serenade* depict the past (in selective colour) reminiscent of an old adventure serial from the 1940s: in a big city we see Jet Black (when he was a cop) and his buddy Fad chasing down some criminals[10] (always with the warehouse setting, always with the dark night, always with the hat and long coats of *film noir*, always with the guns).[11] Jet stumbles into a trap, in which his colleague Fad maims him (Jet was causing too much trouble for the crime syndicate, so he had to go. Note, tho', that Fad doesn't kill Jet – and that plays out later, during the finale, when Fad kills Udai Taxim, but not Jet).

In *Black Dog Serenade*, the theme of the past

9 The final duel in *Sanjuro* (1962) between Sanjuro and the enemy leader on an empty country road in slanting sunlight occurs in a medium two shot, as Sanjuro and the leader face each other; behind them are Sanjuro's nine by now totally loyal followers; the two men stand motionless for many moments before a sudden, fatal thrust from Sanjuro into the enemy's heart; there is a fountain of blood and he collapses (this's some six or more years before the slow motion blood and squibs of *Bonnie and Clyde* or Sam Peckinpah's films). It's an extraordinary ending, the way the two men stand so close to each other unmoving for so long, then the burst into action and the instant death.
10 In the flashbacks, Udai Taxim's design evokes the American jazz era; he might be a saxophonist with the Cab Calloway band. Meanwhile, a muted trumpet plays thru the flashbacks.
11 The setting might be the Lower East Side or near the Brooklyn Bridge in Gotham, or over the river, in Brooklyn.

returning to bite you on the ass is once again trotted out: it's a theme that affects all four members of the *Bebop* crew. Jet Black's past involves brotherhood and loyalty, doing the right thing, and living a criminal life vs. living a lawful life – all classic themes in the gangster genre.

Yes – and *Black Dog Serenade* is also an action-packed episode: the police spaceships arrive in answer to a call for medical help from the hijacked vessel, only to be shot to pieces. Jet Black stages a one-man assault on the prisoner carrier – one of the finest aerial battles in the *Cowboy Bebop* series, climaxing with Jet dodging gunfire and rockets all over the place, and using cables to crash Fad's ship into the prison carrier (the filmmakers exploit cables flying between spaceships to a striking degree in *Cowboy Bebop* – they are sci-fi equivalents for the tentacles beloved of horror and *hentai animé*).

And of course there is the expected climactic duel between Jet Black and the ruthless Udai Taxim, a brutal, very violent grapple, in which Taxim bests Jet. To Fad's credit, he steps in kill Taxim – it's a replay of the flashback scene (which Fad narrates as it runs again: now we see Fad standing beside the search-light with the sniper rifle). But the finale of *Black Dog Serenade* adds a twist that's typical of the *film noir* genre: Fad puts only one bullet in his old-fashioned pistol, and in the final stand-off, Jet snatches up a gun off the floor and shoots Fad. It's one of those endings which metes out poetic justice, so that the guy who betrayed the hero gets to die atoning for his treachery. It's not the greatest episode of *Cobwboy Bebop*, but you can tell that the filmmakers so relish evoking these old *film noir* and gangster stories.

Episode 17. *Mushroom Samba*

Mushroom Samba (episode seventeen of *Cowboy Bebop*), written by Michiko Yokote, is all about Radical Edward Wong Hau Pepelu Tivruski the IV and the dog Ein. Director Shinichiro Watanabe said this episode had been planned from the outset (as had the magic mushroom element). It's fun partly because it has Ed having an adventue of her own, tracking down some bounty (when she's ordered to go and find some food). There are two plots – the mushrooms (and the head trips), and the crime plot.

Set in a 1970s American West (think Arizona, Nevada or California – though it's meant to be the moon Europa),[12] *Mushroom Samba* drew on blaxploitation movies of the 1970s (the three African American characters draw on Pam Grier and the *Shaft* movie), and classic road and criminal-on-the-run movies of the 'New Hollywood' era (such as *The Sugarland Express, Badlands, Thieves Like Us, Vanishing Point,* and *Easy Rider*). And, as in those (road) movies, there are small-town cops, arrests, car chases, gun fights, and internicene warfare among the minor crooks in the wind-blown desert towns. The town in the middle of the desert is exactly like many places in the deserts of the real American West – it's scuzzy and beat-up, it's just a coupla streets and a gas station that's seen better days (the background artists at Kusanagi, Studio Easter andStudio Pinewood have really captured the flavour of the American West).

The combination of road movie and drug comedy is infectious in *Mushroom Samba*. Oh, if only

---

12 The superb, atmospheric backgrounds are laid out in the painterly watercolour-style that *animé* sometimes employs.

the filmmakers of *Cowboy Bebop* could be churning out shows this fun every single week! And there's a terrific soundtrack to *Mushroom Samba*, including a 1990s hiphop track, and a Seventies jazz theme.

The driving motivation in *Mushroom Samba* is food, once again: the characters're so hungry they barely have the strength to eat. They loll about in the den, accusing each other[13] of eating the last of the last resort emergency rations (in a 360° shot).[14] Once again, you have to take your hat off to the writers for making a simple trope like hunger work so convincingly. Having no food and being out of gas[15] – two of the worst things to contend with in the modern, Western world, let alone in the future, or in the rest of the world (hell, Western nations regularly go to war just so they won't be out of gas – the Gulf War, the Iraq War, the 'war on terror', the Afghanistan War, etc).

Mushroom Samba is very silly and a lot of fun: it's fundamentally a comic episode. It features some trippy episodes for Spike, Jet and Faye when they eat 'bad mushrooms' as Ed calls them (Spike ends up on an endless Stairway to Heaven stetching up to the stars, with talking frogs, Jet talks to his collection of bonsai trees and discovers the secret of life, and, best of all, Faye Valentine, in the john, becomes Alice from *Alice's Adventures In Wonderland* swimming in a pool of tears – no, a pool of toilet water and a sea of silver fish).

The comic timing in *Mushroom Samba* is spot-on,

---

13 Jet Black leads the accusations, just like a parent.
14 Turns out it was Faye Valentine who snaffled the food, which was a year out of date. She is punished with piercing sotmach ache!
15 So the *Bebop* ship is just drifting, and gets involved with a hit and run by Domino Walker the drug dealer. And it crashlands on Europa.

too: the filmmakers use the child Ed and the dog Ein for reverse angle reaction shots of each of the three adults acting *very* oddly as they trip out (clever Ed sets up a trap, hiding in a canvas tent set up outside the stranded *Bebop* spaceship while Spike, Jet and Faye take a single mushroom left on a plate on a table: each character reacts to the mushroom in a different way: how Spike, for instance, sidles up and turns his back and lifts the mushroom like it's someone's wallet is classic Spike behaviour.

Meanwhile, Ed, exploring Europa with Ein the dog and, desperately hungry, meets a trio of characters out of 1970s blaxploitation cinema, which includes Domino Walker (Tesshô Genda), a fat guy in a blue boiler suit, dreads and a bowler hat, as the drug pusher selling magic mushrooms which he grows in a spaceship. Then there's Shaft (Houchu Ohtsuka), a tall, skinny and very angry guy who's after Domino, because of the bad mushrooms Domino sold his brother (which killed him). Shaft symbolic-ally drags around an empty wooden coffin, as a reminder. And there's Coffee (Atsuko Tanaka),[16] a sassy, sexy lady (a Pam Grier type), also on the look-out for Domino (Ed and Ein hitch a ride in the trunk of Coffee's car when she stops at a watermelon stand).

Mushroom Samba culminates with a railroad/ car/ bike chase right out of the Marx Brothers, and 1940s adventure serials, and any of 10,000 Westerns. Every gag you can think of involving chases along the top of railroad cars is employed, with Ed magically triumphing (even the cow-on-the-railroad gag is employed, to cap the chase). Guns're employed on the

16 Atsuko Tanaka is the superstar of *Ghost In the Shell*.

train, but in a very comic manner – after all, you've got mid-teen Radical Ed leaping about in the midst of this chase, and it's her show, so you don't want the blood and guts ultra-violence of the Spike 'n' Vicious episodes.

In the end, nobody is killed or even seriously hurt[17] (director Shinichiro Watanabe acknowledged that the action in the railroad was pretty broad and over-the-top). Ed gets her prize – a bag of mushrooms. The cops turn up again but the mushrooms prove to be harmless Shiitake mushrooms (the comic acting from the *Bebop* crew as they try to shut Ed up is brilliant).[18] Thus, dinner that night (cooked again by Jet Black) is mushroom-this and mushroom-that. But of course, *nobody* wants to look at a mushroom again! Except Ed, who tucks in with gusto.

17 Shaft is thrown off the tank, and lands in Coffee's car, still pursuing behind. Altho' the car swerves and blows up (gotta have a car blowin' up in a 1970s road movie, right?), Coffee and Shaft land in a comic heap.
18 The cop even has an electronic gizmo to test the mushrooms! A terrific gag sending up the mandatory testing-of-the-drugs in the crime genre.

Episode 18. *Speak Like a Child*

Many of the twenty-six episodes of *Cowboy Bebop* are absolutely bonkers, in terms of stories, characters, situations and drama. And very funny. About the silliest sequence of many is the one in *Speak Like a Child*[19] (written by Shoji Kawamori, Aya Yoshinaga and Akihiko Inari),[20] where Spike Spiegel and Jet Black travel by hyperspace all the way to Earth just to pick up a television set and a video recorder! Which they want so they can watch a video tape that's been sent to Faye Valentine.

Not only do they venture into the now-devastated Tokyo (how many times has Tokyo has been blown to bits in *animé*?!), the sequence includes every single cliché of disaster movies, action movies, and adventure movies, as Jet and Spike clamber down elevator shafts (avoiding falling elevators), along ducts, wade thru water, leap over abysses, hang off broken ladders, wade thru more water, plunge into flooded restrooms (holding their breath!), slither thru more heating ducts, and crawl thru tunnels. And when they've found the video recorder and TV set in an electronics museum that's built (for some obscure reason!) far underground, they carry them all the way back. It goes on and on, and it's very funny.

At the end of it all, of course the guys have chosen the wrong machine – a VHS video player instead of a Betamax video player (Jet Black was all for getting the bigger one, but Betamax is smaller! It takes geeky

---

19 The title refers to a Herbie Hancock song.
20 The plot of *Speak Like a Child* was used in the Studio Rikka movie *Pale Cocoon* (2005).

Radical Ed to point this out: Ed is on the case with the video machines: the first time, she sends the boys to Earth to a Japanese museum; she does much better when she simply orders a machine to be delivered to the *Bebop* spaceship).

Prior to this, there was a hilarious sequence where Jet Black and Spike Spiegel pay a visit on Mars to a manic video store guy (Shigeru Chiba) running a boutique for ye olde technologies, such as Betamax video recorders (the geek delivers a crazed account of the Betamax <—> VHS wars. And he drools over 20th century TV drama, which he reckons was *so good*, but the extract on show is a vacuous, completely unremarkable TV soap opera, as a dopey sister and brother discuss nothing in particular). The key animators have a great time with the techhead, giving him out-size poses and movements, sending up the whole *otaku,* nerdy thing. The way that the *otaku* goes apoplectic when Spike smokes near his beloved video players is wonderful: especially marvellous is the use of the static pose of total shock when Spike kicks the Betamax player which is scrambling the video tape they've brought.

The Betamax video tape itself (when they finally get to see it!) contains another flashback sequence – another glimpse into the youth of Faye Valentine, perhaps *Cowboy Bebop*'s most enigmatic character. Spike, Jet and Ed watch the home video in amazement, in big, silent close-ups (after they obtain the correct video player, in another delivery)[21] – Jet's forbidden Faye to watch it 'cos she still owes him the dough for the delivery service! We see Faye aged

21 Ordered, presumably, by Radical Ed – in the future of 2071, it would've been a lot easier to order the machine instead of travelling to Earth to find one!

maybe 12 or 13 horsing around with her mates on a beach, being shy in front of the camera, talking about herself, walking in some woodland, standing alone on the beach, and doing some cheers in a cheerleader outfit (note that the imagery is late 20th century or early 21st century – a shot of a jet in the sky and the costumes are the clue: this ain't 2071. This is Faye's childhood from a long time ago).

Rapidly, as the video tape plays, *Speak Like a Child* zooms from comedy to wistful sweetness: Faye Valentine again comes over as a sensitive (and fairly ordinary) kid who somehow was led into a life of crime (but Faye can't remember this girl or her former life at all).

The dialogue is perhaps a little too pointed and on the nail when it has the 12 year-old Faye talking to her older self ten years' hence in terms that are a little self-consciously poetic. But we let that pass because the emotion is tender and poignant. Especially poignant are the reaction shots of Spike, Jet & co. watching the video tape (the scene is played without music (at first) – a surprising choice).[22]

Meanwhile, Faye Valentine has gone off on her own yet again: she's gambling at the horse races, and later at the dog track. These scenes contain some humorous images of Faye in delight at winning, and frustration at losing (the animators have a lotta fun with giant close-ups of Faye zooming from elation to disappointment).[23] Yet Faye can't help phoning the guys on the *Bebop* ship, imagining that they are

22 A Western movie absolutely, definitely would stick sentimental music underneath this sequence. Instead, we hear Faye aged 12 speaking in voiceover.
23 The episode opens with a montage of images of Spike languidly fishing and Faye gambling at the race track, intercutting between the two scenes (while music plays). As the fish escapes from the hook, Faye loses.

worried about her. Note how she doesn't speak to Spike or Jet, but only to Radical Ed (and the dog Ein in another scene!): what Faye would love more than anything is for Spike to say, *hey, come back, we miss you!* Note also how Faye blames her unlucky streak on the *Bebop* crew, as if they've been stifling her.

It's ironic, then, that the quest into the mysterious past of Faye Valentine occurs when Faye has fled yet again. When the delivery craft visits the *Bebop* ship, demanding C.O.D., Faye opts to bolt again: as she hightails it, now all jittery, she wonders what could be chasing her – (her past!). Faye imagines middle-aged men coming after her who demand: 'where's the money?', or they state, 'you're under arrest'! For now, she says, she's just going get away – anywhere! (Of course, when Faye *does* face up to what's chasing her, it's not as scary as she thought – it's not nasty guys coming after her for Woolongs – indeed, the past turns out to be both more mysterious and more banal).

Episode 19. *Wild Horses*

> I watched you suffer a dull aching pain,
> Now you decided to show me the same.
> No sweeping exits or off stage lines
> Could make me feel bitter or treat you unkind.
> Wild horses, couldn't drag me away,
> Wild, wild horses couldn't drag me away.

The Rolling Stones, 'Wild Horses'

Episode 19, *Wild Horses,* written by Akihiko Inari (the title's might be from another Rolling Stones song, but *'Wild Horses'* can refer to all manner of cultural products), focusses on that ol' space opera fave, space pirates (so you know there's gonna be space battles, with Faye Valentine and Spike Spiegel duking it out with goofy dudes). Far more enjoyable are the scenes where Spike is out of gas in the desert again (*Wild Horses* opens with the gag of Spike trying to thumb a lift with a distant spaceship, a jet trail in the big blue far, far above).

The space pirates are depicted rather like the middle-class, loony, would-be rebels found in the movies of John Hughes and other 'brat pack' flicks of the Eighties. They seem way too dumb and silly to be a serious threat – but, what the hey, altho' they manage to get the better of the *Bebop* crew (much to Faye's and Jet's intense irritation!), they die anyway during the finale of *Wild Horses*.

Man, the *Cowboy Bebop* team of filmmaking *love* the American West 🎥 – especially the desert as it's been evoked in movies in the 1960s and 1970s (out comes the bluesy, slide guitar music[24] again (by Tsuneo Imahori) over images of yellowy deserts,

---

24 The slide guitar is reminiscent of the music by Ry Cooder for *Paris, Texas* (1984) and *Performance* (1970).

with a harmonica cue for the *dénouement*). One imagines that the Sunrise/ Bandai team would be very happy if a freak wormhole had transported their cramped offices in Tokyo to somewhere remote 'n' sun-baked outside Flagstaff, Arizona.

With its giant hangars and chunks of planes, helicopters and spacecraft littered about, its heat and dusty roads (like a bohemian, counterculture Edward's Air Force Base),[25] the setting is as familiar as the saloon in a Western or the precinct HQ in a cop show (and there are real places in the American West very much like the ones depicted in *Cowboy Bebop*). And this time we seem to be in the *real* American West – that is, rather than a planet (like Mars) which just happens to look like the mythical Far West.

Doohan (Takeshi Aono) is the grizzled engineer who presides over this backwater garage for planes and jets of every kind (his gaunt visage and shock of white hair were apparently modelled on North American film director Nicholas Ray). Doohan also recalls the characters in *The Right Stuff* (a famous book by Tom Wolfe, and also a marvellous 1983 movie, which deserves to be much better known). Doohan is the familiar old coot and wise veteran of action-adventure tales, a little wizened, who's earned his right to be old and cranky, stern and eccentric.

Doohan's sidekick, Miles (Yoku Shioya), is a black sports fan (the team he follows is the Blue Sox –and he can't stop talking about them, which drives Spike Spiegel nuts when Miles picks him up after he crash-lands in the *Swordfish*). Miles resembles Rocco Bonnaro from episode 8, *Waltz For Venus,* in

25 Some of the production team for *Cowboy Bebop* worked on *Macross Plus*, which included a 'New Edward's Air Force Base', based on a research trip the team took to Komatsu air force base.

temperament as well as visually – a cheerful, well-meaning kid (who puts up with his boss's crabbiness).

So now we're into more boysy stuff in *Wild Horses* as Spike Spiegel takes his beloved but ailing *Swordfish* spaceship back to its maker, Doohan (it's reminiscent of the sequence in *Porco Rosso* (1992) where Marco Pagot, the pig-man hero, travels to Milan to have his smashed plane rebuilt). Men and their machines: what is Doohan tinkering with in his spare time, in the huge hangar, but an American space shuttle from the 1980s (the space shuttle isn't just a throwaway gag – it's used in the finale). *Wild Horses* is a *mecha* wonderland episode – many animators of sci-fi and fantasy shows are hardcore plane freaks.

The gang of space pirates have the upper hand for a while – scuppering all three ships – the *Bebop,* Spike Spiegel's *Swordfish* and Faye Valentine's *Red Tail* (again by using cables to connect physically with the spacecraft). The pirates infect the ships' computers with viruses (much to Radical Ed's annoyance when she can't play her video games).

When the *Bebop* crew catch up with the space pirates[26] and finally trounce them (Jet Black is particularly keen to wreak some revenge for the damage they did to his precious *Bebop*), Spike Spiegel in his newly-refurbished spaceship is cast adrift. It takes some creative manœuvring by the writer (Akihiko Inari) to enable the space shuttle (*Columbia*) to rescue our hero Spike from burning to pieces as he tries to negotiate Earth's upper atmosphere (it's

---

26 Using a rather crude means! – Spike and Faye blast two delivery spaceships with bullets in order to find the right one (the vessel which flees is the one they want, right? Yes – for once Spike agrees with Faye!).

prepped for take-off by a crew of two! – Doohan and Miles. NASA should down-size!), but it's kinda worth it. Jet in the *Bebop* can't get any closer to rescue Spike, so Spike has to try to slow down using any means possible – and all while the *Swordfish* is falling to pieces around him. Of course, the space shuttle rendezvous with Spike just in time, and the *Swordfish* lands inside it.

Do they make it? The *Wild Horses* episode runs out of time to depict the space shuttle landing on Earth in the desert in the conventional manner: instead, they cut to a new photo that's been added to the wall of pictures in Doohan's garage office, depicting Doohan, Spike Spiegel and Miles back on Earth, with the crashed space shuttle behind them (Miles grins, Spike sits on the ground lighting a cigarette).

The gag of Miles listening to a sports game on the radio pays off here: in order to get around being attacked by the computer virus from the space pirates, the *Bebop* crew resort to a simple radio device (Jet Black's idea), which just happens to pick up the Blue Sox game (and, in turn, Miles just happens to hear that Spike's in trouble way up in space as he fixes a motorcycle). Oh, it's long-winded, it stretches belief (just a little!), but, hey, it works to get Doohan and Miles flying to the rescue.

Anyhoo, it's not in the story, once again, that the real pleasures of *Cowboy Bebop* lie, but in the char-acters, the humour, the mood, the atmosphere, the whole vibe.

Wild Horses is overshadowed by some of the flashier (and funnier) episodes in the *Cowboy Bebop* series, but it swings by pleasantly enough, finds something for each of the *Bebop* crew to do (well, not Radical Ed so much), and offers another extended and witty *hommage* to Americana *circa* 1966-1978. And who can complain when there's so much aircraft and boysy stuff on show? If you love *mecha* and flying machines, *Wild Horses* delivers them in spades.

Episode 20. *Pierrot le Fou*

AN ANIMATION MASTERPIECE.

The twentieth episode of *Cowboy Bebop*, *Pierrot le Fou* (written and storyboarded by Sadayuki Murai),[27] is one of the wildest things to appear in Japanese animation. It's *Batman*, it's Tim Burton, it's Walt Disney, it's Tex Avery, it's Buster Keaton, it's *Looney Tunes*, it's *film noir*, it's every gangster flick ever – it's totally *mad*.

When you've seen *Pierrot le Fou* once, go back and watch it again: switch off the subtitles, and marvel at the animation, the editing, the fantastical designs, the colours, the sheer genius of the whole thing. It would win top prize in any animation festival.

Pierrot le Fou is a *hommage* to animation, and it's also a *History of Animation*. The Space Land theme park in the second half contains numerous references to the output of the Walt Disney corporation, but the whole episode is a tribute to classic animation made at Warner Brothers, MGM, and the Fleischers, as well as the greats of Japanese animation, such as Osamu Tezuka.[28]

One can imagine the old heroes of American animation – Chuck Jones, the Fleischers, Ub Iwerks –

27 Yes, the title might refer to the wonderful Jean-Luc Godard movie, but this episode has bugger all to do with the French maestro.
28 Osamu Tezuka is of course one of the major figures in Japanese *animé* and *manga*, creator/ director of *Astro Boy, Arabian Nights, Princess Knight, Triton of the Sea, Kimba the White Lion, Bix X, Black Jack, Dororo, Jungle Emperor Leo,* and *Phoenix* (as well as 21 TV series and twelve TV specials, Tezuka also produced 700 stories and around 17,000 *manga* pages (C, 30). While animators work under the shadow of Disney in the West, in Japan, it's Tezuka. Tezuka was very successful very quickly: by his early twenties, he was 'the biggest selling *manga* artist in Japan' (H. McCarthy, 1993, 13). And he was immensely prolific, creating thousands of pages of *manga* (as well as developing *animé* and running production companies).

just loving *Cowboy Bebop*, because the filmmaking team at Sunrise/ Bandai completely understand what animation is and what it can do. They get the humour, the irreverent genre-bending, the riffing on age-old gags and prat-falls, and the sheer delight in whacking the so-called 'real', physical world into unbelievable contortions and distortions.[29]

In short, in an outstanding animated series, *Pierrot le Fou* may be the most accomplished episode, in terms of animation as creative filmmaking. It's as if the producers told the animation team: *go nuts! Go really, really nuts!* And they did: the producers chained the animators to their desks, ordering them not to leave until they had topped what they'd already done. By any standards, *Pierrot le Fou* is insanely fabulous filmmaking.

Pierrot le Fou is a technical marvel, an object lesson in how to use visual effects in animation. Watch *Pierrot le Fou* and learn how digital elements in animation can be exploited (there is a *huge* amount of computer-assisted animation in modelling in *Pierrot le Fou*). The filmmakers take up one of the chief motifs of the *Cowboy Bebop* series (and all *animé*), the circle shape, are apply it in numerous scenes (where often circles are spinning in the form of carousels, big wheels, platforms, wheels or guns). And as an expresion of lighting, *Pierrot le Fou* is a living wonder: many scenes featuring Pierrot are lit with a very low angle, intense light, creating out-size shadows. And the Electric Parade is a constellation of glowing light.

---

29 More recent animators, such as Ralph Bakshi, James Selick and of course Tim Burton, would probably enjoy *Pierrot le Fou*. In the West, the humour and popular culture sensibility (as well as the kitsch and the Americana and 'adult' themes) of Bakshi's cartoons chimes with *Cowboy Bebop*: *Fritz the Cat*, obviously, and also *Wizards*.

❖

The plot of *Pierrot le Fou* is delightfully thin and *dumb*: the hapless Spike Spiegel unwittingly witnesses a gangland assassination in Downtown Somewhere,[30] and becomes the target of an endless hunt by the portly psychopath Pierrot le Fou. That's it. That's the story. If you think it's just an excuse for yet another shoot-'em-up, you're right. If you think it's another excuse for the filmmaking team to deliver knockabout humour, silly physical gags, and outrageous firefights which build and build up to big explosions, you're right (more firepower is unleashed in *Pierrot le Fou* than in most other episodes of *Cowboy Bebop*, apart from the Vicious/ Red Dragon episodes).

The opening sequence in *Pierrot le Fou* is a *tour-de-force* of animation. The narrative situation – the assassination of a group of gangsters next to their car outside a building at night – is routine crime genre material. But the filmmaking is off the chart. Once again, the stylizations here are of *film noir* cinema (of the 1940s and 1950s, but with fashions from the 1930s), as re-imagined by comicbook artists in the 1960s and 1970s, and then updated by animators in the late 1990s. Deep German Expressionist shadows, harsh, low-angle light, thick, black outlines, selective, sepia-hued colour (the city's in dirty beiges and blacks), and tilted, Orson Wellesian camera angles. (Once the action starts up, the filmmakers introduce saturated reds and oranges, but retain the stylizations of the shadows and the high contrast, reproduc-

---

30 Spike is hustling in a pool hall, and wanders out (after winning a'course), stumbling right into the scene. A case of very, very bad timing. Two minutes later, and Tongpu would've been whirling up into the sky, cackling madly, but oblivious.

ing one of the finest equivalents for a comicbook look you'll see in animation).

The violence is swift and brutal, and the mobsters don't stand a chance against the unstoppable force of nature that is the rotund, demonic Pierrot le Fou. And when the unsuspecting Spike Spiegel saunters out of an alley from his billiards game, he has never encountered a villain like this before! (No one has! Not even the *animé* audience!). Pierrot makes Vicious and the Red Dragon syndicate of earlier *Cowboy Bebop* sessions look like pussies. Spike gets roundly beaten, and seems to have met more than his match. Spike should really die here with Pierrot's gun muzzle inches from his face, but the filmmakers once again have the hero somehow escaping (the sudden appearance of a cat, which makes Pierrot lose it, gives Spike a chance, enabling him to grab a gas barrel while Pierrot shoots up the pussy in a frenzy;[31] but the villain floats thru the ensuing explosions, hurling a knife out of the flames that lands in Spike. Only by apparently diving into the water at the harbour does Spike survive. And with the cops closing, Pierro simply vanishes).

♫

Let's not have the designers and animators taking all of the credit in *Pierrot le Fou* – we can't forget the contribution of Yoko Kanno, Hajime Mizoguchi, the Seatbelts and the music team. Altho' the *milieu* of *Pierrot le Fou* is a *film noir*/ crime genre metropolis that draws on the 1930s, 1940s and 1950s, jazz, bebop, blues and the like are *not* employed. Indeed, the score for *Pierrot le Fou* announces its departure from expectations in the

---

31 And missing – tho' he hits humans every time – you can't kill a cat! No way!

opening sequence: it is highly unusual, dominated by a constant, eerie whine, and industrial noises, scrapes, thuds and jangles. The concept of using abstract, metallic, industrial sounds to accompany the intense firefights and hyped-up cartoon action in *Pierot le Fou* is brilliant. (And the sound effects team are earning their fee by sourcing every gun sound, grenade sound and explosion noise available in the sound production companies in Tokyo).

THE SPACE LAND THEME PARK.

But we're not done yet! – coming up is the totally crazeeee filmmaking that climaxes the *Pierrot le Fou* episode with a visit to a so-zany theme park called Space Land. Ah, how Japanese storytellers *love* theme parks! *Wow*: it's every crummy theme park (Coney Island in the down-at-heel late 1970s), plus every state-of-the-art theme park like Disneyland or Universal Studios. And it's every olde worlde theme park in Europe.[32] And it's every theme park in movies, from *Pinocchio*'s Pleasure Island (the Disney Studios' darkest hour[33] – slave-trading, the

---

32 Such as Gardaland in Verona, De Efteling in Holland, and the Tivoli Gardens in Copenhagen.
33 Richard Schickel calls *Pinocchio* the 'darkest in hue of all Disney's pictures and the one which, despite its humor, is the most consistently terrifying' (*The Disney Version*, 232).

corruption of children and innocence)[34] onwards.[35] (However, *Pierrot le Fou* is not a simple assassination on the Disney Studios or on Disneyland, very easy targets for satirists to send up – consider any episode of *The Simpsons* which alludes to the Disney conglomerate. Because the filmmakers are also clearly fans as well as critics).

As in *Pinocchio*, the filmmakers at Sunrise/ Bandai introduce Space Land at night, and they exploit the creepiness of a fun fair or theme park at night for all of its potential.[36] A *huge* amount of research and thought has gone into Space Land: a team of background artists and designers[37] have spent ages coming up with fun and freaky rides,

---

34 *Pinocchio* features some of Disney's most memorable and powerful villains: beyond con artists Foulfellow and Gideon is the OTT figure of Stromboli, one of the most extraordinary of all Disney villains. A colossal villain, emoting like an opera diva, Stromboli is so dangerous partly because he's so unpredictable. So explosive, you just don't know what he's going to do next. Those three figures would be enough for most movies, but *Pinocchio* adds *two more*: first, the really nasty, creepy figure of the Coachman, a child snatcher who abducts young boys and takes them to Pleasure Island, where they are turned into donkeys (echoes of Circe in Homer's *Odyssey*). And finally a big, bad villain, Monstro the whale.

35 The filmmakers at Sunrise/ Bandai very likely looked at *Pinocchio* (1940) for research, because there are numerous affinities. The fantasyland of Pleasure Island in *Pinocchio* is the first major appearance of a theme park in the Disney canon, though it's definitely not a Disney theme park that would ever see the light of day (yet the Florida Disney theme park contains a Pleasure Island (since closed and re-vamped). It is a form of Coney Island. There are helter skelters, roller coasters, stairways, castle towers, stalls, marquees, a giant pipe surrounded by Native Americans standing before giant cigars, and pavilions – made all the more sinister by being introduced at night, lit up.

36 Of course, theme parks and fairgrounds have been used in *film noir* and crime movies, often for finales, as in *The Lady From Shanghai* (1948), one of Orson Welles' finest movies, or *The Third Man*.

37 Western animation, particularly on television, still employs static backgrounds, as Gilles Poitras pointed out in *Anime Essentials* (58), with characters placed against them, in the familiar foreground-background or *tableau* pattern of Western entertainment, while Japanese animation used dynamic backgrounds (as well as changes in the relation between the foreground and the background). *Cowboy Bebop* wields dynamic backgrounds to the max in its aerial dogfights, and throughout episodes such as *Pierrot le Fou*.

statuary, animatronic critters, stalls, concession stands, elevators, walkways, and out-there decor. Animals of all kinds are employed as the focus – but animals as depicted in the storybook style of late 19th century European Victoriana combined with American 1950s and 1960s modernism. The attention to detail is staggering, as is the beauty of some of the imagery (the background art is as sophisticated and lyrical as in *Pinocchio*). The Electric Parade in particular (a spoof on the Electric Parades at Disneyland) is simply gorgeous to look at – a phenomenal use of silhouettes as well as neon and LED-style lighting, and sweeping disco spotlights (I bet the cels from this scene sell well).

The Space Land sequence in *Pierrot le Fou* intersperses wall-to-wall action, as Pierrot assaults Spike Spiegel every which way he can, with some sinister stuff – at one point, Spike shoots (and kicks) to bits a robotic cast member (who resembles Pluto the Disney dog), with many bullet hits and much violence – like the gag in *The Simpsons* where Bart kicks an overly jolly guy in an animal suit, but much blacker). This sequence also cuts back repeatedly to Jet Black and Radical Ed, as Jet finds out more about Pierrot.[38]

THE VILLAIN: TONGPU/ PIERROT.

As a villain, Pierrot le Fou is a madman in the *Batman* mode (that is, the *Batman* movies[39] from 1989, when Warners revived their franchise): his

[38] We have to forget that there is no security at Space Land, nobody about at all. But with a villain as crazee as Pierrot, he has probably wasted every security guy.
[39] Not only the dark gothicism of the 1989 and the 1992 *Batmans*, but also the two follow-ups, the 1995 and the 1997 movies, which featured cities reminiscent of some of the cities in *Cowboy Bebop* (the use of neon and day-glo colours, for instance).

characterization is clearly reminiscent of the Penguin as played by Danny DeVito[40] in 1992's *Batman Returns* (the corpulent, outsider weirdo bent on vengeance). His design in silhouette is a round ball of insanity – he is Father Christmas as Insanity Clause[41] (his coat opens to reveal an arsenal of weaponry), and in close-up his face is like a spoof on New Orleans, voodoo weirdness, complete with sunken eyes, meticulously trimmed grey beard and a square maw packed with grinding teeth (reminiscent of a death mask or spirit mask).

Mad Pierrot is the id gone wild, an unfettered, parentless child out of control, and now he's killing for the fun of it. He bounces about with a walking stick-cum-gun, and can also fly. He has a Joker-like laugh which echoes around the place, and a Jack Nicholson-on-acid delivery (with many lines spoken in English – 'hello, boy!', 'show time!', 'let's party!'. Credit must go to the voice actor, Banjou Ginga, who makes even simple lines like 'hello, boy' creepy, and does wonders with the demented laughter).[42]

And in true superhero stylee, there's even an origins story for Pierrot the Fool: it involves one of the more remarkable sequences in this remarkable 1998 animated series, as the pitiful figure of Mad Pierrot is

40 Danny de Vito's snarling, grunting Penguin, with his diminutive, lumpy, globular form, his rolling waddle, his penchant for top hats, tails and deadly umbrellas, with his pasty white face, and his pointed nose (a brilliant make-up job from the Stan Winston Studio), is the stand-out character in *Batman Returns*. Richard Corliss called De Vito's Penguin 'a creature of Dickensian rhetoric, proportions and comic depth' (*Time*, June 22, 1992).
41 There is also a whiff of *The Nightmare Before Christmas*, the beautiful, 1993, stopmotion animated move. The design of Pierrot echoes the Mayor, while his demeanour evokes the Oogie Boogie Man.
42 Banjou Ginga must've spent hours and hours recording variations on cackling, evil villain laughter in the recording booth.

employed for scientific military tests[43] (hence his genius with weaponry as well as his superpowers of flight and movement). The visuals in the origins flashback are extraordinary, in palest whites and lilacs, fading out of white and out of black, in a flashback/ montage manner, with a chessboard pattern for the ceiling and floor of Pierrot's cell (life is but a game – and Pierrot is permanently check-mated).[44] Extreme close-ups of syringes filling with blood, of Pierrot's mad eyes, drugs, scientific data, men in white coats, etc.

At the end of it, the nefarious experiments are abandoned, and Pierrot le Fou is left alone in his cell.[45] But… when he's being led along a corridor hand-cuffed to two guards, his teeth start grinding in C.U., his mad eyes start rolling, and pretty soon Pierrot has killed the guards (reminiscent of Tetsuo in *Akira*), and fled (leaving behind a slew of bloody corpses in the hospital).

Most amazing in the flashback, though, is Yoko Kanno's music, a skewed piece of contemporary dance music featuring an electronically treated rhythmic pulse instantly reminiscent of *Dark Side of*

---

43 It's the usual thing of governments developing super-soldiers, and the usual scenes of tests, cloning, of machines strapped to the head and things inserted into the brain, etc. We also see a scientist shooting a gun at Pierrot and the green force field which demonstrates how he can be impervious to bullets.
44 The origins story also incorporates cats – the critters that Pierrot loathes (associating them with the agonizing scientific experiments). The kitty behind the glass is also foreshadowing: cats're involved in Pierrot's demise.
45 A CG-created square of chess squares in waxy violet and white chess squares.

the Moon,[46] the classic 1973 album (that Pink Floyd opus was famously very much about insanity, though from the super-cynical, white rock star's (Roger Waters') point-of-view). There is only the sound of music in the flashback, no local sound, or sound fx (but there is a voiceover, which explains some of Tongpu's back-story. Altho' even that's not really essential, because the filmmaking is already telling the story at the highest level possible).

THE FINALE.

Even more impressive is how the filmmakers interconnect the four main characters: how Faye Valentine contemplates Spike Spiegel in bandages on the couch (again – a call-back to the *Jupiter Jazz* episodes), yet determined to go back to meet mad Pierrot one more time; how Jet Black asks Radical Ed to hack into the ISSP computer to gain access to Tongpu's file (thus, it's Jet who narrates the origins story of Tongpu in voiceover, as well as one of the scientists); and how Faye, who's feeling more caring towards Spike these days, flies in to help him out at Space Land (which he resents – a man don't need a girl's help!).

How can you kill someone who's unkillable and unstoppable? Answer: someone else does it for you. Or, in the case of *Pierrot le Fou,* it's a colossal robot performer at the theme park who stomps on Pierrot.

---

46 As if the producers had gone to Yoko Kanno and said, 'can you give us something reminiscent of *Dark Side of the Moon*?' And she did. Kanno can do anything!
Yoko Kanno's music evokes 'On the Run' from *Dark Side of the Moon,* a mood piece about paranoia, based around the rolling, phasing sounds of the VCS3 synthesizer (the sped-up sequencer forms the basis of 'On the Run'). Other fx in 'On the Run' included: artificial doppler effects on guitar (whooshing from speaker to speaker), treated hi-hat, footsteps, voices, a man panting, and airport announcements.

That ending is certainly unexpected, and exquisitely staged: when Pierrot has Spike Spiegel cornered (and even Faye Valentine turning up to blast the $ß§X! out of the cackling, prancing madman hasn't worked – she ends up crashed on her ass),[47] and when Pierrot has shot Spike in the shoulder, and it seems as if it's going to be curtains for our hero, the filmmakers bring in a number of elements. One: a split-second throw of a concealed knife by Spike just as Pierrot shoots him in the shoulder (it's the blade that Pierrot hurled at him),[48] which stabs Pierrot in the leg. Two: the arrival of an Electric Parade passing just as it looks like it's The End for Spike. Three: the arrival of Faye Valentine. It's as if Pierrot has never been hit before, as if Spike has been the first person ever to get thru his multiple defences and strike him.

When Mad Pierrot breaks down in pitiful wailing at the unexpected pain in his leg, sobbing, 'it hurts! It hurts!', the mood suddenly switches. Spike Spiegel looks on in dumb amazement as Pierrot falls to the ground whimpering (for his momma), and the robotic performers in the Electric Parade pass by, unheeding. One of the players in the procession is a giant, 50-foot tall animal, which unwittingly steps on Pierrot.

And he's gone. Squashed. Just like that.

The unreality and hallucinatory abstraction of this scene (and the meaninglessness of death, the suddenness of death), is enhanced by Yoko Kanno's marvellous music (a spoof on Disneyesque parade music);[49] how Pierrot's hysterical cries abruptly

47 That Faye flies to the rescue is wonderful, and further develops the emotional bond between them. Spike, tho', resents it.
48 And it's a call-back to the face-off with Vicious in the Cathedral, when Spike lobbed a grenade at the last moment.
49 The parade motif was revived in the 2001 *Cowboy Bebop* movie.

cease; how Pierrot's demise is only really witnessed by Spike Spiegel and Faye Valentine; and how it doesn't mean anything in the grand scheme of things: life's parade goes on (the sound mixers also employ selective sound: so that the cheerful but now-creepy Electric Parade music falls away, and slow, low drones come in).

AN ANIMÉ CLASSIC.

However, *Pierrot le Fou* is not about drama and narrative: as with a Tim Burton or Sergei Paradjanov movie, it's really about the mood, the images, the colours, the editing, the designs, the attitude, and the music. Forget the story, just marvel at the out-there imagery and set-pieces that the filmmakers at Sunrise/ Bandai produce. The Surrealists of the 1920s and 1930s in Paris and Berlin would love the full-on madness (and violence – it's *very* violent) of this cartoon.

It doesn't matter if *Pierrot le Fou* doesn't particularly 'mean' anything, or even if it doesn't add up to anything. It's not meant to make 'sense', to be 'logical', 'explainable', and certainly not 'reasonable'! Oh no, *Pierrot le Fou* is *not* reasonable! It's not sitting down in a quiet living room sipping fruit teas and nibbling at cookies in rural Connecticut while talking in a solemn, reasonable way about how the Republican Party can improve its standing in the House of Representatives.

Pierrot le Fou reveals the team at Sunrise/ Bandai and its associated companies working at full stretch. They have really let their imaginations fly with this one. The editing (by Tomoaki Tsurubuchi) is once again pin-sharp, with flash cuts inserted into the already-rapid editing in the action scenes, creating a hallucinatory stream of images. The storyboard artist Sadayuki Murai has let himself go, indulging in extreme angles, grotesque, fish-eye close-ups, and bizarre juxtapositions. Meanwhile, the colour designer (Shihiko Nakayama) and the team have pulled out what seems to be 500 different pots of paint to daub the animation cels in neon-bright hues for the Space Land scenes, and every shade of dirty beige for the *film noir* scenes. And when you add all of the other departments, like costume design, and layout, and sound effects, and photography, and of course music and voices, you have a masterful combination of creativity.

Episode 21. *Boogie Woogie Feng Shui*

Episode 21, *Boogie Woogie Feng Shui* (written – and storyboarded – by Sadayuki Murai and Shinichiro Watanabe), is a Jet Black episode (he narrates it in retrospect – it probably has more voiceover from a single character than any of the other episodes of *Cowboy Bebop*), delving once again into Jet's past, and hooking him up with a cute but rather unconvincing and irritating teenage girl, Mei-Fa (Arisa Ogasawara). Inevitably, the writers (Murai and Watanabe) squeeze some comedy out of the older man and younger woman scenario, with the *Bebop* crew teasing Jet about his new 'girlfriend' – is she his daughter? A love-child? A girlfriend? (Jet's reduced to embarrassment worthy of a spotty teen)

So the subtext or emotional material in *Boogie Woogie Feng Shui* is about parents and children, specifically fathers and daughters (and in this case, absent fathers, fathers who disappoint their children – in this case, absent pa Pao (Tamio Ohki) who lets Mei-Fa down).

Jet Black thus becomes a (reluctant) surrogate father for the duration of the *Boogie Woogie Feng Shui* episode, even doing what daddies sometimes do – eating ice cream on a bench in the park (ah, bless!). I guess it is kinda cute when a gruff he-man like Jet is feminized. But I didn't buy it – I think *Boogie Woogie Feng Shui* is the weakest episode in the *Coyboy Bebop* series (tho' with a TV show this strong, it's still finer than many another show).

Talk about unconvincing: at the cemetery in the Mars capital where Jet Black and Mei-Fa meet (Jet's come to pay his respects to his dead friend, Pao), two henchmen fire at our heroes. They take cover behind daddy's gravestone, a'course. And as they're being shot at, what does Mei-Fa do?: she gets out her *feng shui* prediction board! Very silly.

And then Mei-Fa grabs Jet Black, the veteran of a million firefights and chases, a guy who always knows what to do in such hairy situations, and pulls him down a hill, and onto a bus, with a final leap into a river for the opening action scene chase.[50] But that of course is a dramatization of their relationship, in which Mei-Fa is leading the man.

The bad guys trailing our heroes are modelled on the Blues Brothers from the 1980 Universal movie. *The Blues Brothers* is definitely gonna be a favourite with the Bandai/ Sunrise *Bebop* filmmakers: it's got North America + a big city (Chicago) + soul and blues music + famous rock and pop guest stars + goofy *Saturday Night Live*-style comedy + crime + shady goings-on + of course lots of chases + 1,000 cop cars crashing.

Boogie Woogie Feng Shui is steeped in Chinese culture and imagery, and has some charming moments (the world-building and the background art is incredible), but it's definitely one of the light-weight *Cowboy Bebop* episodes (but maybe that's because it follows the stops-all-out madness of episode 20, *Pierrot le Fou*!).[51] Lightweight as in flimsy and ultimately inconsequential (it might benefit from being placed earlier in the running order), as if the writers were coasting – rather than rollercoasting

---

50 The action draws heavily on the comic stunts of Jackie Chan.
51 If *Pierrot le Fou* was playing at a film festival, you would not want to follow it with your lame-ass documentary about the plight of the endangered Gnzzdhzz insects of Siberia.

(though the MacGuffins of a *feng shui* board and a chunk of moon rock are ingeniously employed. The search for the MacGuffin takes up much of the action of *Boogie Woogie Feng Shui*, with our heroes following the clues, pursued by henchmen from the mob who are also after the 'sun stone', the moon rock. Mei-Fa's dad Pao was another employee of the crime syndicate, and once you're in, you can't get out – as Spike Spiegel discovers).

Jet Black corners the henchmen and strangles the skinny one to get some information out of him. The scene's played for laffs, but at the end of it, Jet twists the guy's neck (there's a loud cracking noise, which always means death in movies), and kills him! Jeez, how about taking the guy to a police station?! The scene doesn't need that, it's vile, it stinks, and it's one of the major mistakes in *Cowboy Bebop* (and with Mei-Fa right there, too: altho' a guy's just been killed, nobody remarks on it: Mei-Fa simply ignores it and asks Jet about her father. What a shitty scene!).

♫

The climax of *Boogie Woogie Feng Shui* is a kinda replay of the climax from episode 4 *Gateway Shuffle*; there is a feeling of *déja vu* when we have Spike and Faye once again in their spacecraft shooting down zillions of enemy vessels as they fly thru the inside of a hyperspace tunnel.

The moon rock MacGuffin is flushed down the toilet (by Radical Ed, of course, because she works out what it is – by staring at its chemical breakdown on the computer, cooing, *ooooh*, as Ed often does), ejected into space, shot up by Spike Spiegel with his plasma canon, creating a wormhole thingy in the side wall of the hyperspace tunnel (as well as blowing up the unmanned spacecraft attacking our heroes).

That paves the way for the emotional climax of *Boogie Woogie Feng Shui,* involving Mei-Fa and her pa, Pao, who's trapped in the wormhole with the oxygen running out.[52] A reunion and an understanding on both sides, of sorts. Well, not really. (It doesn't convince on another level, which's that the *Bebop* crew can't (or anyway don't) rescue Pao, and that Pao has led his daughter Mei-Fa all that way (and with some difficult-to-solve clues) just so he can say goodbye to her! In other words: the script of *Boogie Woogie Feng Shui* needed more work!).

---

52 Father and daughter saying their teary goodbyes thru a video link is reminiscent of *Armageddon* (1998). The scene also recalls Shinji and his troubled relationship with his father in the *Evangelion* series (which was also produced by TV Tokyo).

Episode 22. *Cowboy Funk*

Yet another slice of the American West – the mythology of it, as percolated thru 10 million movies and TV shows (in particular the shows of the 1960s and 1970s) – crops up in *Cowboy Funk*, written by chief *Cowboy Bebop* scribe Keiko Nobumoto. The episode opens with the rapid introduction of the two new charas: the first is the 'Teddy Bomber' (Takaya Hashi, apparently based on the 'Unabomber', Ted Kaczynski), a grizzled, middle-aged terrorist who blows up tall buildings with bombs hidden in toy bears (the disturbing affinities with 9/11 and the Twin Towers seem inevitable. The imagery of skyscrapers blowing up evokes 9/11 immediately, especially if you were there in Gotham, as I was). Another link with September 11 and Osama bin Laden and his crew is that the Teddy Bomber explains at the end that he's making anti-capitalist (and anti-media) statements. (This was another episode not broadcast on its first run).

'Cowboy Andy'[53] a.k.a. Cowboy Andy Von de Oniyate (Masashi Ebara) is the rival bounty hunter who tries to claim the Teddy Bomber, riding into every scene atop a horse (yes, a real, live horse! Andy makes his first, impressive entrance in the opening scene, bursting in to the foyer of the skyscraper) where Spike Spiegel's got the Teddy Bomber cornered. 'Cowboy Andy' is Spike's twin in many respects (they have the same facial features and say the same things), but he's also gormless, dumb, tasteless and

---

53 *Cowboy Funk*'s 'Cowboy Andy' is a character built out of 100s of clichés of the Old West, and also draws on *My Name Is Nobody* (a 1973 Italian-French-German spoof Western produced by Sergio Leone).

shallow. Spike hates him instantly and whole-heartedly, of course, even more than Faye Valentine, perhaps! (even though Faye explains how similar they are, how they behave and think the same; Spike seethes, his eyebrow twitching).[54]

The terrorist plotline in *Cowboy Funk* is a mere backdrop – every time the Teddy Bomber appears, he is upstaged by the on-going feud between 'Cowboy Andy' and Spike Spiegel (and it freaks him out, that he's never able to make his political statement, to the point where he detonates his bombs to get some attention – a wry commentary on terrorism, because with nobody taking any notice of terrorists, they are really failing at their work!).

Despite the issue of terrorism and the images of plenty of buildings being wrecked, *Cowboy Funk* is played as a comedy (in this case, a comedy of rivalry). The 'Teddy Bomber's' terrorist acts form the spine of the narrative, in its top-layer, A-to-B progression, but the meat of the episode is the antagonism between Spike and 'Cowboy Andy' (or it's better to say that between the A-plot and the B-plot, the B-plot, of the rivalry between twins, is far more entertaining).

♫

Spike Spiegel and Jet Black go (in disguise again) to a party where the 'Teddy Bomber' is rumoured to be attending (in a giant teddy bear costume, a'course!). Faye Valentine gets to wear another slinky, *décolleté* outfit, while Jet is dressed as a love-and-peace hippy, *maaan* (with his circular, dark

---

54 In another intricate detail in the scriptwriting of *Cowboy Bebop*, 'Cowboy Andy' has his own brand of snack food. Spike Spiegel, at the beginning of the show, refuses to eat it, but, by the end, as he declaims that Andy isn't in his class, he happily eats the snack along wi' everyone else.

glasses and a long wig, he is a dead ringer for *Cowboy Bebop* director Shinichiro Watanabe – this is probably an in-joke by the filmmakers).[55]

'Cowboy Andy' turns up again, to steal the limelight at the shindig (can't fail, tho', riding a horse, in making an impressive entrance outta the elevator!). When the five charas get together – Jet, Spike, 'Cowboy Andy', Teddy Bomber and Faye – there's bound to be fireworks. Here, cornered, the Teddy Bomber sets off his bombs, causing chaos, then flees in a car. Cue the chase! On horseback! And in a spaceship! Now things're hotting up on the down-town streets (yes *of course* there's a scene in a market with the customary fruit stalls that the car slams into!), but now Spike is chasing 'Cowboy Andy', forgetting about the terrorist (it's played entirely for comedy – Spike is shooting up the Martian (very New Yorkian) city, blowing up buildings, and ignoring for the moment that Faye is on that horse too!).

So super-babe Faye Valentine rides into the sunset with 'Cowboy Andy', and ends up at his place.[56] What a place! A luxurious playboy's yacht! As Faye mutters under her breath, she hasn't seen a more tasteless place (and she's the kinda girl that's probably been to a few!). The background designers (at Easter, Kusanagi and Pinewood studios) excel at delivering a room stuffed with kitsch junk (rivalling the tackiest Las Vegas hotel suite), with red leather seats, a fake marable horse trough, and photos in frames everywhere of – what else? – Andy himself![57]

---

55 Later, Ed puts the wig on Ein the dog.
56 The scene reminds me of the famous one in *Some Like It Hot*, on the yacht, with Faye in the Marilyn Monroe role and 'Cowboy Andy' in the Tony Curtis role (but with the roles reversed).
57 When Andy offers Faye Valentine his chat-up line, it's: 'here's looking at my reflection in your eye', delivered over a close-up of Faye's eyes and Andy's reflection in it to sell the joke.

No, Faye's not going to get it on with 'Cowboy Andy' (who's as stupid as he is sexless, and talks about himself). All of the 'Cowboy Andy' scenes're played for comedy, including the climactic duel with Spike Spiegel.

With immense wit and skill, the Sunrise/ Bandai team recreate a gun fight to climax the *Cowboy Funk* episode atop a wrecked skyscraper, turning the debris from an explosion into a painted desert scene of cacti and sandstone pillars *à la* Monument Valley, and lit by a molten, red-orange sun. It's smart and amusing, and full of great jokes; the setting enables 'Cowboy Andy' to ride off into the sunset, after he's given up being a cowboy (he becomes, in the final gag, a samurai warrior on horseback, one of a number of references to samurai culture in *Cowboy Bebop* – and of course some of the *Cowboy Bebop* team went on to produce the marvellous *Samurai Champloo anime* series).[58]

♫

Also worth noting: running thru *Cowboy Funk* are the marvellous *hommages* to the music of Ennio Morricone from Yoko Kanno and her band the Seatbelts, in particular the cult scores that Morricone composed for the 1960s Westerns directed by Sergio Leone (including the familiar whistling, the slide guitar, and the harmonica). Kanno and co. also deliver a send-up of *jidai-geki* music from the 1950s for the samurai-on-horseback skit.

Another note: a character says, in English, the phrase *See You, Space Cowboy*, which closes most o'

---

[58] And how intricate are the jokes in this series: notice that Jet 'n' Faye don't believe Spike's story of a man on a horse. Now, Jet quips, if it had been a samurai instead of a cowboy. And 'Cowboy Andy' becomes a space samurai in the final scene.

the episodes.

Another note: the *Cowboy Bebop* movieee of 2001 takes place between this episode and 23: *Brain Scratch*.

Episode 23. *Brain Scratch*

'Mind fuck' or 'brain fuck' or 'mind game' are typical terms for the kind of crazy narrative and religious cult presented in *Brain Scratch*, written by Dai Sato. *Brain Scratch* centres on a mad spiritual cult (called Scratch) which promises eternal life or salvation or immortality by digitally transforming the soul so it can live forever in the network or in cyberspace. This's a notion found in science fiction, and also in *animé* (the *Ghost In the Shell* series, for instance, has explored this idea (in the *2nd Gig* series), and Major Kusanagi in the first *Ghost In the Shell* movie (1995) enters the cyberspace network at the end of the story).

The bonkers Scratch Cult is headed by Dr Londes (Chikao Ohtsuka), a middle-aged guy with a scary, ugly face and beady (purple) eyes – as unappealing a poster boy as you could imagine for a cult which is head-hunting potential victims. The Scratch Cult leads to suicides, again a recurring theme in Japanese animation (both of the two *Ghost In the Shell* TV series featured suicide cults).

It's all quite insane – literally. Turns out that the Scratch Cult in *Brain Scratch* is really the mastermind of a teenage kid in a coma in a hospital – he's dreaming all of this up, including Dr Londes, who's a fictional character (Londes only ever appears in photographs or on television – so he's another of those artificial characters which regularly crop up in postmodern art and cyberpunk. You fake photos and video recordings, then you manipulate a digital persona on television or online – which's what movies do all the time, of course).

The Scratch Cult in *Cowboy Bebop* was partly based on the Heaven's Gate religious cult which also involved suicide, and was led by Marshall Applewhite, whom Dr Londes resembles. There are of course many other religious cults of recent times (including suicide cults in Japan). The Sublime Truth (Aum Shinrikyo) sect, the Hindu-Buddhist cult led by Shoko Asahhara, was thought to be behind the nerve gas attacks in Tokyo's subways of 1995 (as well as killing opponents and plotting to overthrow society. Aum's leader was in prison). In animation, *The Simpsons* delivered a wonderful spoof about cults.

Rather predictably, the means that the Scratch Cult employs, and the target of the episode's satire, is television. Yep, once again television is singled out as a form of mind control, hypnotism, tranquillizer, whatever, in which the media turns people into vegetables for four hours every night. Well, at least part of that is true: millions of people around the world right now *do* sit and stare at a machine for hours on end, in a light form of trance (25-40 hours per week is average for TV and radio consumption in the West).

Thus, when Faye Valentine and later Spike Spiegel enter what appears to be the villain's HQ, the run-down building is dominated by a giant mound of television sets (looking rather like a piece of contemporary installation art – visit a few art galleries in any affluent metropolis, and you'll come across monitors playing back summat weird). The disturbing ugliness of Dr Londes appears on every screen of the TV sets in the pile, intoning his religious bullshit about God and immortality, about transcending the body and living as a soul in an eternal realm. Unfortunately, the broadcasts have a sinister effect on the viewer, ending in suicide at worst, and starting with blurred vision and los of motor control (the filmmakers at Sunrise/ Bandai reprised this blurry, debilitating device for the 2001 *Cowboy Bebop* movie, and had already included summat like it in episode one, *Asteroid Blues,* with the effects of the drug Red Eye. It's TV as a drug).

Faye Valentine goes to collect the bounty on Dr Londes in *Brain Scratch* (undercover), only to fall victim to the sanctimonious cult (she appears in a scene to be fleeing, but the deleterious effects of the broadcast make her collapse). It's up to Spike Spiegel to save the day, when he turns up at Scratch's HQ to find Faye unconscious on the ground. These two share a touching moment when Faye comes round (after the broadcast has ceased, when Jet Black and Edo pull the plug in the hospital), and Spike is waiting for her, sitting beside her: this time there's no doubt about it: Spike really has come to rescue her, just as Faye came to help Spike in his struggle with Pierrot le Fou (leaving Jet to finish off the detecting work of finding out who Dr Londes is).[59]

But, in the end, it's actually Jet Black and Radical Ed[60] who nail the culprit in his coma in the hospital (putting on an amusing father and daughter act, in order to get past the security guard to see the ill youth, with Edo appearing for the only time in

[59] There are scenes where Spike chats to the youngsters on the city streets promoting the Scratch Cult to passers-by (notice that they are surrounded by junked leaflets on the ground). The cultists don't take too kindly to Spike being less than devoutly respectful, and demanding to meet a guy who's dead.
[60] Ed does her bit by hacking into the police files, to discover that Londes doesn't exist. It's great that a teenage kid can achieve what the security services in the Solar System can't do.

Cowboy Bebop in a flouncy dress; the guard wonders if Edo is a girl). Jet, faking tears, explains that she went kookoo when she found out what happened to her brother.

The two narrative strands of *Brain Scratch* are cleverly intertwined in the finale, when Spike Spiegel talks to the avatar of Dr Londes on the mountain of TV sets. Londes rattles off the usual traditionalist, conservative, and old-fashioned contempt for television and the media (which he calls the new religion, the best and worst thing invented by humanity). Spike shoots at the TV sets with his gun, of course (exactly what you'd expect Spike to do!). But the broadcasts are having a injurious effect on Spike, he's stumbling, his vision's going foggy (in point-of-view shots).

The sequence is repeatedly parallel-cut with Radical Ed and Jet Black at the hospital, where they discover that the youth, Ronny Spangen, a master hacker, has created the Scratch Cult and Dr Londes: as they re-configure the computer interface, so that the kid can't control things remotely anymore,[61] the Londes avatar appearing on the TV screens panics and is eventually switched off (hopefully the audience will recognize the irony – that Dr Londes was only ever a creation of the very media he condemned. Just an image, in the end).

♬

Alongside all of this nonsense, however, there are some entertaining swipes at television: *Brain Scratch* opens, for instance, with a continuous and outstand-ing five-minute TV montage, in which the filmmakers

61 Jet Black handcuffs Spangen, but any major corporation would hire him instantly. Anybody who can create a cult of religious fanatics by remote while in a coma in hospital is priceless!

send up all the shows you love to hate (such as a cheesy confession show *à la* Jerry Springer, where a woman shrieks about someone she's lost to the religious cult, and of course countless nauseating TV ads for utterly unnecessary items). [62] The guys see Faye on their TV, being interviewed as one of the cult's new recruits, wearing the shapeless overalls of the cult[63] and looking very spaced-out. And of course the filmmakers also use the television to deliver tons of exposition (from a news channel, in the usual manner of using TV in movies).

Brain Scratch in fact delivers an *enormous* amount of visuals – not only fake ads and fake TV shows, but parody news shows (including on-the-spot reports), fake websites, posters, leaflets, etc. Organizing all of this material is a huge undertaking in itself – the filmmakers use multiple screens in some images, plus numerous video effects and visual effects.

And some thought was put into just how the Scratch Cult would advertize to itself: thus, the episode opens with a Scratch commercial, in which Dr Londes appears in the lotus position to intone about immortality, God and the body that wears out, while the imagery is spacey and trippy (plus some symbols from the history of magic, like pyramids, and eyes in pyramids, and eagles, and suns, and clouds, and sparkly oceans. And the psychedelic, rainbow colours of rave culture, and tessellated patterns reminiscent of holograms. And rapidly-cut photojournalist images of wars, catastrophes, well-known events in recent history, and famous works of

---

62 Such as an exercise machine in which you can become a DJ at the same time.
63 The worst outfit Faye has to wear in *Cowboy Bebop*!

art such as Leonardo da Vinci). Dr Londes promises an escape from the cycle of violent humanity (multiple images of conflicts from history are displayed, in the form of real photographs), by transforming the spirit into digital form ('electronic transcendence', it's called).

Episode 24. *Hard Luck Woman*

It's a girlie episode – the two girls in the *Bebop* crew – Radical Edward Wong Hau Pepelu Tivruski the IV and Faye Valentine – are the leads in this session of *Cowboy Bebop*. It's a fairly out-there episode in an already Out There television series: both Ed and Faye are on quests to discover their pasts, to discover an emotional connection to their roots, and to meet their childhood selves. So Faye is exploring the home video she (and others) filmed as a youth (which cropped up in session 18, *Speak Like a Child*).

The writer of *Hard Luck Woman*,[64] Michiko Yokote, includes narrative elements that don't quite gel. Well, that's putting it nicely: in any other TV show, the script would be rejected by the producers and the commissioning TV channel with the familiar response:

'What is this shit?'

It's *Cowboy Bebop*, that's what it is, sir!

It doesn't fit, it doesn't gel, it doesn't hang together at all. Yet, somehow, the filmmakers make it sing. And that talent for mashing together a bunch of ill-fitting, eccentric, and downright *weird* ingredients is precisely what makes *Cowboy Bebop* so impressive, and so entertaining.

To make sure the audience gets that this session, *Hard Luck Woman*, is gonna be *maaad* as a March Hare, the filmmakers insert a kiss on the mouth for our two girls in the post-credits, pre-title teaser: Faye Valentine is on her bed[65] examining her home movie

---

64 A title like that has to come from a pop song, and it does, from Kiss.
65 Our first look at Faye's bedroom – and our last!

video tape on TV in great detail, losing herself in her childhood self, as the camera cuts in closer and closer between Faye's eyes and the grainy home video (the filmmakers fetishize the video image here, like many other filmmakers, as if they're re-playing the 100s of hours they spent as kids watching TV). Ed appears scarily from nowhere, right next to Faye's shoulder. The dialogue, as always with Ed, is part gobble-degook (the kid's more spaced-out than ever!), but the scene climaxes with Faye grabbing Ed, stretching her face comically, teasing her to find out where the home video was filmed, and finally giving her a smackeroo (they fall comically out of frame. It's typical of this oddball *animé* series that the only on-screen kiss for the heroine should occur with a teenage girl, and not with Spike Spiegel, or any of the (many) guys who hit on Faye!).

The two lines of inquiry in *Hard Luck Woman*, embodied in the quests of Faye Valentine and Radical Ed, follow plots established earlier: Faye's goal is to discover who she really is, where she came from, and what happened to her youth, to her life, that she seems to have lost (her memory is still only coming back in fragments). Ed's quest is the familiar parent quest (in this case, a father quest), of teenage and children's literature.

The quests are both about origins and identity (and thus take place on Earth),[66] familiar from story-telling the world over, but given the *Bebop* twist. Which means that nothing plays out quite as you'd expect, and along the way there're all sorts of bizarre goings-on. The wackiest element in *Hard Luck Woman*

66 The *Bebop* ship was supposed to be heading for Mars, but Faye Valentine detours it to Earth (much to Jet Black's annoyance, until Faye gives him a silent, reproachful look).

is probably the portrayal of Ed's father, Appledelhi Siniz Hesap Lutfen (Kenji Utsumi),[67] 7and his young, long-suffering assistant, Macintyre (Shigeru Nakahara), who are on Earth searching for meteorites and exploiting them by digging and mapping them. Mad. Right out of *Alice's Adventures In Wonderland*. Mapping meteorites where they land! (it seems Earth's receiving a meteorite every minute or so in *Hard Luck Woman*). Doesn't make sense (when Appledelhi explains what they're doing to Spike Spiegel and Jet Black (who've arrived to haul in Appledelhi for a bounty), the guys stand there in disbelief. Their shock is even more extreme when they discover that Appledelhi is Edo's father!).

♬

There's also an interlude in an orphanage in *Hard Luck Woman*,[68] which's overseen by – what else? – a nun. Here's where Radical Ed was sent by her father (who's been searching for her ever since, or he says he has been, at least for some months). Faye Valentine had taken Ed with her to find the place with the large lion statues that spout water, where the home video was filmed (but, in true *Cowboy Bebop* style, Faye doesn't carry Ed beside her in the cabin of her spacecraft – she ties Ed on the roof with rope, so Ed can see where to go! And Ed, of course, is happy to be there).

The nun runs an orphanage filled with bouncy, running wild kids, in which meal times are the focus (note the weird items in the dishes on the table – Ed's has something like a lizard's foot sticking out of it.

---

67 The wonderful Kenji Utsumi (1937-2013) played Alex Armstrong in the *Fullmetal Alchemist* series, the scary demon Nosferatu Zodd in *Berserk,* and appeared in everything from *Dragon Ball* to *Dr Slump.*
68 Ed detours Faye Valentine because she's hungry – that's classic *Cowboy Bebop*!

Faye Valentine meanwhile is given a bowl with a whole fish in it. Maybe wisely, she doesn't eat anything.)

The reunion of father and daughter in *Hard Luck Woman* is as OTT as the duel between Spike Spiegel and Radical Ed's father[69] moments before (Ed dives off the *Bebop*[70] into her father's arms like an Olympic swimmer – he catches her by her legs as she stays rigid. Then they horse around in fine style, with Ed being hurled into the air, while Spike and Jet try to make head or tail of the revelation that the guy they're after for the bounty is actually Ed's father.[71] And it turns out that Ed manipulated the bounty, so the adults would take her to her father: it was for 50 Woolongs, not 50 million – a full stop instead of a comma! Clever Ed!).

But the father quest for Radical Ed comes to an abrupt and inexplicable end, when another meteorite hits the desert nearby, and Appledelhi and Macintyre drop everything to dash away to investigate it (in the distracted, careless manner of fuddy-duddy scientists or, once again, Lewis Carroll characters). Although Ed's father claimed he'd been searching his child for ages, it comes to nothing, and Ed is abandoned once again ('gone', she says mournfully as she watches the guys zip away in their yellow amphibious vehicle. Another example of fathers disappointing their daughters – like Mei-Fa and Pao in *Boogie Woogie Feng Shui*).

However, at the end of *Hard Luck Woman*,

69 Spike gets his ass kicked soundly (where is Jet Black during the fight? Oh yeah, Appledelhi throws eggs at Spike and Jet!).
70 Ed has manœuvred the *Bebop* spaceship to land in the desert, hurtling towards the camera – a reprise of the scene in *Jamming With Edward* (notice how Ed's father stands immobile to face the oncoming vessel, while Spike flees).
71 Her father calls Ed Françoise Appledelhi.

Radical Ed is seen leaving the *Bebop* and striking out on her own: leaving home, in short, exactly like a fairy tale character who moves out into 'the wide, wide world', as fairy tales put it (tho' Ein the dog runs after her and catches up). And that's, sadly, the last we see of the amazing Radical Edward Wong Hau Pepelu Tivruski the IV: walking off into the sunset (and a big, beautiful, fiery sunset of red, golds, oranges and yellows it is, with Ed a skinny figure framed in silhouette against it). Ed doesn't appear in the final two episodes, *The Real Folk Blues* parts one and two (perhaps because those sessions concern Spike Spiegel above all, perhaps because they are extremely violent, and it wouldn't be quite right that Ed was involved, but perhaps also because if Ed's going to find her way in the Wide, Wide World, it ought to be in an episode where she finally meets her father).

SEE YOU, SPACE GIRL!

❖

Faye Valentine's journey into the past in 24: *Hard Luck Woman* is even more ambiguous and unresolved: she encounters a former school chum, who's now a grandmother in a wheelchair (a grand-daughter also appears). Parts of the past come back to Faye in frag-ments (as Faye lies on her bed, lost in reverie, and then in the shower, there is a rapid montage delin-eating a space flight above the Earth that's involved in an accident, with glimpses of the moon out of the window.[72] We also see Faye's parents briefly (sitting next to her). The long-suppressed memory returns to

72 Suggesting that the incident was linked to the hyperspace gate explosion 50 years previously.

Faye finally as she takes a shower – and, again, the sound mixers use the sound of the shower prominently, instead of music).

Faye Valentine's story in *Cowboy Bebop* is also to run away: she runs away and comes back to *Bebop* repeatedly. She wants to find *home*, and eventually recognizes that it is the *Bebop* spaceship and the gang of misfits there. Which is sweet, isn't it? *Kawaii*, yeah? I guess.

In *Hard Luck Woman*, Faye Valentine understands finally where she lived: the episode cuts between Faye Valentine in the present day (in full colour) and her childhood self (in pastel hues: the editing and the visuals are reminiscent of the switches between the past and the present in *Only Yesterday*, a marvellous 1991 *animé* directed by Isao Takahata. Indeed, this part of the Faye Valentine story echoes *Only Yester-day* in other ways). Faye's is thus a *shojo* story, drawing on *shojo manga*.

As the adult Faye and the childhood Faye (at different ages) run up a hill to some gates, the destination is a very grand, Italian-style mansion with red, tiled roofs. This appeared to be home for Faye, but it's not certain if she had very wealthy parents[73] who could afford a house as opulent as this (it's possibly a boarding school or private school. It seems to be Singapore. However, the satellite map consulted by Appledelhi is of the Tokyo Bay area, very familiar to *animé* fans. And the views of the flooded city look like Tokyo, too).

But now it's all gone – only the foundations, the water fountain and a few bits of rubble remain. Yep, folks, you can't 'go home', you can't 'go back'! 'Cos

73 So it's ironic that Faye is now skint and reduced to bounty hunting!

when you do there's nuttin' left 'cept a pile of trash. Faye Valentine then acts a little oddly (well, not odd for Faye! Or for *Cowboy Bebop*!): she takes a stick and draws the outline of where her room would've been on the ground, then she lies down.

Something is shifting in Faye Valentine emotionally and psychologically, and the emotional shifts occur across the 1998 series, not in any single episode. In *Hard Luck Woman* there's a scene between Faye and Spike which demonstrates how their relationship is developing towards summat closer and more intimate: Faye is on her way back from the shower, in her dressing gown (thus the meeting already has an erotic component).

Faye Valentine bumps into Spike Spiegel (very Freudian!),[74] and (after an awkward pause) apologizes. Spike can't believe that Faye just *said sorry*! (Spike's reaction shots are very funny). Faye struggles to express something, but can't. Look at the design of Faye's face – it's a softer, rounder, and younger face, which only at the end of the brief scene switches back to the harder, tougher Faye face.

The sweet scene has Faye Valentine on the verge of reaching out to Spike Spiegel emotionally, but being unable to make the final move. It wouldn't work unless there was some feeling on Spike's part, too. Which there is.

---

74 You know what Sigmund Freud says about people you accidentally bump into!

THE FINALE OF *COWBOY BEBOP.*

Cowboy Bebop is going to end its astonishing 26-episode run with a bang, right? With a big, stops-all-out, action-jammed episode, eh? Of course: plenta bangs, plenta action, plenta wildness. Like the other double outstanding episode (*Jupiter Jazz*), it's a two-parter, written by head writer Keiko Nobumoto. It has another muso title: *The Real Folk Blues.*[75]

This is a masterpiece of screenwriting: in episode 25 – and in just 22 minutes! – Keiko Nobumoto orchestrates a *ton* of plot, *plus* several flashbacks, *plus* languorous and moody conversations and tales, *plus* four action set-pieces, *plus* more characterization and back-story. How in hell does Nobumoto and the Sunrise/ Bandai team fit all of this into twenty-two minutes?! It's quite, quite remarkable.

The Real Folk Blues rocks, it explodes, it does not disappoint! Keiko Nobumoto wheels in arch villain Vicious and the gangland warfare (centred around the Red Dragon syndicate), that was introduced in the fifth session, *Ballad of Fallen Angels,* and continued in the two *Jupiter Jazz* sessions. Vicious and the crime firm feuds are simply too good to leave aside, and if you're gonna give Spike Spiegel a really good villain, it's best to tie him into the other parts of Spike's murky past: the crime gang (Red Dragon), and of course the woman he lost (Julia). (However, throughout the series, Spike has been pitted against plenty of nasty villains, right from ep one, *Asteroid Blues*!).

---

[75] The title prob'ly comes from the series of blues albums put out in the mid-1960s. Or from 'The Real Folk Blues' by John Lee Hooker.

If every element in the two *The Real Folk Blues* sessions is a cliché, and was already a cliché in cinema by 1925, who cares? Yeah, it's cops and robbers, it's gangs 'n' shoot-'em-ups, it's a solitary hero taking on an entire crime syndicate, but *it works*. (Using clichés is inevitable in this kind of genre outing, even if it is mixing together a number of genres – space opera, Western, crime thriller, comedy, etc. But it's how you *deliver* those clichés, how you make them anew, how you shape them to suit your purposes. And when clichés're depicted with such esprit and skill, the audience doesn't mind, because they're being exceedingly entertained).

As this is largely Spike Spiegel's show, the others don't have so much to do in *The Real Folk Blues*. They warn him off his death-seeking path, though: Jet Black, who's wounded in the leg in the first episode (which importantly renders him effectively out of action for the rest of the episodes),[76] cautions Spike repeatedly (as he often does thru the *Cowboy Bebop* series). Jet's advice is very sound, and very useful: *let it go. Let the past go* ('turn back', Jet tells Spike). Because Spike is facing and heading directly for danger: there is certainly a death-wish element to it, an egotism, a self-centredness. It is not an essential quest that Spike needs to be take: he'd be so much better off lazing on the couch and complaining about the inedibility of Jet's cooking (which he gobbles up anyway, as Jet points out).

Jet Black has good reason for being so stubborn about Spike Spiegel letting it go – because early in

---

76 However, Jet is up and about later, and there's even time in the final episode for Jet to visit the Native American witch doctor Bull, to find out where Spike might be (and, a'course, Jet doesn't receive a straight answer from Bull!).

episode 25 he's involved in yet another shooting match in a bar, when heavies from the Red Dragon mob target Spike (cue more shattering glass in the grand, Hong Kong action cinema manner, and more gouts of blood *à la* John Woo). It's here that Jet's injured, and Shin (Lin's brother) helps them flee.

SPIKE AND FAYE.

There's a tender scene between Spike Spiegel and Faye Valentine, the real romantic couple of the *Cowboy Bebop* series, when Spike returns to the *Bebop* briefly (following the death of Julia and before he leaves to confront Vicious). It's by far their most emotional scene. Here Faye tries to voice her feelings for Spike (by saying that she had nowhere to go, and came back to the *Bebop*. She doesn't say to come back to him, but it's implied).[77]

It's a terrific scene, brilliantly written by Keiko Nobumoto, loaded with emotional subtext, solidly storyboarded by series director Shinichiro Watanabe (tricky angles here would be too distracting), expertly directed by Watanabe & co. (Ikuro Sato was the episode director), and marvellously and emotionally voiced by actors Megumi Hayashibara and Kôichi Yamadera.

Well, it's as close to a declaration of love as you're gonna get from Faye Valentine! She's just not the kinda girl to come out with a dick-ass line like, 'I love you'! Faye will *never* say, 'I love you'! What a scene, coming after 25 episodes of this simply gorgeous *animé* series! Note the way the animators

[77] In an interview, director Shinichiro Watanabe said that sometimes people ask him about how Spike feels about Faye: 'I think that actually he likes her quite a bit. But he's not a very straightforward person so he makes sure he doesn't show it'.

have blocked the characters, having them facing away from each other at right angles, or with their backs turned. It's wonderful – the way that Faye holds a gun to Spike when she corners him at the start of the scene (following his warm reunion with Jet Black), and the way that Faye repeatedly fires her pistol in frustration as Spike walks away (that works so much better than screams of fury, altho' Faye can scream like the best of 'em! And Faye, at the end, is weeping, when the episode briefly cuts back to her and to Jet, absent-mindedly cleaning a window, as Spike flies away for the final time).

The scene's in two halves: the first half deals with Spike Spiegel and his unfinished business with his past and the Red Dragon crime mob. The second half is about Faye Valentine: as Spike is walking away, she tells him she got her memory back. That stops him in his tracks. She then says something very important for the theme of the past in *Cowboy Bebop*: recovering the past wasn't what she thought it would be, Faye recounts, and it wasn't as useful as she hoped it would be.

But the bubbling-underneath-the-surface, will-they-won't-they romance between Faye Valentine and Spike Spiegel is not resolved, and that's partly because Spike has unfinished business with his old flame Julia (as well as with his former comrade-in-arms, Vicious). And partly of course because on-off romances mustn't be paid off until right at the end (*Cowboy Bebop* <u>begs</u> for a second series! A tenth series! Oh, if *only* a show as matchless as *Cowboy Bebop* were running every week!). But we know, also, that when Spike returns from his unfinished business with Vicious and crime syndicate, he and Faye are going to fall into each other's arms with a passion (I like to think they do!).

SPIKE AND JULIA

Most of the Spike-and-Julia scenes play out as expected, right down to Julia dying in yet another shoot-out, as she and Spike flee along a rooftop.[78] They meet in a graveyard in the rain (which provides the cliffhanger for episode 25), Julia pulls a gun on him (as forced to do by Vicious),[79] but then they embrace ('course she ain't gonna kill Spike! No way!).[80] They talk about escaping from it all – 'let's just get away from this world!' – but of course they don't. (We also saw Spike and Julia in some blue-toned flashbacks, which concentrated first on Julia, before introducing Spike – where the topic is again escape. Spike wants to leave the cold, rainy Mars[81] city, but Julia says she has to stay).

So the Spike-Julia scenes're necessary, and entertaining, but also rather routine, dramatically (we do need to see Spike and Julia together, to see what their relationship was like: and it does seem as if Spike loses some of his *oomph,* his 'Spikeness', you might say, and becomes rather too much like any other regular guy when he's with Julia). Notice that when Julia embraces Spike, he doesn't move: it's the first time we've seen Spike with a woman romantic-

---

78 That their romance seems doomed from the outset is suggested in many ways. Not least, their arrangement to meet in a graveyard! Jeez, that's a really fun place for a date! They talk about the future, about fleeing this world (that is, Mars), but the *mise-en-scène* of the grey cemetery, seen in long shot, suggests endings and deaths.
79 Earlier we see Vicious holding a gun right at Julia's head for a long time while he talks – this is one mean motherfucker. Yet Vicious was one of Julia's lovers.
80 Women pulling guns on men is a recurring motif in *Cowboy Bebop*.
81 For a red planet, Mars sure is cold and blue and rainy much of the time!

ally, in the foreground, present tense of the series, but he is oddly (perhaps understandably) unmoved. Maybe Julia doesn't have as much a hold on his heart as he thought.

For Faye Valentine, Spike is being a sap over Julia, as *film noir* movies put it (but then, Faye thinks that most guys are saps. And she can never find a decent guy). Julia is Spike's weakness, as he admits. Is she worth it, in the end? Jet Black and Faye would say, no. Definitely no. But in the scene between Faye and Jet, she's generous enough to talk up Julia, even though Julia's her romantic rival (and Faye perhaps also realizes she hasn't a chance with Spike while he still has unfinished business with Julia). (Similarly, the price of going back to the crime syndicate to deal with the past is also too high, for Jet and Faye: they also advise staying away.)

FAYE AND JULIA.

Thus, one of the more intriguing scenes in *The Real Folk Blues* two-parter is the *Thelma and Louise* girls-on-the-run sequence,[82] where Faye Valentine saves Julia from some heavies' pursuing cars (by shooting out their tyres with skilful accuracy), in a fun car chase (with Julia driving a giant, red, 1950s open-top auto with fish tails – is it a Ford Galaxie?).[83]

---

82 Of course the *Cowboy Bebop* filmmaking team are gonna love *Thelma and Louise* – the American West, the desert, girls with guns, girls on the run, an old-fashioned road movie, lotsa cops chasing the heroes, a silly OTT ending – hell, it's tailor-made for *Cowboy Bebop*!
83 How Julia drives by and Faye simply leaps into her car at the airport is, well, not wholly convincing. Yes, it gets the two women together, and on their way (they're still being pursued by heavies), but would Faye do that? Maybe Faye recognizes a woman alone in danger, and sympathasizes with her. Maybe Faye, who's at a lowpoint in her life, thinks, what the hell, and goes for it. Maybe Faye knows or guesses it's Julia.
However, the hoods do also shoot up Faye's beloved spacecraft, which's a good enough reason for Faye to want some payback.

Faye quite likes the idea of being on the loose with a woman as a partner, and suggests the notion to Julia (who declines). But that is Faye's life already, isn't it? However, Julia is ahead of Faye, and guesses who Faye is b4 Faye finds out who Julia is.

In the *Thelma and Louise* scene the audience is invited to compare the two women, both tied intimately to Spike Spiegel. While Julia is a terrific character, tender, loving, determined, and independent, she is not a patch on the incredible Faye Valentine, one of the funniest, kookiest, wildest and sexiest characters in all of Japanese animation.

Indeed, when Faye Valentine is right there in the *Bebop* spaceship throughout much of the *Cowboy Bebop* series, you have to wonder why Spike Spiegel pines so much and so deeply for Julia (Julia is talked about much more than shown, so she hasn't got a chance against Faye!). The filmmakers suggest the bliss of the romantic relationship which Spike yearns for with flashbacks (most are in rapid montage style), but even that doesn't compete for a second with the craziness of Faye, in her truly mad, yellow croptop and shorts combo. Gimme Faye any time!

At one point, in a quiet scene between Spike Spiegel and Jet Black, Spike tries to voice what he feels for Julia. Jet is astonished – more perhaps by the fact that Spike is talking like this, never mind that he's talking about Julia. (Here, Spike admits that Julia represents something that he's lost, and he's he's simply got to go to her).

This is a new Spike, an emotionally wounded Spike. The running gag of storytelling is employed, too: Jet Black tells a story (Kilimanjaro + hunting + Ernest Hemingway), saying at the end that he hates that story (it's macho bullshit about heroic deaths). Jet tells Spike *to let go of the past*. Later, Spike tells a story (a reprise of the previous scene) about two pussies who loved each other – one died, then the other cried a million tears and died. Spike then says he hates that story, and hates cats (Spike is also compared to a kitty with many lives, but maybe this time there won't be a resurrection).

At Annie's place, when the gangsters catch up with Spike S. and Julia and another fire fight begins, Spike apologizes to Annie (now dead) that he's going to make a scene. At that moment, just when the fight's about to start, the filmmakers cut back to Jet B. and Faye V. in the *Bebop* ship, for an intriguing (and unusual) two-hander scene. They both denounce Spike in loving tones, unable to disguise their fondness for the guy. He's acting crazy, but they can't help loving him: the misfit family is thus now at its strongest.

The insertion of the emotional bonds between Faye and Spike, and between Jet and Spike, makes the following scene, the shoot-out at Annie's store, even more poignant (when Julia dies).

ACTION.

One action set-piece follows another in *The Real Folk Blues*, and the filmmakers at Sunrise/ Bandai deliver two sensational sessions to close their *Cowboy Bebop animé* series, rightly regarded by many viewers as the number one *animé* show (yup, even despite *very* strong competition, *Cowboy Bebop* remains an absolute fave with so many fans). No need to explore the action scenes that climax *Cowboy Bebop* – just go watch them again! But it's worth noting just how skilfully the filmmakers have woven in 100s of references to earlier movies and TV shows, as well as adding their own unmistakable and unique spin.

The Real Folk Blues contains all the expected elements, and then some: Clint Eastwood Spaghetti Westerns, John Woo, Hong Kong action movies, martial arts movies, Sam Peckinpah Westerns, *The Godfather* (and other Italian-American gangster flicks), American TV cop shows from the Seventies (*The Rockford Files, Kojak, Hawaii Five-O*, etc).

The two episodes *The Real Folk Blues* open with a bloody battle (in a bar, where Jet Black and Spike Spiegel are ruminating on their fate – now that 'the women', as they put it, have gone). With the sixth sense of seasoned street punks, Jet and Spike dive for cover seconds before machine guns spray bullets everywhere (note the pinball machine in the bar, another reference to the 1960s among the 1,000s dotted throughout the series). Here writer Keiko Nobumoto brings in Shin (Nobuyuki Hiyama, who's basically the same character as Lin – he's Lin's younger brother), in order for Spike to have a little help (tho' Shin is inevitably sacrificed (like Lin) in the final showdown at the skyscraper).

The massacre in the Red Dragon headquarters is amazing (and, for *animé* made-for-TV, amazingly bloody). Of course, we know that Vicious is not going to die in the execution ordered by the three mob Elders (bizarre figures who're just too patronizing and smug for their own good). Wrinkly, old sages in temple settings are a staple of Japanese animation, and the execution of Vicious takes place in just such a quasi-religious setting (with Vicious manacled to the wall in a Crucifixion pose below carvings in stone of the Red Dragon's emblems and mottoes).[84] Pretty soon it's guns going off all over the place, with Vicious taking up his precious samurai blade, and using it to cut the Elders to ribbons. (How is Vicious going to get out of this one? – chained to the wall while a firing squad raises their machine guns? The filmmakers come up with an inventive gag: Vicious' pet bird[85] has a bomb in it! It flies down, explodes, creating chaos. One of the guards crosses sides, and shoots at the Elders' guards, and so it goes on, in a very violent sequence).

But the Red Dragon Elders massacre is just one of numerous action set-pieces in the two-parter *The Real Folk Blues*. One truly stupendous piece of animation and action is the dogfight in the space above Mars as Spike Spiegel and Faye Valentine try to defend the *Bebop* spaceship from the crime syndicate's craft. To out-do the incredible aerial battles of the earlier episodes (not easy!), the filmmakers at Sunrise and Bandai employ rotating camera and many skewed and upside-down camera angles. The editing throughout this sequence (by Tomoaki Tsurubuchi), and all of the *Cowboy Bebop* series, is sharp as a slash across the chest from a samurai sword (the dogfight is cut in parallel action with the Red Dragon massacre, *Godfather*-style. Editing is the secret, invisible weapon in *Cowboy Bebop*, as it is in all TV). Visually, the filmmakers drench the aerial dog-fights in beautiful, saturated blues and reds (delivering a bit of *Macross Plus*'s high style).

---

84 Altho' we're in the 21st century, organizations such as the Red Dragon crime syndicate are as conservative and traditional as the Catholic religion or Buddhism.

85 The filmmakers cut to the crow a number of times, to reinforce the *deus ex machina* rescue to Vicious. Those bird shots also function as 'pillow moments'.

Speaking of which, what does the 26-session *Cowboy Bebop* series close with? A one-man army, of course, as Spike Spiegel storms the Red Dragon skyscraper downtown single-handed (at night, of course), battling his way to the top against overwhelming odds (and 100s of henchmen), to take on the bad guy, skinny, white-haired, slit-eyed psychopath Vicious (single-handed, but multiple-gunned, and he has grenades, a'course, lobbed all over the place, and bombs on timers which he sets off on walls and escalators).

Blood is splattered all over the place as Spike Spiegel takes out henchman after hapless henchman, with the filmmakers employing every gag ever invented for firefights,[86] using the elevators, the escalators, the doors, the columns, anything they can think of (Spike opens the salvo with a grenade nonchalantly kicked as he enters the foyer form the street – no walking in the back way for Spike!). There are plenty of deaths in the final two episodes of *Cowboy Bebop*: Annie dies, Shin dies, Julia dies, Vicious dies, the Elders die, and loadsa henchmen die (so that *The Real Folk Blues* has the atmosphere of grand opera or a Shakespearean tragedy).

The colossal throne room at the top of the skyscraper (lit in shadowy reds) is the setting for the expected duel which uses that old staple of thousands of Japanese movies and TV shows, the gun versus the samurai sword motif. Hell, if it worked for all those zillions of other shows, it'll work here. And it does.

The first part of the incredible duel closes with

---

86 The sequence looks as if the producers encouraged the animation team to go nuts – use every gag you've ever wanted to use in a big action scene.

the weapons on the ground.[87] Cut to the long shot (which acts as a breather), then back to the close-ups: the rivals agree to end it all, and kick their weapons over to each other. Vicious snatches up his samurai sword in the final gag and slashes at Spike, but Spike has also plugged the freak with a bullet. Just one bullet. It's enough to kill people in so-called 'real life', though not in movies. Thankfully, and rightly, there's only time in a 22-minute show for a one-bullet-death (but in the climax of the *Cowboy Bebop* movie, the fight btn Spike and the villain Vincent includes many, many gags and firings – a few too many, I think – b4 Vincent finally dies). Here, Vicious is killed and he collapses immediately (so we know *he's* dead).

THE ENDING.

When Spike Spiegel emerges triumphant but wounded from the duel and collapses on the enormous staircase up to the throne, after staggering down it slowly, the *Cowboy Bebop* series closes with a lengthy, high angle zoom out (on a pastel-hued scene after the Gothic darkness of the preceding sequence). Just prior to the long shot, we zip into Spike's mindscreen very briefly, with a clever return to the dying words of Julia on the roof: now we hear them: it's just a dream… a bad dream… (from the flashcuts, the screen washes to white, enabling the seamless transition to pastel hues for the final shots).

Not dead, of course. What, kill the hero? No way! Actually, there are many indicators that Spike's

---

87 Vicious also has a throwing star which he hurls against Spike.

collapse is not meant to be interpreted as death[88] (and besides, we've seen Spike crawl free from so many battles, often bandaged up like a mummy. And there's the running gag of Spike 'dying' and returning to life. And comicbook characters like Spike, or Lupin III, never die, although they appear to die, many times).

It's a suitably Big Finish, leaving the audience with the one demand: *more, please!*

88 Death can be regarded as the ultimate badge of honour for a hero in *animé*, because it's motivation that counts, more than the end result or the cause. 'For the Japanese, death is the final proof of the hero's selflessness, of the purity and altruism of his motives,' according to Antonia Levi (105). That is, if you interpret the scene that Spike dies!

CONCLUSION.

Ah, if only all television were this good, this classy, this funny, this wild.

And, once again, the *mix* and the *tone* of *Cowboy Bebop* is simply spot-on. Drama where drama is required, and light-heartedness where necessary, with comedy, *not* tragedy, under-pinning everything. The balance of elements is so accomplished in *Cowboy Bebop* you can't believe how good it is. And *pauses*: don't forget those classic *animé* 'pillow moments'.[89] *Cowboy Bebop* demonstrates how to *stop* action, again and again, to *stop* and to *savour* moments – to relish poses, gestures, facial expressions, lines of dialogue, colours, sunsets, skies... and jokes!

Cowboy Bebop isn't good, it's *fantastic*. The animation is astonishing, as are the designs, the layouts, the invention of the whole secondary world, but it's all tied firmly to tremendously skilful storytelling, compelling characters, themes and situations, and a tone and an attitude which's impossible to resist. *Cowboy Bebop appeals* to you – you can't help but ♥ this *animé* show: it appeals to the viewer on so many levels, wittily and cleverly getting under your skin with its 10,000 cultural references, its tongue-in-cheek, let's-*not*-be-serious approach, its visual panache and its utter confidence in its own brilliance.

SEE YOU, SPACE COWBOY!

---

89 Even in the slambang climax of *Cowboy Bebop*, there's time for a C.U. shot of flowers in the rain.

The 'Big Shot TV show in Cowbow Bebop

Cowboy Bebop is a richly designed show –it's virtually
an entire history of graphic design. Above is a title card
from the famous opening crredits.

06

COWBOY BEBOP: KNOCKIN' ON HEAVEN'S DOOR (2001) THE COWBOY BEBOP MOVIE

The movie version of *Cowboy Bebop: Knockin' On Heaven's Door* (2001) is as enjoyable as any action/ adventure/ sci-fi/ comedy movie, with some truly outstanding action sequences – a gun battle on a monorail train over the sea, a dogfight between jets and a spacecraft, a grocery store hold-up (which opens the movie),[1] and numerous fist fights and martial arts duels. Totally confident filmmaking – *Cowboy Bebop* includes blood and guts and drugs, and the movie is strong enough to slow down to quiet conversations for quite a few scenes, an hour into the piece, after the monorail action scene.

Quite, quite awesome. Deliciously awesome.

Another way of putting it: there's nothing *not* to

1 This is an outstanding action sequence, which doesn't add much to the rest of the movie, narratively, but it does serve to introduce the major characters in a flamboyant, zinging manner. The scene's designed, perhaps, to introduce audiences who haven't seen *Bebop* before to the characters.

like and enjoy in the movie of *Cowboy Bebop*. It all works. The elements have been assembled from every place, but they all fit together.

If you know the *Cowboy Bebop* series, you'll love the movie; if you don't know the *Cowboy Bebop* series, you'll still love the movie (though it definitely enhances the experience of the movie if you've seen the TV series).

PRODUCTION.

Many in the team who produced the *Cowboy Bebop* movie worked on the series: it was produced by Sunrise, Bones and Bandai,[2] co-directed by Yoshiyuki Takei, Tensai Okamura[3] and Shinichiro Watanabe, the series' director, and written by Keiko Nobumoto, the chief writer on the series. Also back were Yoko Kanno and the Seatbelts composing the music (it couldn't be anybody else, could it?), and sound director Katsuyoshi Kobayashi. The 2001 movie was produced by Takayuki Yoshi, Ryohei Tsunoda, Masuo Ueda, Masahiko Minami and Minoru Takanashi, key animator and character designer was Toshihiro Kawamoto, mechanical animator was Masami Goto, colour designer was Shihiko Nakayama, set designer was Shiho Take-uchi, mechanical designer was Kimitoshi Yamane, and it was released in the West by the Sony corporation.

The voice cast (*seiyu*) in the 2001 movie is thankfully the same as the TV series: Kôichi Yama-dera (Spike Spiegel), Unsho Ishizuka (Jet Black),

2 Synergy contributed to the *Cowboy Bebop* movie; Synergy was founded in 1998 by Minoru Okazaki, Minoru Maeda and Hiroshi Wagatsuma.
3 Okamura handled the Western within the movie, and Takei did the opening credits. Hiroyuki Okiura designed the credits images.

Megumi Hayashibara (Faye Valentine), and Aoi Tada (Radical Ed). It just couldn't be anyone else, could it? It can't be *Cowboy Bebop* if it's not Yamadera voicing Spike, or Hayashibara as Faye, or Tada as Ed or Ishizuka as Jet.

The new charas included:

> Tsutomu Isobe (Vincent)
> Ai Kobayashi (Electra Ovirowa)
> Yuji Ueda (Lee Samson)
> Hiroshi Naka (Jovin)
> Jin Hirao (Antonio)
> Juurouta Kosugi (Harris)
> Kinryuu Arimoto (Captain)
> Mickey Curtis (Rashid)
> Miki Nagasawa (Judy)
> Nobuo Tobita (Murata)
> Renji Ishibashi (Rengie)
> Rikiya Koyama (Steve)
> Takashi Nagasako (Caster)
> Takehiro Koyama (Laughing Bull)

Among the companies involved in producing the *Cowboy Bebop* movie were: Studio Alpha, Studio Elle, Studio Kuma, Studio Toys, ACCEL, Anime House, Anime Roman, Anime Torotoro, Anime World Osaka, Bee Train, Beijing Xie Le Art Co., Ltd., C&S, Doga Productions, Dr. Movie, Gainax, Ingres, JEM, Last House, Marsa Inc, Radical Party, Radix, Sonsan DeenStudio Fantasia, Studio Line, Studio Takuranke, Studio Wombat, Synergy Japan, TASK, TNK, Xebec, Tokyo Laboratory, Flying Dragon Cartoon Studio, Light Foot, M I, Marsa Inc, MSJ, Multi Access Company Time, Peacock, Sonsan Kikaku, Studio OM, Aomori Works, and Studio OZ.

Many *animé* TV shows produce movies by re-editing the existing episodes (some shows, such as

Ghost In the Shell: Stand Alone Complex, have episodes which form an over-arching storyline, so they're readymade for cutting into feature length). *Cowboy Bebop* could easily have re-cut episodes to make a movie – the ones involving Spike, Vicious and the crime syndicates are an obvious choice: episode 5, *Ballad of Fallen Angels,* the two-part episodes 12 and 13, *Jupiter Jazz,* and the final two-parter, episodes 25 and 26, *The Real Folk Blues* (indeed, the viewer could watch those five episodes of the home video and DVD releases and they'd make a great movie).

Instead, Sunrise/ Bones/ Bandai opted for a new story and new animation: a wise choice (altho' many elements from the TV series were included, and the story had been an idea for an unmade episode).

PLOT.

Director Shinichiro Watanabe confirmed that the plot for the 2001 movie of *Cowboy Bebop* was drawn from an idea for the TV series. You can see how the story and characters reflect the first TV episode, *Asteroid Blues*, for instance, the one about the criminal couple who're selling a dangerous drug called Bloody Eye. Asimov, the tall, dark, gangly villain recalls the main villain Vincent (in his attitude, too), while Katrina recalls Electra (both women flirt with Spike Spiegel, are strikingly attractive and independent women, that Spike is charmed by, but they end up sticking with the bad guys).[4] The drug in *Asteroid Blues*, too, has affinities with the effects of the nano-robots in the 2001 movie (for example, the filmmakers employ an extreme subjective vision for the drug's effects, employing

4 The charas are clearly designed by the same artist – Toshihiro Kawamoto.

handheld camera and altered colours).

Apart from the gang of four misfit bounty hunters, there are three other main characters in *Cowboy Bebop: Knockin' On Heaven's Door*: Vincent, the insane villain, his assistant, computer whizz Lee Samson, and Electra, his former girlfriend. Although set in the future (in 2071), the characters're very much of the time, the late 1990s: black, computer hacker Lee Samson, for instance, is a detailed depiction of an *otaku*, a nerd, the kind of geek who hangs out in amusement arcades playing shoot-'em-up games,[5] or plays old school computer games 'cos they're quaint.

To show just how alienated *otaku* Lee Samson is from reality, the 2001 movie employs a startling juxtaposition: as he and Vincent're driving to a harbourside warehouse, Samson is playing a video game and he loses, and the game avatar dies. Samson says dopily, 'oh no, he's dead', like a child. When Vincent blows away a security guard at the warehouse at point blank range, instead of being shocked/ disturbed/ saddened/ angry/ terrified/ mortified/ whatever, Samson merely uses the same inane line: 'oh no, he's dead'. Delineating Samson's *otaku* alienation from the world is important, so that when Vincent kills Samson (as nasty villains seem to do to their henchmen in action movies), it's not the murder of a wholly innocent guy: Samson is involved with Vincent's plan from the beginning. (The way that Vincent kills Samson seems a little silly as he uses one of the blue balls full of nano-machines – it would be much easier and far cheaper to shoot Samson.

---

5 There's a great moment when Faye uses her real gun to shoot up the arcade game. As Faye says, she prefers the real thing to virtual reality – a wry commentary on the *otaku* culture of playing games (such as shoot-'em-up video games), and watching TV, instead of living.

However, there is a plot point here: as Samson staggers around the apartment, choking and dying, Vincent isn't affected. So Vincent, who's already a spectre from beyond the grave, has some special protection from the nano-machines).

The *Cowboy Bebop* movie includes many aspects of the 1998 TV series and skilfully integrates them into the fabric of the piece, so that it works for fans, but also for folk new to the world of *Cowboy Bebop* (in fact, the 2001 movie picks over story elements from almost every episode). For instance, it's important to establish that the *Bebop* crew are a bunch of misfits who're looking for the Big Score: they wanna eat (they're surviving on instant noodles). That worked so well for the TV show – having Spike Spiegel complain about not eating enough protein (meat) – and it works in the movie, too.

If you know the 1998 TV series, watching the 2001 movie is a delight as you spot so many of the elements the writers, producers and filmmakers have culled from the 26 episodes of the TV show (that the movie was released three years after the show probably helped – at least in retaining many of the same key people who worked on the TV series).

In the *Cowboy Bebop* movie, the band of misfits are still not working as a team[6] (the movie would've taken place between two of the later episodes – 22: *Cowboy Funk* and 23: *Brain Scratch*, according to director Shinichiro Watanabe). Well, they are, but only sorta: they *do* look out for each other, but they also pursue the mystery of bad guy Vincent, his accomplice Lee Samson and the nano-machines in

---

6 There's a quiet moment when Jet Black ruminates on the notion of the 'family' of the *Bebop* spaceship. It's a scene that a Western movie would probably cut.

their own fashion (the key moment is when, goofing around in the living room of the *Bebop* spaceship, the TV news announces that the bounty on the perpetrators of the explosion on the freeway is 300 million Woolongs (= $3m). 300 million! That's enough for stop anybody horsing around and get focussed!).

The bounty hunter TV show *Big Shot* makes a brief appearance – only for the TV presenters to sheepishly admit that there are no leads whatsoever on the 300 million Woolong bounty of the terrorists currently spooking Mars.

Faye Valentine is pursuing Lee Samson (aided by Radical Ed), tho' at the end of the first act of the *Cowboy Bebop*, neither she, nor Jet Black, nor Spike Spiegel have got anywhere, really. Jet has done his detective work by simply chatting to his former I.S.S.P. buddy Bob, while sitting down and watching a cowboy movie. Spike's method has been much more pro-active: infiltrating a chemical plant posing as a cleaner. And Faye has hunted down Lee Samson, only to have him elude her in an amusement arcade in a shopping mall.[7] Meanwhile, little Ed, aided by the ever-faithful dog Ein, does some Sherlock Holmes-ing of her own (that dog sure is clever! It recognizes that the data on the élite Mars military team features Vincent, a man who's supposed to have died two years ago). Ed manages to track down Samson (despite some trick or treating escapades which go wrong – there's an irate guy with a gun, and a burly tranny). However, after this, Ed sadly disappears for much of the movie.

---

7 That Samson evades the resourceful and determined Faye by simply turning out the lights and running, is a bit lame.

MAIN TITLES.

Before the 2001 movie introduces us to the *Bebop* and the rest of the crew, and before the main titles, there are some short scenes which set out some of the characters and scenarios: Vincent, the chief villain, and the nasty little balls of nano-robots (the film's MacGuffin), are introduced (notice also the butterfly fluttering by in the scene). The main prologue scene is the grocery store hold-up, which introduces Spike Spiegel and Jet Black.

The *Cowboy Bebop* TV series featured an incredible main titles sequence, along with an outstanding black-and-white prologue (which was about Spike's backstory). The 2001 *Cowboy Bebop* movie combines the black-and-white approach with the main titles. Over a catchy song ('Ask DNA'), the opening credits feature short shots of people on the streets of the Mars city (the characters and the settings are almost wholly New Yorkian).

Following the credits, which climax with an ultra-cool shot of – who else? – Spike Spiegel (in a pose reminiscent of classic American photography, such as that famous photo of James Dean huddled up in his Winter coat, by Dennis Stock),[8] the movie shifts to a regular form of narration: Spike and Jet playing chess on board the *Bebop* (and both bored out of their minds), Ed and the dog, and Faye Valentine in her spacecraft *Red Tail* flying towards the Martian city (so that it's Faye, not Jet or Spike, who first sees Vincent).

---

8 This is where Shinichiro Watanabe has his director's credit.

MUSIC.

Music is huge element in the 2001 movie of *Cowboy Bebop* (including its title).[9] *Of course* it is! With Yoko Kanno and Shinichiro Watanabe, you have two people who foreground music often in front of everything else. And right from the get-go, too, with the song 'Ask DNA' that plays over the opening credits. For example, when Faye Valentine is first introduced, she is scanning thru the airwaves on the radio in her spacecraft until she finds some music she likes: the pop song plays as Faye flies into the Martian city along the freeways (tho' why would a spacecraft fly so low over a freeway? 'Cos it looks cool! Actually, there *is* a good reason: Faye's hunting down her bounty).

The 2001 *Cowboy Bebop* movie includes many pop songs on the soundtrack, which are skilfully integrated into the piece (often by shifting into a pop promo/ MTV mode, and using montages of action). The jazz and blues scoring goes a long way in delivering *Cowboy Bebop* as a super-cool product. When the music's starts up, it's 90% of the effect of the piece.

By ten or so minutes into the 2001 movie, a variety of music has been played, from introspective, melancholy pieces (for Vincent's scenes), to the pop-rock of the opening credits, to Faye's pop song, and to the Arabic/ Moroccan music (reminiscent of North African *rai* music), which's used in the *souk* scenes.

---

9 The song *Knockin' On Heaven's Door* was written by Bob Dylan for *Pat Garrett and Billy the Kid* (1973), one of Sam Peckinpah's finest movies (*Pat Garrett and Billy the Kid* certainly chimes with *Cowboy Bebop* in terms of setting (the American West), attitude (a bleaker version of the Peck's tough guys in crisis), look (grizzled old cowboys), the era (1970s), and music (Country & Western and blues).) *Knockin' On Heaven's Door* has been covered by many acts – two of the most well-known are Eric Clapton and Guns 'N Roses.

Especially satisfying are the montage sequences in *Cowboy Bebop: Knockin' On Heaven's Door* – the early one, for instance, which follows Spike Spiegel as the foot-sore detective following up leads all around the city. The filmmakers conjure up a series of marvellous vignettes, as finely observed images of a modern city as you'll ever see in cinema: watching kids body popping and break dancing in a back alley;[10] Spike play-fighting a black kid in front of a grafittied wall; grizzled stall owners; and Spike eating lunch on a bench. This is incredible animation, brilliantly observed and evoked.

SETTINGS.

The setting of the 2001 movie of *Cowboy Bebop* is mainly Mars, and it's a giant, sprawling metropolis. But within it, there are sections that're wholly New Yorkian, with the famous skyline, the Brooklyn Bridge, and the giant signage that artists love.[11] In fact, Mars in the movie is *very* Gothamite, with street scenes accurately evoking Greenwich Village and the Bowery, the business district around Wall Street, and of course the canyons and skyscrapers. There is a shot of the beautiful Flatiron Building, one of the great New York landmarks, plus the Empire State Building and the Chrysler Building. (Yet almost all of the people in the many companies working on the *Cowboy Bebop* movie would *not* have visited Gotham: when *animé* shows depict New York, or London, or anywhere, really, outside of Japan, they do it from

---

10 Break dancing is a key ingredient in the *kung fu* moves of Mugen in *Samurai Champloo*.
11 The flashback in the Jet Black episode *Black Dog Serenade* evokes a familiar Gotham setting around Brooklyn Bridge. Director Watanabe wanted the flashback to have the 'atmosphere of a classic hard-boiled movie'. And it did.

photos, research, etc, while sitting in a Tokyo studio. Yet the recreation of a New Yorkian city in *Cowboy Bebop* is absolutely remarkable).

Meanwhile, with the over-arching story being about terrorism, and the movie being released on September 1, 2001 (in Japan), and with images that include many famous New York views, including the Twin Towers,[12] the *Cowboy Bebop* movie takes on added layers of meaning. Vincent might be working alone, and his motivation might be more metaphysical or Existential than ideological or political, but there is no doubt that the *Cowboy Bebop* movie explores aspects of terrorism.

The *Cowboy Bebop* series had already explored terrorism and groups using viruses in episode 4: *Gateway Shuffle*, and bombs in 22: *Cowboy Funk* (and also religious cults, in ep 23: *Brain Scratch*).[13] The *Cowboy Bebop* movie thus also references the Heaven's Gate religious cult and the Sublime Truth (Aum Shinrikyo) sect.

Cowboy Bebop took place in a diaspora world, a post-colonial universe, with an emphasis on the frontier spirit (plus of course the culture of the Wild West as manifested primarily in American movies). But the 2001 *Cowboy Bebop* movie also happily takes the characters to other areas, including one that's wholly Moroccan,[14] complete with *souks*, stalls,

12 And lengthy visits to a Middle Eastern district, with one of the dodgy charas (Rashid) dressed in a *djellabiah.*
13 In *Brain Scratch*, the fake religious cult is created by a teenage *otaku* reminiscent of Lee Samson.
14 Director Shinichiro Watanabe wanted something truly alien and exotic, and chose Arabic/ Moroccan culture for that reason (he also visited Morocco for research). Morocco has been employed by European artists and musicians for inspiration for decades. Morocco was a favourite destination with rock music acts of the 1960s (such as the Stones, one of Watanabe's favourite rock bands, and Led Zeppelin), as well as Brion Gysin, William Burroughs, the Beat poets, and many other literati and bohemians.

casbahs, sheesha pipes, and denizens in *djellabiehs*.[15] And the climactic fight takes place in a recreation of the Eiffel Tower.

CITY LIFE.

The *density* and *intricacy* of the futuristic city life evoked in *Cowboy Bebop* is just stupendous: it goes way, way beyond the city life portrayed in famous and celebrated city movies such as *Star Wars, Batman* and, yes, even *Blade Runner*, the god of future city movies for Japanese animators. Yep, it's even more accomplished and insightful than *Blade Runner*: because the city in *Blade Runner* was always stylized and fake like a ad-man's vision of the future (Ridley Scott claimed he had filmed about 2,000 commercials by the time he directed the Philip K. Dick adaption released in 1982). It looked amazing, but it didn't have the depth of life and truth and *real people* that *Cowboy Bebop* has (in *Blade Runner*, everything looks staged for the camera, like a Hollywood musical: in *Cowboy Bebop*, the camera is an observer of street life).

Cowboy Bebop comes across as if the filmmakers have spent hours and hours on buses and trains and cars and sidewalks in Tokyo, New York, London, L.A., Paris, Seoul, and Hong Kong: looking out of the window, watching, taking pictures, sketching, and writing notes (the background art was by BIC Studio, Digital Works, Green and Team's Art Productions). Certainly the 2001 *Cowboy Bebop* movie looks as if the filmmakers had enough of a budget to have a research trip to Gotham for the key personnel. (And the *love* of the Big City comes across: no matter how scuzzy and

---

15 It's in Morocco town that Spike Spiegel encounters Rashid (Mikki Kachisu), an ambiguous informer who's first introduced lighting a cigarette for Spike with a lighter in the shape of a grenade!

cynical the stories and characters might be, the filmmakers, as with *Akira* and *Ghost In the Shell*, still adore these cities).

There's a futuristic drive-in scene, a giant parking lot where people watch movies from their spacecraft (and Jet Black meets an old cop buddy to find out about the virus story). What's playing on the screen? A Western, of course, from the 1950s,[16] which evokes American stars like John Wayne and Gary Cooper (of course, the scene included in the drive-in is the climactic shoot-out on the main street, and of course the final shot is the horseman riding off into the sunset).

ACTION.

The *Cowboy Bebop* movie has action set-pieces that are truly awe-inspiring. The shoot-out on the monorail hurtling over the sea between different parts of the Martian city is just incredible. That would suffice for the ending of many an action movie, but not *Cowboy Bebop: Knockin' On Heaven's Door*: there is more. Lots more.

For instance, there's a truly astounding dogfight with Spike Spiegel out-witting (though at great cost) a bunch of military top guns.[17] It's a very lengthy and intricate aerial battle, but it works partly because the heroes are rushing to the city to prevent the villain Vincent from releasing the killer virus.

The filmmakers at Sunrise/ Bandai/ Bones seem to be aiming to out-Miyazaki Miyazaki in the dog-fight: they throw in every possible gag and move in an

---

16 In very scratchy black-and-white, as if it's been rescued from a dumpster outside a cinema.
17 Some of the team worked on *Macross Plus*, as well of course as the *Cowboy Bebop* TV show, and they draw on their expertise here.

aerial duel that takes place everywhere: alongside towers, down below enormous walls, in and around elevated freeways, thru skyscraper canyons, five feet over water, above bridges, and partly in space. Spike Spiegel has to use every trick he's ever learnt to evade the military jets that just won't quit. Intercut with other action cenes, the dogfight sequence the *Cowboy Bebop* movie leaves pretty much every other aerial battle behind (except, of course, for Hayao Miyazaki's movies!).

There's a terrific kickboxing duel (followed by a chase) between Spike Spiegel and the attractive agent Electra in the corridor of a chemical plant,[18] an *animé* heroine who can hold her own in any situation.[19] Unfortunately, she falls for the wrong guy – Vincent (just as Faye Valentine picks the wrong guy repeatedly). The 2001 *Cowboy Bebop* movie could've made quite a bit more of the romantic triangle between Spike, Electra and Vincent – she's certainly a character worth more screen time (and Spike likes her – and she's his kinda girl, of course – she can handle herself, is a fierce fighter, carries a gun, etc). Needless to say, had *Cowboy Bebop* been like some of its inspirations – *James Bond* and *Lupin III* – Spike and Electra would certainly have got together.

THE MONORAIL SCENE.

The monorail sequence involves shoot-outs from movies directed by John Woo and Hong Kong action movies, with the famous Mexican stand-offs that

---

18 When the duel begins, in comes the lively jazz music.
19 There's a scene where Electra stands before her boss, who tells her, in no uncertain terms, that Vincent and Lee Samson must be stopped and killed. We don't know the back-story yet of the relationship of Electra and Vincent, but when the movie cuts to a close-up of Electra, we can see, in retrospect, that it's going to be tough for her to kill Vincent. Which's how the finale plays out.

Woo's pictures specialized in: you can also spot references to *The French Connection* (1971), with its celebrated subway train chase. It is a meticulously staged sequence: out-size action, assuredly, but marvellously achieved. There are face-offs with guns, fire fights, and of course fist fights and martial arts; Vincent, incredibly, shoots his former lover, Electra (!),[20] and he bests Spike, hurling him outta the window of the speeding train.

The filmmakers of *Cowboy Bebop: Knockin' On Heaven's Door* are happy to borrow from anywhere for inspiration (and not care if anyone notices). Thus, after the monorail action sequence ends in a giant explosion (how else can a chase that amazing end?), where does Spike Spiegel wind up, but rescued from the sea by a Native American, complete with teepee, open fire, and totem wolf! And of course, the Native American guy (it's Laughing Bull again, played by Takehiro Koyama), is a shaman: Spike has come back from death (when he really should be dead!), the shaman tells him, and the movie shifts into a trance-like state, along with Spike, with images of stars in the night sky (the Native American trope had been introduced in the first episode, *Asteroid Bllues*, and also appears in the *Jupiter Jazz* episodes of the 1998 TV show).[21]

The shifts in genre and tone that *Cowboy Bebop* makes are a big part of the fun of the show, and the movie capitalizes on that. To move from a hi-tech, all-out shoot-out on a futuristic monorail (where the hero

---

20 His excuse – or her excuse for him – is that he didn't recognize her. Yet in his dying speech, he tells her that his time with her was the highpointj of his life.
21 The dream/ trance that Spike experiences as he comes back to consciousness is a very effective and skilful blend of subjectivity and storytelling.

is shot thru the chest),[22] to a back-from-the-dead scene out of a revisionist Western movie from the 1960s or 1970s (when Native Americans were portrayed more sympathetically), is remarkable. But it works.

FAYE VALENTINE.

Faye Valentine's great – she's basically a girl with a gun, and that pretty much always flies. That was Jean-Luc Godard's famous Sixties maxim, of course (*all you need to make a movie is a girl and a gun*), and 100s of movies and TV shows have followed that tactic (and they still do). As Hayao Miyazaki noted, a girl with a gun is somehow more intriguing than a boy with a gun.

And Faye Valentine isn't jammed into tired, old romantic plots: sure, she's a babe – come on, I mean, a *super-babe*! – but she isn't chasing boyfriends, stressing over love and romance (how boring!), and also isn't hit upon by guys (well, she is, but not so often. When Faye enters a dingy dive, sure she turns heads). Faye embodies independence, and gets spikiest and snippiest when the guys on the *Bebop* ship make remarks about romance, love or women (there's a moment in episode 3, *Honky Tonk Women,* when Spike Spiegel decides he's going to tell Faye, who's gone for a shower, that she's gotta leave: the camera stays with Jet in the den, and gunshots're heard offscreen: Faye is exactly the kinda girl who'd take a gun into the shower!: it's a funny gag to end the episode).

Faye Valentine's look is pure, masculinist fantasy – a tomboy with large eyes, a pouty mouth, large, firm, round boobs, l-o-n-g legs, and a tight ass,

---

22 When Spike Spiegel falls back in slo-mo, it's a replay of the incredible episode *Ballad of Fallen Angels*, where Spike falls backwards out of the Cathedral.

all displayed to great effect by a costume that includes a wrap top exposing her midriff, and short shorts.[23]

VINCENT, VILLAINS AND VIOLENCE.

There's a crunching, nasty element to the violence in the movie of *Cowboy Bebop*, as there was in the TV show. That meant that only 12 episodes were broadcast in Japan during its original airing, due apparently to the elements of violence (and drug-taking – the first episode, *Asteroid Blues*, features drugs and violence; clearly the filmmakers wanted to announce their intentions Big and Loud from the get-go). Movie versions of TV shows are typically more graphic, and the movie of *Cowboy Bebop* is no exception.

Vincent is a particularly vicious villain: he's another of the tall, dark, spindly figures of *animé*, a close cousin of the vampires,[24] wizards and samurai warriors of other *animé* shows (note also the affinity of the names Vincent and Vicious, the chief bad guy in the *Cowboy Bebop* TV series). There's a desperate nihilism embodied in Vincent: he is literally a walking shadow, a figure of Death. The despair that emanates from Vincent is palpable: this is negative stuff: Vincent really does seem to hate life itself.

Many movies attempt to depict a villain who resents everybody, has a major chip on his shoulder, and plans to kill kill kill. In Vincent, due to the way the character's written and played (by Tsutomu

---

23 Faye Valentine's design was not based on anybody in particular, noted designer Toshihiro Kawamoto. Originally, he wanted to have her wear a Chinese dress, but that was vetoed (although the dress does appear).

24 When Vincent transfers some of his blood to Faye Valentine, it makes her immune to the nano-machines – making him reminiscent of Dracula, and Faye a victim like Lucy.

Isobe),[25] there is a genuine feeling of nihilism and misanthropy. He's a monster, but not a 'natural' monster, like a dinosaur who's running amok. Vincent is humanity in its twisted, isolated manifestation, humanity which has turned its back on humanity, to the point where it doesn't value human life anymore.

Vincent is scary because you can believe he's a terrorist who would get into a plane and fly it into the Twin Towers, killing himself in the process (the movie was released ten days before that happened on 9/11/2001). But not for an ideological or political purpose, not to make a statement against North America, or the West, or capitalism, or imperialism, but because he hates himself even more than everyone else on the planet. Self-loathing is one of the most difficult problems to deal with.

Vincent is a portrait of someone utterly alienated from the world and from humanity. We first see Vincent playing the solitaire board game with the little, blue balls of nano-robots, in the opening scene of *Cowboy Bebop: Knockin' On Heaven's Door*: he's on his own, and the voiceover informs us about his isolation. Later, Vincent's first dialogue is about purgatory, Catholicism's limbo for souls somewhere between heaven and earth. And again, Vincent is depicted in an empty room playing solitaire, on his own in that scene (*don't be alone*, and *don't live in false or virtual realities* is one of the messages of the 2001 movie).

The thriller plot of *Cowboy Bebop: Knockin' On Heaven's Door* involves Vincent releasing a virus of

---

25 The animators also give Vincent a flattened, non-3D look to his features, as if he is not a rounded person anymore, but has had life beaten out of him.

killer nano-robots (nano-technology being big news in the 1990s, and perfect for a futuristic *animé*). But the 2001 movie goes further, providing Vincent with a back-story set on Titan (the moon of Saturn) that explains not only how he got to be so nasty (he was unloved, poor thing, so Electra tells Spike in the jail scene), but is also intended to evoke a little sympathy for the guy (he was the victim of a scientific experiment[26] by Dr Mendelos – who's actually Rashid).[27]

Well, no sympathy from me: he is a mass murderer, who by the end of the picture has killed hundreds of people (and at the beginning of the picture, he kills and maims masses of folk in the freeway explosion). We also see him dispatch a number of victims, and he also either possibly rapes Faye Valentine or comes close to it (there's a creepy moment when he kisses her, against her will, right after he's defeated her, and later he threatens her with a knife, using it to cut open her clothes, including the croptop, as she lies bound on the floor. Thus allowing for several 'fan service' scenes of Faye nearly topless on the floor, with her breasts jiggling about).

Creating an ambiguous villain is typical of Japanese *animé*, of course: the movie of *Cowboy Bebop* goes quite far in depicting Vincent as a victim as well as a villain, a guy who didn't ask for the horrors that happened to him on Titan following the scientific experiment (the flashbacks to Titan recall the origins stories of characters in the *Cowboy Bebop* TV show such as Wen in episode 6: *Sympathy For the Devil*). The movie goes far, too, in subverting the romantic

---

26 Recalling Pierrot in the TV series, Vincent is subject to experiments (this time with nanomachines).
27 The scientist who's developed the nano-machines is Dr Mendelos. I wonder if the name Mendelos is a reference to the nasty ex-Nazi doctor played by Laurence Olivier in *Marathon Man* (1976).

subplot, and having Electra choose Vincent over Spike (even though Electra and Spike seem tailor-made for each other, and Vincent shoots Electra when they first meet! But, no, Electra chooses Vincent over Spike, and sheds a tear for Vincent when he dies).

♪

The flashback sequence for Vincent in the *Cowboy Bebop* movie very cleverly intercuts (by editor Tomoaki Tsurubuchi) several scenes occurring at the same time. As Spike Spiegel talks to Rashid/Mendelos in Morocco Town, and they discuss Vincent, Vincent is talking about himself to Faye Valentine (who's tied up on the floor). This handily explains Vincent's origins to two of the main characters (Spike and Faye), and also allows the explications of the back-story to comment upon each other.

The marvellous editing by Tomoaki Tsurubuchi also weaves in many other scenes around this point in the *Cowboy Bebop* movie (at the 100-110 min mark) – such as Electra being questioned by her superiors about Vincent and the nano-machines.

THE FINALE.

The climax of *Cowboy Bebop: Knockin' On Heaven's Door* involves the expected face-off between the hero and the villain: it's a big scene in every way, taking place during a Hallowe'en Parade,[28] Macy's Day Parade-style, with giant, floating inflatables of pumpkins, spectres and witches, crowds in the streets, music, and punters in trick or treat costumes (these are impressive, multi-layered scenes, involving many extras, shots which're nightmares to animate – and you have to add the indiviudualized Hallowe'en

28 There's also a Hallowen'en parade in 2000's *Blood: The Last Vampire*.

costumes to that workload).[29]

As well as extras, the finale of the *Cowboy Bebop* movie includes generous amounts of visual effects animation, plus rain, plus smoke (all of which significantly drive up the budget). Meanwhile, the production designers and directors (Shihoko Nakayama, Shiho Takeuchi, Atsushi Morikawa) and the DP (Youichi Oogami) have staged the finale in late afternoon, going into sunset, and finally night, allowing for those incredible washes of hot colours like oranges, golds and yellows, which Japanese animation has made its own.

The *Cowboy Bebop* movie jacks up the level of spectacle and action in the finale with big crowd scenes of the I.S.S.P. (the cops) getting involved, followed by the Army. Well, these scenes (of the agents and S.W.A.T. teams searching out terrorist bombs or devices), plus plenty of aircraft and vehicles, aren't wholly necessary (partly because they divert attention from our heroes, and partly because they take *Cowboy Bebop* too far away from its dramatic core).

Incidentally, it's Spike Spiegel who takes command in the finale – sending Faye Valentine to the weather control facility, and Jet Black to drum up any air support he can; meanwhile, Spike heads off in his faithful *Swordfish* to nobble Vincent).

The fight takes place on the Eiffel Tower,[30] no less (and recalls the finale of the Jackie Chan actioner *Rush Hour 3*). Of course it is an extended fight and

29 The *Pierrot le Fou* episode of the *Cowboy Bebop* series had featured a similar procession, but to much greater effect.
30 There's a famous replica (1958) of the Eiffel Tower (Tokyo Tower) in downtown Tokyo, 1080 feet tall, which you can see in many *animé*, such as *Tokyo Godfathers* and *Ghost In the Shell: Stand Alone Complex* (and you can visit the observation deck).

kickboxing duel between Spike Spiegel and Vincent,[31] very much in the Hollywood stunts-and-gags mode, with plenty of Hong Kong martial arts (realism is chucked away – both Spike and Vincent should be knocked unconscious or dead not far into the fight!).

Of course Electra shows up, and it's she (quite rightly) who finally wastes the villain[32] (poor Electra, she really picked the wrong guy this time). Electra also saves Spike, because our hero's defeated, crouched on the floor, while Vincent holds a gun to his head (a woman killing a man, yes – but Electra closes her eyes as she pulls the trigger).

The effects of Vincent's air-borne virus are spectacularly evoked with amazing, handheld, subjective shots as the victims stagger about (unusual in *animé*, and a technical marvel to witness). A genius touch has yellow butterflies materializing when the victims're close to expiring – heavily symbolic of *mono no aware,* the fleetingness of life (and very Japanese), but it works (thus, 100s of butterflies appear at the climax, when Spike's close to death. For me they recall the fireflies in the matchless *Grave of the Fireflies*).

The rain helps to spread the vaccine that the old coots drop from ancient warbirds (including the three poker-playing old guys who recur in the TV series – Antonio (Jinsho Hirao), Carlos (Toshihiko Nakajima) and Jobim (Hiroshi Naka)). This section of *Cowboy Bebop* allows the *mecha* nuts[33] in the production to indulge themselves in some old school

---

31 The absence of Jet Black during the whole finale is notable. But the filmmakers clearly wanted this to be between Spike and Vincent.
32 However, Vincent has already been shot by Spike in this duel – but a bullet from a former lover is gonna hit the mark.
33 Kimitoshi Yamane was mechanical designer. Masami Goto was mechanical animation director.

mecha outings (they include all of their favourite planes), the kinda flying machines that Hayao Miyazaki loves. (Rounding up the warbirds gives Jet Black summat significant to do in the finale, too, and adds some moments of humour: the ancient planes are museum pieces, and some of 'em fall to pieces even before they've left the ground. Meanwhile, Faye Valentine is sent to the weather centre of Mars, to order up some rain).

Vincent is humanized at the end of the *Cowboy Bebop* movie: he not only gets a death speech, he also admits he didn't shoot because he recognized the only person he ever loved (when Electra appears). The humanizing of such a ruthless mass murderer is unusual: even Spike Spiegel seems to feel some sympathy with the villain, even though Vincent's just tried to kill him, has already killed and maimed hundreds, has tormented and possibly raped Faye Valentine, and has just released a virus of nano-robots which will kill thousands (especially the old anf infirm – before the rain spreads the vaccine).

♫

The end credits of the *Cowboy Bebop* movie revisit some of the amazing background art from the movie (plus images of Faye Valentine at the races (and losing), Jet Black with Ein the dog, Spike Spiegel passing another hooded woman in Morocco Town, and Radical Ed fishing on the deck of the spaceship). There's a final judgement of Vincent from Spike Spiegel (now back in his favourite spot – the couch of the *Bebop* spaceship). *Don't be alone* is the message of the movie, it seems (the signing-off caption says something about living in reality).

RECEPTION.

Animé expert Helen McCarthy reckoned that the *Cowboy Bebop* movie was half-an-hour too long. I don't think so – partly because the animation is stellar, because the movie is so entertaining, and the whole package is so appealing. It's true, though, that the 2001 movie does spend more time with the villain Vincent than is necessary, and also that after the monorail action sequence, which would work as a finale in any other movie, the picture does slow down and meander somewhat. (You can see how the final climax replays the monorail action scene; you can also see how the movie could end with the monorail chase and shoot-out, complete with Spike Spiegel seeming to die (after averting catastrophe), but being rescued by Native Americans, right down to the beat where Jet Black appears, to take Spike back to the *Bebop* spaceship).

If you know the *Cowboy Bebop* TV show, you might find the *Cowboy Bebop* movie just a little too serious, or maybe it's that there are too many long gaps between the comedy (and Radical Ed has too little to contribute). A more accurate reflection of the *Cowboy Bebop* TV series would have been an action comedy movie; but the filmmakers opted instead for an action movie with occasional comic moments. Which isn't the same. If you didn't know the TV show, I can imagine that the action and drama would work very well indeed, because the movie is fabulous in that respect. And the design, the multi-cultural world, and the genre mixing, is all stupendous. But I reckon the characters and their relationships might perplex some newbies. And if you don't know the *animé* series, a character such as Radical Ed is going to appear odd (there are no equivalents in Western cinema, for instance).

In the U.S.A., the *Cowboy Bebop* movie fared well at the box office, compared to most *animé*. The *Pokémon* movies have generated the biggest ticket sales in North America ($85 million gross in 1999, for the first Pikachu flick). The *Cowboy Bebop* movie was in 11th place, behind Studio Ghibli's *Spirited Away* (it made around $10m).

Illustrations

Images from the 2001 *Cowboy Bebop* movie.

Images from the Cowboy Bebop movie
(this page and following pages).

Electra

Vincent, an extremely nasty villain, captures the heroine, Faye Valentine

COWBOY BEBOP

APPENDICES

SAMURAI CHAMPLOO
SAMURAI MANGA
MACROSS PLUS

SAMURAI CHAMPLOO

The samurai genre connection with *Cowboy Bebop*
would bear fruit in 2004-05, when Shinichiro
Watanabe, director of the *Cowboy Bebop* series,
helmed the 26-episode series *Samurai Champloo*. This
is the closest thing to a sequel to *Cowboy Bebop*. Fuji
TV and Manglobe produced; the show aired from
May, 2004 to March, 2005 on Fuji TV.

Samurai Champloo was written by Shinji Obara
(chief writer), Keiko Nobumoto (*Cowboy Bebop*'s head
writer), Dai Sato (who wrote some *Cowboy Bebop*
episodes), Seiko Takagi, Ryota Sugi, Touko Machida,
Uwadan Shimofuwato, and director Shinichiro
Watanabe. The music was by Fat John (an American

producer), Force of Nature, Nujabes (a Japanese DJ) and Tsutchie. Shing o2 and Nujabes ('Battlecry') appear in the opening titles of *Samurai Champloo*, and Minmi ('Song of Four Seasons') over the end credits. Animation directors included Kazuto Nakazawa,[1] Yumiko Ishii and Shinji Takeuchi. As well as Watanabe, many others directed episodes[2] (see the Anime News Network for the most detailed credits to *animé* online). Among the voice cast, Kazuya Nakai was Mugen, Ginpel Sato was Jin, and Ayako Kawasumi was Fuu (they were outstanding – voice director Tsutomu Kashiwakura coaxes wonderful comic performances from the trio).

Executive producers were: Hideki 'Henry' Goto, Sanae Mitsugi, Shinichiro Kobayashi and Shiro Sasaki. The producers were: Takashi Kochiyama, Takatoshi Hamano and Tetsuro Satomi.

Character design was by Hideto Komori and Kazuto Nakazawa. Takeshi Waki was art director. Mahiro Maeda was *mecha* designer. Kazuhiro Yamada was DP. Eri Suzuki was colour designer. Background art was by Studio Green and Feng Animation. Shuichi Kakesu was the editor. Yoshimoto Ishikawa was music producer (at Victor Entertainment).

Samurai Champloo is without question one of the most *intelligent* of recent *animé* series: the amount of research, wit, knowledge and self-awareness on display is formidable. The team who put this show together know their history, their art history, their

---

1 Born in 1968, Kazuto Nakazawa's credits include *Blood +, Record of Lodoss War, Moondrive, Ergo Proxy,* and *Sweat Punch*.
2 Along with Akira Yoshimura, Hiroyuki Imaishi, Kazuki Akane, Kazuyoshi Katayama and Tsukasa Sunaga.

political history, their literary history, as well as their pop culture (and their music!) inside-out.[3] A number of workers in the team have clearly spent a *long* time immersed in books, documentaries, articles, websites and the like about the Meiji and Edo periods in Japanese history (*Samurai Champloo* is set *circa* 1650-90). And the designers and background artists (at Studio Green and Feng Animation) have also devoured 100s of textbooks, exhibitions, and yet more movies and TV shows, in order to recreate this rich visual world.

Sam Champ is a wholly successful update of the samurai genre, I think, which works at the level of reclaiming the action, art and politics of the samurai genre,[4] and also as a postmodern commentary on the genre (and other action-adventure genres), and an analysis of (*animé*) entertainment itself.[5] *Samurai Champloo* happily deconstructs itself and every other *animé* show before your eyes.[6] It also takes apart the mechanics of storytelling, and characterization, and lit'ry notions such as issues, themes and motifs.

Samurai Champloo, I reckon, is a masterclass of examining what narrative entertainment is, what it does, why we love it, and why it's still so successful. The biggest TV/ movie/ DVD/ web shows and products, globally, are still built around *stories*. Movies, *animé*, television, novels, plays, operas,

---

3 There is more historical research on show than in *Ninja Scroll, Dagger of Kamui, Samurai X* or any other historical show for Brian Camp (334).
4 *Samurai Champloo* 'successfully reclaims the samurai drama for modern teens – a bold affirmation that stories about Japan's past do not have to be boring, staid Sunday night NHK epics for Dad', as Helen McCarthy and Jonathan Clements put it (2006, 559).
5 For Helen McCarthy and Jonathan Clements, *Samurai Champloo* is 'at heart, a crushingly old-fashioned show, with a studied punkish-ness dating back to the Vietnam-era *Monjiro*' (2006, 559).
6 The samurai genre had been sent up before in a pop culture manner (in shows such as *Samurai Gold*).

ballets, cartoons – they're all just *stories*. Stories – one of the great pleasures of *Samurai Champloo* is its deep awareness of what storytelling is (you find this self-conscious deconstruction of storytelling in other *animé*, such as *Mushishi* and *Fullmetal Alchemist*).

Samurai Champloo is drawing on a really *huge* retinue of movies made about samurai and gangsters: beyond the well-known samurai movies and TV shows there are literally hundreds if not thousands of others. The samurai genre has been updated many, many times: it's a genre that never goes away in Japanese culture.

Like *Cowboy Bebop, Samurai Champloo* was notable for its use of pop music, cinematic allusions and popular culture references. This time, the teams at Fuji TV and Manglobe employed hip-hop music (there's a big close-up of a vinyl record spinning on a gramophone in the title sequence). But not only hip-hop – there is a wealth of music in *Samurai Champloo*, including folk singing and *biwas* (there's some plaintive acoustic guitar, for instance, in episode 11: *Gamblers and Gallantry*).

Samurai Champloo's a lotta fun, a hyper postmodern take on the samurai genre, couched here in the form of an action comedy. Set in the Edo period (a.k.a. the Togukawa era), it has numerous links to the *Cowboy Bebop* series,[7] including the group of misfits that comes together, the comic banter and franxious alliance between them, the fast-paced action, the jokey pop culture references, the high art and high culture references, and humorous direct addresses to the audience (in the form of handwritten notes). It was a samurai action show for an internet generation, a

---

7 Another forerunner is *Samurai X* (a.k.a. *Rurouni Kenshin*).

downloading generation, a post-*manga*, post-comicbook generation, with its flashy editing and jacked-up stylizations.

Philip Brophy describes the style of the show in *100 Anime*:

> Abstract graffiti patterns and neo-mod website layering are merged with Edo scroll colouring and printing techniques. Blaxploitation score interludes are laid over rural historical locations where a wah-wah would never have sounded. Vinyl scratching erupts on the soundtrack to sync to cross-cuts and scene transitions, forming the *anime* into a remix of itself. It's like a hip-hop crew has been warped back to Edo to tell the story of *Samurai Champloo* like a wildstyle *kamishibai*. (2005, 201)

As Brian Camp pointed out in *Zettai: Anime Classics*, altho' *Samurai Champloo* used 'all sorts of playful design touches and contemporary visual and audio tricks with assorted dejay and hiphop references', as it aimed to appeal to a modern, youth audience, it was still possesed 'a genuine respect for its historical subjects', and encouraged viewers to 'further research the numerous real-life figures and incidents cited' (18). For Camp, every story in *Champloo* is 'worth telling and is beautifully written and planned, with seeds planted early that sprout later with great effect' (333).

Samurai Champloo is a very clever and witty way of delivering a *jidai geki* (historical genre) and *chambara* (samurai genre) to a postmodern, seen-it-all-before audience. When you present something with such style and flair, as well as intelligence and humour, you can't help being won over by it. Shinichiro Watanabe and the team are masters at *mixing* styles and genres, at smashing together elements which really don't belong together at all. The *confidence* of the filmmaking is apparent from the first frames.

And, let's not forget, there is a ton of amazing visual spectacle on display: from the 'eye-catches' or bumpers for the commercial breaks (each one different) to the background artwork, *Samurai Champloo* is a very high class product. It looks stunning, as if the filmmakers have consumed the whole history of Japanese art (and cinema) from 1600 to the present day, and transformed it to their own purposes. You can bet that the production team at Fuji TV/ Manglobe spent 100s of hours studying reference books (and the web), as well as, if their budget allowed it, visits to museums and the countryside.

Samurai Champloo is also *very* Japanese: the deployment of American crime genre ingredients or American Westerns or American hip-hop music, for instance, were only part of the mix. Because numerous elements of *Samurai Champloo* were self-consciously Japanese, and some flash past the audience at light speed. *Samurai Champloo* is a show, like *The Simpsons*, that assumes a high intelligence factor in its audience.

For Helen McCarthy and Jonathan Clements, *Samurai Champloo* is sometimes too clever, too self-parodic for its own good, which hides the slightness of some of its episodes:

> The show is so stylish, so manically energetic and so involved in its own mythology that it's easy to forgive its lack of substance, but it is an interesting experiment rather than a complete success' (2006, 559)

While it's true that *dramatically* or *narratively* some of the episodes in *Samurai Champloo* are distinctly thin and lacking in substance (as well as misguided and misconceived), this is not true of the series as a whole, nor is it entirely what the series is about. *Samurai Champloo* works on many other levels apart from that of story, character, themes and issues (tho' on those level it's superb, too). Or put it like this: *Samurai Champloo* is operating on so many levels, that to find several layers as lacking doesn't damage the show, because there are so many other layers to consider. A poor series is soon let down by lacklustre stories and unengaging characters, if there isn't much else going on. Not *Samurai Champloo*. It has so much going on simultaneously, when it doesn't work in one area, it is on fire in other areas. (It's true, tho' that *Samurai Champloo*, like *Cowboy Bebop* or *Fullmetal Alchemist*, *knows* it's good, but you can forgive such self-assurance or even arrogance when the show is so entertaining). *Samurai Champloo* is desperate to be cool (like *Cowboy Bebop*), but it really does achieve it.

> Dark glasses and earrings, rap music and hip-hop, graffiti and baseball invade the Edo period in *Samurai Champloo* with hilarious and un-expected results [writes Stefano Gariglio in *Manga Impact!*]. The direction is virtuoso but never forced, with a prevalence of wide angle and tilted shots (which enhance Mugen's acrobatics) and a syncopated editing style that intertwines parallel events with scenes changing to the sound of a vinyl scratch.[8]

The credits sequence of *Samurai Champloo* (directed by Mamoru Hosoda) is a classic, as with

---

8 Quoted in C. Chatrian, 169.

Cowboy Bebop, a brilliant montage of visual art and animation to a hip-hop beat ('Battlecry' by Nujabes and Shing 02). The retro feel of the Pop Art graphics is wittily updated for a 2000s audience. Like the typical title sequence in *animé*, it acts as a trailer, a commercial, and a summary of the show. The *attitude* of *Samurai Champloo* is right there, as with *Cowboy Bebop*, in the opening credits. And it's the *attitude*, an almost impossible thing to define, or manufacture, that's so important to the success of *Samurai Champloo*.

Some of the episodes in *Samurai Champloo* run together, tho' each episode always closes with the caption 'TO BE CONTINUED'. Yes, and don't you wish that the filmmakers at Fuji TV/ Manglobe could continue for years and years!

Only one aspect of *Samurai Champloo* marred it for me, and that was the OTT level of violence: oh, sure, like, *duh,* a samurai TV show is gonna be violent – hell, anything with samurai warriors is probably gonna be violent. But in *Samurai Champloo* the brutality sometimes went on too long, and was too vicious, and included nasty shit directed against women (including the heroine, Fuu, who's tied to crosses and brutalized in more'n a few episodes). It unbalanced the show, and worked against the comedy.

And the animation, though as accomplished as ever for a high profile Japanese animation series, contained aspects of digital ink and paint which were everywhere in animation of the 2000s period: a new flatness coupled with ugly, thick black lines around characters, reminiscent of German Expressionist woodcuts. The approach recalled stained glass and early comicbooks.

There're three characters in the oddball team in *Samurai Champloo:* Jin – the super-cool, calm, Buddhist samurai warrior, taciturn, withdrawn, unflappable. He is pale, thin, tall, and wore blue kimonos and round spectacles (like the director Shinichiro Watanabe!). Mugen[9] – the reckless, crude, gauche, rebellious, eccentric, breakdancing swords-man, wearing shorts, a sort of Afro haircut, earrings and tattoos (the relation to Spike Spiegel is obvious).

And there's 15 year-old Fuu – a total ditz, feisty, tough, romantic, sensitive, determined, a delightful comedienne with large *animé* eyes wearing a long, red dress. Fuu is the heart of the piece, dramatically more necessary than either of the two samurai misfits she teams up with (in fact, some of the best episodes are those that concentrate on Fuu, not the two guys. And of course it's Fuu who is introduced first, and it's she who sets up the team and the quest in the first episode).

Sam Champ's three misfits are always broke, and always hungry – situations that aren't always easy to make convincing to those lucky folk in the audience of *animé* who have lots of money and plenty of food. It's a staple of the historical genre, though, that people are often poor and often hungry. And *Cowboy Bebop* made it a central premise.

Apart from hoping to get a good meal (the film-makers squeeze a *lot* of mileage out of that predica-ment!), and trying to get by without any dough (the filmmakers also exploit that to the *max*), there is an over-arching (and very silly) quest, one of oddest in

9 The name Mugen, as well as his characterization, owes plenty to the samurai tradition in *manga* and *animé*.

all *animé*: Fuu's desire to find the samurai who smells like sunflowers (there is some effort by the script-writers Dai Sato, Seiko Takagi, Shinji Obara and others to set up how Fuu falls in with Jin and Mugen and persuades them to join her quest to find the sunflower-scented samurai warrior, but it's not very convincing. It doesn't matter, tho', because in a show like *Samurai Champloo* you just accept conventions like that. Only late in the series does Fuu deign to reveal that the samurai they're looking for is her father. Instead, *Samurai Champloo* simply withholds inform-ation about the motives and layers behind the central quest. But father quests are central to many *manga* and *animé*).

The opening episode of *Samurai Champloo* (*Tempestuous Temperaments*, broadcast on May 20, 2004), rightly throws everything that the filmmakers have at the audience: rapidly introducing the three main characters (with Fuu the first to be seen), staging scenes that evoke their personalities, building up a series of action scenes, throwing in postmodern jokes, hip-hop music, and self-conscious cinematic tech-niques (like the retro transitions between scenes, accompanies by vinyl scratches from hip-hop).

And all of this is achieved before the commercial break at the eleven minute mark! This is *fast* story-telling – yet also completely clear and direct, and it doesn't hurry thru vital pieces of information.

The obstacles/ villains in episode 1: *Tempestuous Temperaments* is a domineering prefect of a town who abuses his power by tormenting citizens. Jin, the do-gooder, self-righteous samurai *ronin*, objects to this maltreatment, and takes on the prefect's ace bodyguards (and of course slices them to pieces). Thus're our three heroes aligned with under-dogs and peasants.

In the other fight scene, intercut with the Jin scene by the river, Mugen wanders into the restaurant where Fuu works as a waitresses, offering to deal with the roughnecks who're causing trouble for the customers in return for dumplings (food is a Big Deal in *Samurai Champloo* for the three misfits. It's typical that Mugen wants to be paid in food, and is perpet-ually hungry!).

Splitting the samurai hero into two, Mugen and Jin, means that a variety of aspects of the classic warrior character can be explored. Jin, for example, embodies the Buddhist, *bushido* aspects of samurai culture, where the emphasis is on proper action, humility, nobility, integrity, respect, deferrence, right action and training in martial arts schools (*dojos*). Mugen is the total opposite of all that! – he's untrained, rebellious, antsy, wild, and uncouth. His background is shady, linked to crime.

In the second half of the *Tempestuous Tempera-ments* episode, the writers make the bond between the three main charas a strong one by having Fuu helping to rescue Jin and Mugen from execution (it has to be a solid connection in order for the relationships to work throughout the 2004-05 series). There is a *giant* action sequence in which Mugen and Jin go up against hordes of town guards, while Fuu hurls a coupla bombs from a nearby roof.

One thing strikes you immediately about the first episode of *Samurai Champloo*: it is *extremely* violent. We see both Mugen and Jin killing several people with little forethought (and their motives are dodgy, too). Rather than teaching the bullies in the restaurant a lesson by beating them, Mugen has no problem with slicing off one guy's arm, and killing some o' the others. Jin, meanwhile, cuts the three bodyguards of the prefect to pieces.

In the finale of episode 1: *Tempestuous Temperaments*, the body count on screen is enormous, and the blood is flying all over the place as the swords of Jin an' Mugen flash and dice. *Samurai Champloo* seems to go out of its way to impress the viewer with just how vicious it is going to be. Meanwhile, when the heroes are captured by the prefect, they are tortured the night b4 the execution by the prefect's lackeys, with a series of gruesome acts (seen in a rapid montage).

The second episode of *Samurai Champloo*, *Redeye Reprisal* (also written by chief writer Shinji Obara), depicts the fall-out from the mayhem of the first episode, *Tempestuous Temperaments*, as the victims of Mugen's and Jin's antics demand some retribution. Sasaki Ryujiro (Otoya Kawano), who had his arm chopped off by Mugen, has hired an assassin[10] to deal with Jin, and an ugly giant Oniwakamaru (Seiji Sasaki) to nobble Mugen (as well as a hooker, who during sex with Mugen poisons him, while Hotaru (Masako Katsuki) has the antidote. This is also a staple of *jidai geki*). And this demonstrates one o' the challenges of producing a samurai show (or any action show): you have to keep creating villains for the heroes to battle against (and if you've split the hero into two, and made 'em both hotshot swordsmen, you have to come up with greater and greater

---

10 In the baths at night, a gay subtext is introduced when the assassin makes an approach to Jin as they bathe (who promptly exits the pool).

foes, and one for each character). And you also have to find summat for the heroine, Fuu, to do (often Fuu plays the princess who needs rescuing).

The solution in *Redeye Reprisal* has the assassin duelling Jin in a bamboo forest (a mandatory setting for any *chanbara*), while Mugen is soundly beaten by the ogre next to a river (another classic samurai genre location – rivers crop up *many* times in *Samurai Champloo!*). Thus, Fuu gets to play Beauty to the warrior Beast, taming him a little (so that he turns on his master, the very nasty Sasaki, and strangles him. Which's apt, because Sasaki has hit poor Fuu not once but twice).

The evocation of transience and impermanence – *mono no aware* – is one of the staples of Japanese philosophy and poetry. Here, *Samurai Champloo* includes entrancing images of fireflies at night. Oniwakamaru, as he dies, reaches up to the flickering, green insects in an image that recalls *Grave of the Fireflies*.

Style-wise, episode 2: *Redeye Reprisal* has jettisoned most o' the flashy, hip elements of the first episode of *Samurai Champloo*, as the 2004/ 2005 series settles down to alternate more conventional storytelling episodes with the gimmicky, postmodernist installments.

In the third episode of *Samurai Champloo*, *Hellhounds For Hire* (part one of a double-header), Fuu can't help chattering on and on about the guys always fighting each other, and how she's always hungry, and is desperate for a bath. They can't take any more of her whingeing, and flee, in opposite directions.

But of course, they are soon bumping into each

other: there are two yakuza gangs fighting for supremacy in the nearby town. Mugen becomes involved with the Nagatomi, the newer, cooler but also crueller gang (of course!), and is hired as a bodyguard, and Jin is attached to the older, more traditional gang (having saved the boss Daiguro's (Katsuhisa Houki) son Sousuke (Mayumi Yamaguchi) from the rival gang's henchmen).

Poor Fuu, meanwhile, arrives in town some time after her bodyguards, and ends up in a brothel in a rather unconvincing series of events (well, yeah, putting Fuu in a whorehouse *is* predictable! But it *is* also part o' the *chanbara* genre. And it's repeated). Needless to say, we only see Fuu in a comic scenario with a customer (a wrinkly, old man): she is plotting escape, but is dismayed that the woman who joins the brothel at the same time, Osuzu (Sayuri), the sister of Sousuke, can't leave because the *yakuza* will punish her father).

In the second part of *Hellhounds for Hire*, the rivalry between the gangs reach its apogee with a dice match. It takes some finangling by head scripter Shinji Obara (1) to get Fuu into the scene, (2) to play the part of the dice thrower, (3) to have Jin playing the *yojimbo* (bodyguard) to the mob patriarch Daiguro, and (4) to have Mugen returning to (A) save Fuu, and (B) fight some more guards because he's, well, bored. So there is, of course, a giant bust-up in the gambling hall, with Jin and Mugen in the centre of the ruckus. (And yet another duel, when Mugen and Sasaki settle their quarrel).

In the midst of it all is the kid, Sousuke, thoroughly out of his depth (but desperate for payback against the rival Nagatomi mob), the scheming leader of the rival *yakuza*, plus assorted gnarly hired guns, old restaurant owners, and imperious brothel madams. Writer Shinji Obara is trying to squeeze a 100 minute feature story into two 22 minute *animé* episodes (and succeeding, by and large).

Samurai Champloo is also, like *Cowboy Bebop*, highly intellectual, with numerous high culture references alongside the pop culture ones. Fr'instance, episode five, *Artistic Anarchy*, opens with a montage of close-ups of paintings by Vincent van Gogh (though re-imagined by the production team at Fuji TV/ Manglobe). A voiceover (from a grizzled old cop, Inspector Manzou,[11] played by Unshou Ishizuka, who is Jet Black in *Cowboy Bebop*, on the trail of white slave traders), talks about the influence of Japanese art on Paul Gauguin and van Gogh. *Artistic Anarchy* also explores other ingredients, such as the culture of *ukiyo-e* (woodblock prints) in Japanese art,[12] the artist and the model (and nude modelling, of course!), and the links between mainstream art and erotica (another Japanese speciality – 'this girl's getting it on with an octopus!' quips Mugen, referring to the famous print by Katsushika Hokusai). It assumes a high level of cultural knowledge on the part of the audience.

As if that isn't enough for one 22 minute episode, 5: *Artistic Anarchy* also brings in the white slave trade (of young women), with Fuu inevitably being a

11 There are one or two recurring charas in *Samurai Champloo*, such as Inspector Manzou, and the sports commentator Ichiemon.
12 The influence of the art of famous Japanese artists such as Katsushika Hokusai, Kitagawa Utamaro and Hiroshige Utagawa on Japanese animation is easy to spot: their woodblock prints (*ukiyo-e*) are some of Japan's most distinctive artworks. Masahiro Emoto made the *ukiyo-e* works (Emoto's credits include *Jin-Roh, Millennium Actress* and *Ghost In the Shell*).

victim, plus the uneasy alliance between Western nations and Japan in the Edo period. But all of that cultural stuff is allusion and subtext, because *Artistic Anarchy* also has to deliver a dramatic episode, with some comedy, as well as the mandatory samurai vs. bad guys duels.

While Mugen careens around the place like a broken, wind-up toy samurai with a ravenous appetite, Jin gets to play *shogi* with the villain of the piece, the slave trader Masaaki Tsukada, who's using as a front for his crimes a book and print store (run by his imperious wife, Sawa – Yayoi Nakazawa).

There's some comedy squeezed outta Fuu being persuaded to pose as a model by the artist Moronobu Hishikawa[13] (Shinichiro Miki), a hapless, scrawny individual (but he's a good artist). Until she's kidnapped by three *yakuza* (who're also inept), which provides *Artistic Anarchy* with its mandatory action-based finale (and cop Manzou rounds up the criminals).

Episodes 6 to 8 further explored high art references, with *kabuki*, geishas, *bushido*, and early novels about homosexuality. At times it was striking just how many intellectual pursuits and references *Samurai Champloo* managed to cram in to its 22 or so minutes.

As with *Cowboy Bebop*, *Samurai Champloo* explores different forms of sexuality from the heterosexual norm. The episode *Stranger Searching* (number 6) features a European in disguise as a samurai (this was the historical period when Japan closed itself off from outsiders). During a visit to a magical *kabuki*

13 Hishikawa (1618-94) was a real artist of the period, and one of his works is included.

show, the European, a Dutchman, who insists he is a Japanese guy called Jouji (his real name is Isaac Titsingh, and he's a prominent merchant),[14] is revealed to be gay (inevitably there's a joke made at the crossdressing of the lead kabuki actor, Yamato Nadeshiko, but a double joke, because Jouji the Dutchman likes men, after all).

The first half of *Stranger Searching* features an eating contest (which the crew of the *Bebop* spaceship might've entered). Jin bows out early on (as expected), Mugen does very well, but collapses with a bloated belly (as expected). The perpetually-starving Fuu is close to winning (as expected), but swats a fly, a gesture misinterpreted as giving up. The winner is of course the Dutchman Jouiji (he wins Jin's beloved swords. This is the narrative hook which has our heroes teaming up with the unlikely figure of Jouii).

There's a very humorous interlude where the hapless Dutchman Jouji is shown in a field of tulips (surrounded by windmills, of course), back in the Netherlands, holding a flower (like Narcissus in Greek mythology), and contemplating at length on what it means to be homosexual in a society where no one understands you. There are plenty of jokes being played here about gay culture (for instance, the irony that Holland is now famously laid-back and tolerant and welcoming of alternative sexual identities), and also an in-depth dip into the work of Japanese author Saikaku Ihara (it's like watching a mini-lecture, because the filmmakers also include a piece on *bushido*, the ethics of samurai culture, and its relation to homosexuality. Jouiji narrates this long side-story, so that *Samurai Champloo* becomes a TV documentary

14 In the Edo period, the only nations trading with Japan were China and Holland.

on the Edo period's attitude towards sexuality for a few minutes. The postmodern, melting pot format of *Samurai Champloo* allows for this sort of diversion which halts the narrative and has only a tangential relation to the main story).

Stranger Searching is also a send-up of tourists and tourism, and Japan's ambiguous view in the Edo period of foreigners (which still persists): Jouji is a gross caricature of a white, European man, with blue eyes, red hair and a ridiculous facial design. Jouiji is crazy about Japanese culture, while the locals take it all for granted. Jouji is 'other' in every respect, from his appearance to his national, political and sexual identity.

In episode 7: *A Risky Racket*, that staple of the crime genre, a youth getting in over his head in the criminal underworld, was explored (*Cowboy Bebop* had used it in *Waltz For Venus*). So Shinsuke (Shigeru Shibuya) is a petty thief who snatches some opium and becomes involved with gangs and cops. However, he has a sick mom, and is thieving to buy medicine for her; so he's not a bad boy after all.

A Risky Racket focusses very much on Fuu, and how she becomes linked to Shinsuke (Shinsuke snaffled her purse at the top o' the show – dough that the trio won, yet again, from gambling). While Jin and Mugen want some payback for going without the noodles they were so hungry for, Fuu develops a soft spot for Shinsuke (she overhears him talking to his mom in their home, and realizes he's trying to help her). Things turn out badly in the finale, when Shinsuke takes Fuu hostage and inevitably comes to a sticky end at the hands of the authorities (there's a

siege sequence, a rooftop escape, and of course a Big
Fight, with Mugen smashing down the doors to get at
the thief who did him out of a really yummy bowl of
noodles).

Every narrative turn, character and situation in
A Risky Racket is predictable and obvious, and we've
seen all of this many times before. But it's an entertaining enough episode, tho' lacking the invention and
eccentricity and humour of the better *Samurai Champloo* episodes. (However, there is a dream sequence,
where Fuu remembers her past: entering a room
where a dead body lies in state – presumably this's
the samurai who smells of sunflowers. Only later do
we find out that it's her dead mom).

Among the most amusing sequences in *Samurai
Champloo* are those which use the tropes of hip-hop –
how a singer will use a 'mic', even tho' they haven't
been invented yet, and the backing musicians will
perform the drum beats and bass of hip-hop with
their mouths. In episode 8: *The Art of Altercation*, a
trio of youths deliver the exposition of a folk tale –
which woulda been done with a wizened, old crone
in previous *jidai geki* – as a hip-hop trio.

The chief new character in ep 8: *The Art of
Altercation* is a completely over-the-top diva of a
wannabe samurai hero and ruler of Edo, Nagamitsu.
He's one of those obnoxiously arrogant, look-at-me
guys who reads aloud from his autobiography,
strikes ridiculous, heroic poses, but is a total meat-
head. Nagamitsu sports a 1950s quiff and 1970s
custom car fire flashes on his jacket, a delightful
mash-up of the kitsch, Fifties Americana of *American
Graffiti* and *Grease* with hip-hop stylings in *jidai-geki*

setting. It shouldn't really work, but it does, and episode 8: *The Art of Altercation* is one of the funniest in the *Samurai Champloo* series.

The story of episode 8: *The Art of Altercation* isn't really worth bothering with – you just go along for the ride to see how far the filmmakers are gonna take this postmodern riffing. Well, all right, there *is* a story to episode 8, involving Nagamitsu searching for Jin, the killer of the *sensei* of his *dojo,* Mariya Enshirou (tho' of course, it wasn't part of Nagamitsu's background, but another guy's – but Jin did accidentally kill his *dojo*'s leader); Nagamitsu falling for Fuu; Jin and Mugen getting hustled with poisoned wine by a housewife with a bouncy cleavage in a bar (a motif already employed in episode two); the trio pawning their valuables (then performing some street entertainment to raise some dough); the trio being ravenously hungry, etc.

❖

Episode 9: *Beatbox Bandits* was a crazy outing of *Samurai Champloo* which began with (1) an old man remembering back 30 years to the time when he worked at a check-point, and an infamous getting-across-the-border scene (involving obtaining permits),[15] and ended up (2) with a stops-all-out, druggie, Summer of Love, psychedelic fantasy. Along the way, the filmmakers staged some wild duels, a prolonged and inventive chase, a big, revolutionary mass meeting, and a climactic battle. Did it make sense? Nah. Was it fun? Oh yeah! And in amongst the comedy and action, there was some gorgeous back-ground art (of Edo period Japan, including temples), send-ups of political movements, and some unusual

---

15 Getting thru borders is a staple scene of Edo period *chanbara.* A great one appears in the *Blade of the Immortal manga.*

turns in the plotting.

Bizarrely, the State fascists at the border gate crucify victims[16] – so this episode 9: *Beatbox Bandits* includes repulsive images of poor Fuu, near-naked, on a cross, having spears thrust at her breasts. Really vile stuff, where the filmmakers go WAY too far. You can't crucify your heroine, *for fuck's sake!*

The story of *Beatbox Bandits* wasn't the point of the show, but it did cram a whole lotta narrative beats into 22 minutes. It involved Mugen being given a quest to travel many miles – and he had to be back by sunset, otherwise his chums, Jin and Fuu, would be executed (a sort of dare/ quest out of Western fairy tales). So off Mugen goes, pursued by masked ninja – these are the fabled Tengu, warrior priests of old who've somehow survived into the Edo era. They are revolutionaries, too: there's a lengthy mass meeting where their leader rouses the mob with some zealous rhetoric.

In the finale of episode 9: *Beatbox Bandits*, the burning of a field which turns out to be cannabis in the midst of a heroes-versus-ninja action sequence resulted in some of the wildest animation in the *Samurai Champloo* series (it was reminiscent of the *Pierrot le Fou* episode in *Cowboy Bebop*).

Psychedelic drugs are an excuse for animators to go nuts (but some animators don't need LSD, DMT or Ecstasy – they're already there!). And the team at Fuji TV/ Manglobe delivered a wild ride of post-Robert Crumb, post-*Fritz the Cat*, post-*Easy Rider* trippiness (and those colours, *maaan*, so cool!).

---

16 Crucifixion was taken up in the feudal era as a means of torture and death, tho' its depiction in popular Japanese culture doesn't automatically mean a Christian reference.

Episode 10 of *Samurai Champloo* – *Lethal Lunacy*
– is a much more conventional *chambara* piece, with
fairly straightforward (i.e., non-gimmicky, non-
flashy) evocations of samurai warriors, and *ronin*,
and *dojos*, and *bushido*. Two new characters're introduced – a former samurai Zuikou (Shibui Matsuno-
suke) who's now a Buddhist priest,[17] and his one-
time pupil, Shouryuu (Sho Hayami), who turns, you
might say, to the 'Dark Side of the Force'. Shouryuu is
a life-loathing, miserable excuse for a man who uses
the special martial arts he learnt somewhere overseas
(i.e., China) to kill people. The technique involves
controlling *chi* to burst the internal organs of unfor-
tunate victims, so 'they bleed from every orifice' (as
one of the characters graphically puts it). The *chi*-
based martial arts was reprised for the final episodes
of *Samurai Champloo*.

Mugen thus finally finds in Shouryuu an opponent worthy of his time and energy: so the most
enjoyable segments in this rather solemn episode of
Samurai Champloo are those depicting Mugen undertaking a rigorous samurai training routine delivered
as a Jackie Chan montage (running up the temple steps
carrying weights, flying kicks at dummy enemies
chalked on a trees, handstands on thumbs, and even
meditation under a waterfall. Ah, no, Mugen decides
he *isn't* gonna do that last one! Instead, Zuikou the
priest does).

For the finale of *Lethal Lunacy*, there's a duel by
moonlight on and under one of the lovely, curved
wooden bridges that're mandatory in any *jidai-geki*.
Of course, Mugen is victorious, giving Shouryuu back

---

17 To demonstrate just how old-fashioned *Lethal Lunacy* is, the writer
(Touko Machida) uses that old staple of the travellers working for
their food and board by cleaning the Buddhist temple.

some of his deadly *chi*, and knifing him as he rushes him.

The middle episodes of *Samurai Champloo* include a Jin episode (11: *Gamblers and Gallantry*), where Jin meets and hopes to save a woman, Shino (Hiromi Tsuru), who is forced to become a prostitute (she has a violent husband with large gambling debts). Well, we've been here before (we've already had heroine Fuu put in a brothel in *Samurai Champloo*), but *Gamblers and Gallantry* was at least a chance to get to know Jin better (not that he gave away much! – Jin-in-love is still Jin!). A kind-hearted episode, a slice of *very* under-stated melodrama, in which the samurai/ fighting elements are unnecessary and appear kind of tacked-on.

A boorish, violent husband, a woman who wants to do her duty and not ruffle any feathers, a silent *ronin* who hopes to save her from the brothel and from her husband. A thousand clichés piled up on top of each other here (which should really smother the drama with boring familiarity), but the *Gamblers and Gallantry* episode was delivered with an entertaining knowingness, so it didn't matter.

There is action in episode 11: *Gamblers and Gallantry*, of course – Jin pounds away at the brothel's security guards (without his swords), for instance, as he and Shino flee. Mugen and Fuu hurry to his assistance, and more poor sods hit the deck – *Samurai Champloo* gets through a *lot* of henchmen and bodyguards! (Mugen thinks that Jin is pathetic, doing all of this just for a woman. But of course, if there's a fight, Mugen is always up for that!). Jin attacks more guards at the riverside.

Gamblers and Gallantry closes with a kinda happy ending: Shino finally says her piece to her total loser of a husband, and leaves him. As she floats away on a boat, she stands and stares at Jin (and weeps), while Jin watches her. (The show also includes hints of romantic jealousy, as Fuu is stunned that Jin has left their group for a woman. *I should be enough for him!* she huffs (Fuu is great when she's huffy and sulky). As the *Samurai Champloo* series progresses, the unspoken feelings between Fuu and Jin're developed further – but not, alas, to a Grand Union of Lovers).

Episode 12: *The Disorder Diaries* was a clip show,[18] narrated by Fuu, and acting as a typical mid-series summary (using the narrative device of her diary, which Jin and Mugen take a peek at, while Fuu's enjoying a hot bath). So we see segments of the previous episodes, linked by Fuu's voiceover. And we were reminded of the central quest of *Samurai Champloo:* to find the samurai who smells of sunflowers (now we discover that we are on our way across Japan to Nagasaki).[19]

The continuous story of episodes 13: *Dark Night's Road* and 14: *Misguided Miscreants* were Mugen episodes, in which, just like Spike Spiegel in *Cowboy Bebop*, Mugen becomes embroiled in a criminal organization he used to work for (and placed halfway thru the series, as the two *Jupiter Jazz* episodes were in *Cowboy Bebop*). So, again, the past comes back

---

18 There's a reference to Harumachi Koikawa, a dime novelist of the Edo period.
19 Of course the filmmakers acknowledge the historical significance of Nagasaki.

to bite Mugen on the ass, which he doesn't want at all. Of course, the guy who entices Mugen back to do one more job (a heist, natch), Mukuro (Kiyoyuki Yanada), is an arrogant, deadly, double-crossing prick, and there's also a girl (Koza[20] – Ai Maeda) involved (ain't there always!). So we get to learn a little about Mugen's shady past, and, this being a Mugen episode, there is *lots* of action and fighting (!). Meanwhile, Jin and Fuu look on in horror and disbelief as their colleague falls for the spiel of Mukuro, and joins the pirates holding up a gold-carrying ship at sea (probably a nod to the incredible finale of *Ninja Scroll*, 1993).

Some of the narrative devices of episode 13: *Dark Night's Road* beggar belief – like the fact that Mukuro and his gang just happen to be lying in wait for Mugen, Jin and Fuu to turn up on the beach. However, the structure of 13: *Dark Night's Road* has a satisfying flashback format which reveals quite a bit of Mugen's misspent youth (on a hell-hole of an island – a sort of Japanese Alcatraz or pirate island, tho' not as much fun as the pirates in *One Piece*!). The filmmakers at Manglobe/ Fuji TV are certainly audacious in *Samurai Champloo* – for example, they stage a version of the 'death race' in *Rebel Without a Cause*, but with horses! On a cliff overlooking the sea! (So the horse and riders topple over into the drink). It's completely ridiculous, but somehow *Samurai Champloo* gets away with it.

And the action finale of episode 13: *Dark Night's Road* delivers an impressive series of set-pieces during the sea-bound, nighttime heist of the gold, which tumble across the screen very much in the

20 Koza's design is reminiscent of the character designs of Satoshi Kon.

manner of the New Wave of Hong Kong cinema (it's reminiscent of the incredible *Once Upon a Time In China* movies starring Jet Li and directed by Tsui Hark).

Misguided Miscreants (Part 2) (a.k.a. *Dark Night's Road* 2) is a fun, fast-moving episode, big on action but also comedy, and yet it also has its serious side. By now, the filmmakers at Fuji TV/ Manglobe were really getting into their stride with the *Samurai Champloo* series, making the mix of action, comedy and characterization look so easy. (And the music continued to be 21st century hip-hop, while the contemporary references were numerous).

In the episode 14: *Misguided Miscreants,* part two in the on-going story, just like Spike Spiegel in *Cowboy Bebop*, Mugen appears to die. And, as he dies (drowning, following the catastrophe on the ship), there is a fantastic, multiple, musical montage (as with *Cowboy Bebop*), detailing Mugen's past life, as well as elements of the current plot, plus scenes involving Fuu and Jin. When the filmmakers at Fuji TV/ Manglobe and its associated companies launch into an extended montage, and let the music and the images do the talking (instead of the talking doing the talking), the results are marvellous. Look at the variety of imagery conjured up here, the use of colour (saturated reds, oranges and yellows), light, composition, movement – and cut together (by editor Shuichi Kakesu), with that magical feeling for pace that characterizes the finest Japanese animation.

We are in a realm of pure filmmaking here, in which storytelling is only part of the deal (tho' *Samurai Champloo* is definitely still telling a story, and still filling in characterization). And thus pure filmmaking – music-and-images – is one of the reasons why Japanese animation is the finest fantasy filmmaking in the world, as well as some of the most wonderful filmmaking of any kind.

We see flattened images of the ocean, we see molten skies filled with giant suns and atomic-level orange colours, we see giant close-ups of Mugen's eyes as he floats into the depths, deeper and deeper, we see Jin standing there, impassive as always, we see sheets of rain in a steel-grey sky, we see flash cuts to a former criminal job… When, it turns out, the same thing happened, and Mugen was betrayed by Mukuro.

We also see Mugen emerging in a sort of heaven, but upside-down (with the surface of the sea on top). There's a line of dead samurai extending into the distance (like the lines of aircraft in the WW1 flash-back in *Porco Rosso*). Mugen rightly decides that, no, he's not ready yet for the Big One, and wants to return back to life, to finish off business.

In the end, both Mugen and Jin are played for saps by Koza and her true beau, Shiren – this is the guy who was behind the gold heist. Koza begs Jin (in her timid, pitiful voice) to kill Mukuro, which Jin duly does (*Samurai Champloo* stages the inevitable gun vs. sword duels of the *chambara* genre several times – Mukuro has been waving gun around for ages). Mukuro's demise is spectacular (and, as he was such a despicable character, kinda satisfying). But then Jin finds out that Koza and Shiren have fled.

Meanwhile, Fuu has discovered Mugen washed up on the beach, and nearly dying. She takes care of him. Not one to laze about for too long if there's (1) a

fight or (2) food or (3) revenge in the offing, Mugen
hobbles along the beach in search of Shiren and Koza.
The finale is played like a Spaghetti Western, with
shots of the two parties facing each other held and
held, and a shot of Mugen limping along is held and
held. The outcome is a foregone conclusion: Mugen
wastes Shiren in a flurry of slashes, and proceeds to
walk right past Koza (she, pathetically, begs him to
kill her).

Episode 15: *Bogus Booty* of *Samurai Champloo* is
as mad as some of the craziest *Cowboy Bebop*
episodes, with a story of a crime organization forging money as the (rather flimsy) basis for some
brothel scenes, chases, and some incendiary, incredibly rapid action scenes.

Episode 15: *Bogus Booty* opened with a super-fast
chase involving mystically-skilful ninjas (a regular
animé motif) zipping thru trees and forests at night
(pursuing a thief who's lifted some counterfeit coins
and high-tailed it into the woods). The sequence is not
only cut with razor-sharp rapidity by editor Shuichi
Kakesu, it's also concocted as a challenge to the
animators: just how *fast* can you make the action?
How *few* cels can you use to make an action read
clear and exciting? (If it's *too fast*, you risk losing the
audience. Like those martial artists, such as Jackie
Chan and Jet Li, who can move too fast for the camera
to pick their movement, and have to slow themselves
down).

In episode 15: *Bogus Booty,* the background story
of money counterfeiting overseen by a gangland boss
is ultimately predictable and uninteresting – and it
plays out pretty much as you'd expect. So, our hapless

heroes discover a bag o' fake coins and spend 'em: Fuu buys food (of course!), and balloons up to the size of Nebraska (the TV series depicts the bloated Fuu often). Jin an' Mugen take their dough and head for the red light district (which's designed like Las Vegas, complete with the Stratosphere Tower). Here, women aren't allowed (much to Fuu's irritation), and most of the geishas look like something found in a live bait store (as Woody Allen might put it in one of his stand-up routines). But there is one babe among 'em – Yatsuha (Noriko Hidaka) – and Mugen is smitten.

Mugen and Yatsuha (who turns out to be a super-spy – and the Shogun's daughter), are involved in a lengthy whorehouse scene: Mugen is rapidly becoming the star attraction in *Samurai Champloo*, this rough-and-tumble, frizzy-haired *ronin*, the stand-in for the fantasies of the male members of the audience (he's super-cool, super-lazy and laidback, and a super-brilliant fighter). Played largely for laffs, the brothel sequence in episode 15: *Bogus Booty* is an extended, comic, seduction scene (Mugen wants it, she doesn't (sound familiar?!) – she repeatedly smashes him on the head, runs away from him, grapples with him, kicks him in the balls, and generally finds him impossible to shake off. Mugen, like Spike Spiegel, just keeps getting up).

◆

Written by the head writer of the *Cowboy Bebop* series, Keiko Nobumoto, the next episode in *Samurai Champloo*, 16: *Lullabies of the Lost (Verse 1)*, is another two-parter, with another big argument, another break-up (of the trio), and another near-death-by-drowning. 16: *Lullabies of the Lost* is an episode that looks as if it was the result of a bunch of writers spending a drunken night in Shinjuku and coming up with the most ludicrous plot twists they could think of (for instance, they have a silly legend of a monster or summat that's spooking the mountains, and the exposition is delivered in a very funny scene featuring three guys doing a rap, carrying wooden boxes like beatboxes on their shoulders).

Episode 16: *Lullabies of the Lost* (broadcast Sept 16, 2004) summarizes the threesome's goals, motives and characters: just what are these trio of misfits doing together? Looking for a samurai that smells of sunflowers? Eh? What's that all about?

Thus, the centrepiece of the episode is a lengthy argument up in the mountains, which results in each of 'em going their separate ways (Fuu is griping about a taking a shortcut that seems to be going nowhere). *Lullabies of the Lost* fragments into separate storylines, but focusses very much on the lovely, trusting Fuu: and, *finally*, we have *images* that go along with Fuu's quest for the samurai who smells of sunflowers. It's conceived as a flashback as Fuu is drowning (sound familiar? – it's Spike Spiegel in *Cowboy Bebop* all over again! And Mugen!), as she slips and falls off a cliff into a river, and we see a younger Fuu in a field of sunflowers, while a guy walks away from her, oblivious to her cries. What this is all about, we don't know yet – all we know is that these are images of separation and loss.

Fuu is subsequently saved by a guy, Okuru (played by the incredible Akio Otsuka – Batou in *Ghost In the Shell*), and helped back to life on the riverbank at night beside a fire (again, echoes of *Cowboy Bebop*, with the scene where Spike Spiegel's revived by the Native American shaman Bull – but it's also a staple of the action-adventure genre). That Okuru appears to be part of an older Japanese culture, such as the Ainu (he might've stepped out of *Princess Mononoke*), is intriguing (and he seems indestructible, another ghost on the mountains from the folktales – he is engulfed in flames in the episode's finale, and leaps off a cliff into a river, but Mugen muses that they'll probably be seeing him again).

Meanwhile, Mugen seems glad to be rid of silent, withdrawn Jin and talkative, whingeing, impossible Fuu (yet of course he also misses them – and, darn, he forgets to kill Jin, as he's sworn to do). And Jin, torn between going back to look after Fuu and striking out on his own, runs into an old student of his *dojo* (which precipitates yet another sword fight – gotta have a duel in every episode of *Samurai Champloo,* right? And the motive for the fight? The sub-plot of Jin killing the *sensei* of the *dojo*). At the end of the fight, Jin turns and leaps into the river, which's ridiculous (well, he does hear Fuu's scream, so presumably he's going to rescue her, but it's still dumb).

As a Fuu-led episode, *Lullabies of the Lost (Verse 1)* is highly entertaining – *Samurai Champloo* really comes to life whenever it places Fuu at the centre of things (and Mugen, of course!). Because the film-makers're putting an unarmed, young woman in the midst of the samurai genre, and when it's someone with a personality like Fuu's, it's great fun. Because Fuu is feisty but gentle, determined but lazy and hungry, eccentric and ditzy but lovable (accompanied by her little critter, Momo). With Fuu, you're not getting a wild card, samurai warrior like Mugen, the archetypal selfish criminal, or the super-restrained, silent and brooding *ronin* Jin, whose episode-long broods suggest great depths of Zen Buddhist meditation on the Meaning of Life. Instead, with Fuu you're getting a character completely attuned to the present day (of 2004-2005, when the show was made), without any historical baggage (altho' Mugen, of course, could walk down Gotham's Seventh Avenue or Venice Beach (!) in his funky, black shorts and red shirt and frizzy hair and nobody would bat an eyelid).

◆

In the following episode (17: *Lullabies of the Lost (Verse 2)*), the events in the forested mountain are resolved, with extended fight sequences and action which brings our three heroes back together again. The writers (Ryota Sugi, Keiko Nobumoto, Shinji Obara *et al*) have to work hard to draw the characters and the plots together, and the viewer has to suspend quite a bitta disbelief, as everybody just happens to be in the right place at the right time (to overhear this, or witness that). But it works, largely due to the sheer force of the animation, the staging, and the brave decision to set so many of the scenes in these episodes at nighttime in forests and mountains.

So, it turns out that the warrior from the North, Okuru, lost his wife and child to a wasting disease which also took his whole village.[21] To prevent the disease spreading, the authorities simply torched the whole place (a reference to the My Lai massacre in the Vietnam War, perhaps, tho' some *manga* have depicted similarly apocalyptic incidents).

The showdown in *Lullabies of the Lost (Verse 2)* occurs between Okuru and the authorities, deter-

---

21 This may be an allusion to the plague scene in *Ninja Scroll*.

mined to hunt down Okuru because he's a witness to their atrocity. Our intrepid heroes, after being uneasily re-united, get involved (Mugen, furious with being mistaken for Okuru, lays into the officials, then tracks down Okuru, changing his mind after hearing his side o' the story about the village). [22]

Meanwhile, Jin re-unites with Fuu (with a subtly played awkwardness which masks their feelings for each other). Romantic jealousy, for example, is kept bubbling underneath the Jin-Fuu scenes in a very under-stated manner. Unfortunately, Jin's rival from the *dojo*, Unkimaru, turns up, providing the expected duel (which's intercut with the showdown between Mugen and the officials). Of course, Jin is victorious.

By the end of the *Lullabies of the Lost (Verse 2)* episode, our trinity are back together again (tho' standing and facing pointedly in different direct-ions). The guys instantly forget why they quarrelled, and walk off looking for food. Fuu shrugs and smiles and follows them off into the sunset (into multiple images of a staggeringly gorgeous sunset – *animé* producers seem especially fond of late afternoon and early evening light, when the sun's low, casting very long shadows, and the colours glow).

◆

Episode 18: *War of the Words* is a very amusing exploration of graffiti and tagging, and associated cultural forms, such as hip-hop and rap music and break-dancing. How can you transplant the very contemporary form of graffiti and street/ urban

---

22 Okuru plays a *biwa*, up in a tree, (which also sounds over the flashbacks). Mugen makes one of the key statements of *Samurai Champloo*: that he is familiar with the music from the North of Japan, even tho' he coms from the Southern islands. Music is one of the primary passions of director Shinichiro Watanabe: the statement that music is a universal language is absolutely fundamental.

fashion to Edo period Japan? The filmmakers at Fuji TV and Manglobe come up with a simple solution: be as bold and silly as possible! So we have a bunch of grungey, ex-samurai dudes (led by bickering brothers Kazunosuke (Akio Suyama) and Tatsunoshin (Hiro Yuuki) who go around armed with paintbrushes (no spray cans yet!) tagging walls, ceilings, bridges, roofs, anywhere. Blue and black, red and black, the familiar spiky lettering, and the abstract shapes of graffiti that you see in big cities all over the contempo world.

The true stars of 18: *War of the Words* are the animators and the animation directors (Sayo Yamamoto was storyboard artist and episode director, Masaki Yamada was animation director). Seldom have so many extraordinary pieces of out-size, insane acting styles in animation been crammed into a single show. The animators have been encouraged to indulge themselves in their wildest fantasies as far as movement, behaviour, characterization, gesture and timing are concerned. There is a dynamism and kinetic power in the animation of the characters in *War of the Words* that really does give many of the great works from the history of animation a run for their money.

This episode, *War of the Words*, has clearly benefitted from the filmmakers and writers sitting around for hours in Tokyo coming up with ideas on how to combine contemporary urban forms like graffiti and tagging and fashion (and piercing/ tattoos/ jewellery) with :(1) the samurai genre, with (2) the Edo historical period, with (3) comedy, with (4) our characters (Mugen, Jin and Fuu), and with (5) our story. Not easy. But why make things easy for yourself?! – when you've already done everything in *animé* anyway (as many in the production team of *Samurai Champloo* have done).

As with many other *Samurai Champloo* episodes, part of the pleasure of *War of the Words* derives from how wittily and imaginatively the filmmakers have come up with placing contemporary motifs into a historical context. For instance, there's a camp Andy Warhol-a-like art guru/ fashion designer (with a platinum blond, Warhol wig and fey mannerisms), another bunch of (former) samurai who act like break-beat-lovin' street punks, and the litters which're carrying officials have flashing lamps on 'em to stand in for cop cars.

Meanwhile, as Jin gets all uppity that a cele-brated martial arts *dojo* (school) has become a run-down shell (with no respect for the founder/ father, and his former teacher!), and Fuu looks on in bemuse-ment as the boys act… like boys, Mugen embarks on a bizarre bid to catch up on his education – by learning to read (at the start o' the episode, our heroes're in yet another restaurant – food is a *big* deal in *Samurai Champloo*! – but Mugen admits he only knows one letter. So he always orders what Jin has).

But, this being a postmodern, comic and rebellious spin on the samurai/ *jidai geki* genre, it can't be Mugen going back to school, no, it has to be Mugen and his teacher Bundai (Norio Wakamoto) engaged in an epic struggle of macho histrionics (yelling, bragging, scuffling). Bundai is one o' the craziest characters in a series stuffed with crazies, a teacher with a truly scarily passionate committment to education! And the writers (Dai Soto, Shinji Obara and the team) twist the plot of *War of the Words* into a corkscrew of unbelievability by bringing the two plot strands together in an outrageous manner in the finale: the ex-samurai brothers're having a graffito duel on Hiroshima Castle, no less, to see who can tag in the most dangerous setting (as judged by Fuu and Jin), only to have Mugen besting them by racing to the top of the castle, in a seriously manic action finale.[23] It's played for extreme, knockabout comedy, as the authorities close in on all sides, rushing to overwhelm the brothers as they daub the castle walls and roofs, higher and higher.

The quality of the screenwriting in *Samurai Champloo* in some of the episodes is very high: you can see just how much work the team have put into episode 18: *War of the Words*. For instance, even after that remarkable action finale, with Mugen posing against the full moon with his paintbrush and giant, white symbol for infinity, the writers have developed the concept of writing and grattifi even further (now Mugen is painting his infinity signature everywhere, including on the clothes of Fuu and Jin, much to their irritation).

The best episodes of *Samurai Champloo* pack the scenarios with so much detail and asides, giving the shows the narrative density of *Cowboy Bebop*. Too much, really – the writers go far beyond what is required to deliver an enjoyable half-hour piece of television.

The *Samurai Champloo* series rarely puts a foot wrong, even when it's being *waaay* over-the-top and insane (apart from lapses in violence). But in episode 19: *Unholy Union,* it slips up big time, with a story

---

23 Mugen's tag is the symbol for infinity.

involving 'hidden Christians', a cult that meets secretly in a cave which's being used by criminals as a front for a gun manufacturing and gun running business (overseen by zealous Catholic priest Father Xavier (Juurouta Kosugi), who turns out to be the chief bad guy).

Why do animation companies in Japan never get Christianity right? They use its symbols all the time – crosses, statues, Cathedrals, angels (how they love angels!) – but not one cartoon creator understands the theology, issues or spiritual aspects of Western religion. The Christian religion is clearly utterly foreign to Japanese filmmakers. All *animés* use Christianity cosmetically, exotically: *Fullmetal Alchemist, Macross Plus, Ghost In the Shell, Cowboy Bebop, Hellsing, Vampire Knight, Escaflowne*, etc.

And *Samurai Champloo* is no different – so we have Christianity portrayed as a twisted, furtive cult which has little relation to historical Christianity, or any reality (and there're still only a tiny number of followers of Christianity in Japan).[24]

It doesn't work.

This episode is also cack-handed when it comes to delivering an action-adventure yarn in the manner of a run-of-the-mill, menace-of-the-week episode in an adventure serial, or a bad episode of *The Young Indiana Jones Chronicles*. None of it convinces. And you also get *sick* of seeing the bad guy Xavier smash Yuri (Megumi Toyoguchi, his bride-to-be) in the face repeatedly, hurling her to the ground, and pointing a gun in her face. Xavier is a ridiculously nasty villain

24 Yes, there is a message about blindly following religion here – which Mugen makes in the opening sequence, when he says he doesn't like anyone telling him what to do. But, come on, this is a useless attempt at delivering that very familiar statement.

– not only is he a cackling madman, with a preposterous disguise (so he can look Spanish), we're also supposed to believe that he's capable of leading a large, religious group. It takes forever for Xavier to receive his comeuppance (with a gun blowing up) – but not after he's aimed or shot that gun at just about everybody.

◆

But the following episode – 20: *Elegy of Entrapment (Verse 1)* – redeems (or simply wipes out) the previous episode, with a return to form for the *Samurai Champloo* series. Now we're back in the historical aspects of the samurai genre, with another emphasis on music. Here, it's the haunting *shamisen*[25] player and singer Sara (Sakiko Tamagawa). She's blind, enigmatic and – whaddya know! – attractive (thus, Mugen is smitten).

Elegy of Entrapment (Verse 1) – another two-parter – delivers an appealing mix of comedy, romance, drama and action. But the most striking element in the narrative recipe for this episode of *Samurai Champloo* is the music, with Sara singing two songs, and captivating her audience in the taverns along the way – and also the animators, because they rise to the challenge and come up with one of several mesmerizing musical montages in *Samurai Champloo*. As in *Cowboy Bebop* (and shows such as *Escaflowne*, *Macross Plus* or *Moribito*), when *animé* producers allow their filmmaking teams to ditch dialogue and go with wall-to-wall music, and to use a montage form of editing, the results can be marvellous. In *Elegy of Entrapment (Verse 1)*, it's a kind of music

---

25 *Biwas* and *shamisen* are staples of the historical genre; *Samurai Champloo* also employs 'em – inevitably – as electric guitars played with plectrums.

promo, and also a travelogue, with the filmmakers cutting back to Sara singing on stage, in different places along the route (with Jin and Mugen comically acting as her security team, throwing out hecklers).

The narrative of *Elegy of Entrapment (Verse 1)* moves along winningly, but we're not quite sure where all of this is going. We see the three misfits teaming up with Sara the blind woman, and acting as her road crew, in a way, for a tour of restaurants and inns in Edo period Japan (food of course plays a big part in this adventure). There is a marvellous festival sequence that's tossed in so casually – yet in many another TV series, this would be a celebrated piece of filmmaking.

Along the way, we learn that Sara has a child, that the boy's father is dead, that she is swamped by a cosmic melancholy which is more'n just the sadness and frustration of being blind. Mugen is very taken with Sara, and there are several scenes of Mugen's rough style of courtship (which irritates Fuu no end – Fuu is the only person who can whack Mugen on the head and get away with it).

Fuu speaks more of the samurai who smells like sunflowers (now she's not hiding that he is her father, and that she's gonna punch him when she meets him). And Jin? Well, if you view the *Elegy of Entrapment (Verse 1)* episode again, you'll notice that Jin barely says anything to Sara (other than to ask her about the charm she has hanging from her *shamisen*, which's linked to her son. This's a clue – because Sara's being blackmailed with her son's life).

So who is this enigmatic woman Sara? The final minutes of the episode reveals all, when it suddenly ramps up into a major action sequence, on a rope bridge across a canyon at night. Sara turns out to be an assassin[26] – hence providing our cliffhanger: has Jin met his match?!

The *Elegy of Entrapment* episodes are beautifully put together, in every department. Forget about the story, themes and characters for a moment, and just relish the quality of the filmmaking in this stellar *animé* series. If this was a 'serious' drama – a poetic meditation on Hiroshima, say, or an adaption of an Edo period classic story – *Samurai Champloo* would be applauded as an exquisite artefact, an animation gem, and showered with awards. Because it's comedy (or much of it is comedy), and because it's playful and postmodern and parodic, nope, sorry, it doesn't get the kudos, the affirmation, the critical jamborees of a serious, solemn drama.

But this happens to comedies and parodies everywhere: even tho' the demands of comedy are often even higher than that of drama – for the producers, directors, actors and, above all, the *writers* – comedies're usually placed well below dramas critically.

That doesn't matter with *Samurai Champloo,* tho', because *we know* it's good.

It's also entertaining in these later episodes of *Sam Champ* that Fuu is beginning to assert herself more and more, taking to calling Jin and Mugen 'her bodyguards', and castigating them like a mother when they're late or mess around. And Fuu's fondness for Jin – eternally unspoken and undemonstrated, of course – is also fuel for comedy (such as when Fuu asks Jin to accompany her earlier, inaugur-

26 The scenario recalls the Chinese, martial arts epic *House of Flying Daggers.*

ating the first time the unlikely trio's been split up by design, hoping that he'd say no, so Mugen would have to do the job. Note that it's Fuu who suggests breaking up the trio, just as it was Fuu who brought them together in the first place. And it's Fuu who goes on ahead to the island to meet the samurai who smells of sunflowers in the final episodes).

Of course, we know that Jin must feel a little something for Fuu in return (tho' he never lets on anything in his manner or speech). Because he always manages to be nearby to rescue her (which, being the young woman (i.e., the princess) in this misfit trio, is required from time to time).

The cliffhanger at the end of the first *Elegy of Entrapment* episode (the 20th) is a duel between Sara and Jin on a rope bridge: any action series has to come up with formidable villains for our heroes to go up against. Indeed, one of the challenging things for any action show is inventing villains who can be introduced, seen in action, and trounced by the heroes at the end. And in show after show (even more difficult when your two heroes are incredible warriors!).

In *Samurai Champloo,* the producers and screenwriters decided to go for the impossible: a villain who can beat both Jin and Mugen (and we've seen, so far in the series, that *no one* can, ultimately, best our heroes). Well, Sara can. Not only that, she is a woman, and she is blind! Arrrgh!

Being a woman means that neither Mugen or Jin will be allowed to kill her. No, of course not (not by the rules of the *chambara* genre, even when *Samurai Champloo* has been so transgressive of them at times). In the end, Sara, who is being used by somebody to murder Mugen, Jin and Fuu, opts to allow Mugen an opening in the final, frantic duel, and in doing so dies. A kind of suicide, then. (Because Mugen, altho' he uses Jin's advice of moving with the flow of the universe, which the fisherman taught him, still isn't able to defeat Sara. At the end of their fight, she has a moment when she can stab him, but holds back).

So, in the rope bridge duel (at night – it's a pure samurai genre cliché), in *Elegy of Entrapment (Verse 2)*, Jin slashes the bridge rather than face any more of Sara's impossibly quick parries and thrusts (she uses a sort of short spear, not a sword). And Mugen repeatedly attempts to take on Sara, with disastrous results (in the first duel, he is soundly beaten, despite deploying all of his tricks. It's as if Sara can sense his moves just before he performs them).

So our Fuu is nursing both badly-beaten-up guys (Jin is lost in the river and waterfalls for a while, only to be rescued from near-death by yet another enigmatic warrior/ teacher/ nature man/ philosopher). In that sequence, *Samurai Champloo* turns in its own riff on the old chestnut of the crusty, old philosopher living in the wilds who rescues a youngster who becomes a kind of pupil for a time. Gurus and students, wizards and novices – it's a staple of many forms of fiction. Here, *Samurai Champloo* portrays the fisherman as a gnarled, somewhat kooky nature-man who stands in the river catching fish with his bare hands while talking about sensing the flow of the water. Jin is impressed (tho' he finds the fisherman's prankish methods a little odd. The fisherman places a bowl of food some distance from Jin's bed, for instance, so that Jin has to crawl to reach it – only to find it's empty).

Meanwhile, the mystery of just who has hired a highly skilled assassin to kill our three heroes (and why?) is left unsolved in *Elegy of Entrapment*. The only hints are the vaguely menacing masked man who appears at festivals with spinning, toy windmills, and speaks to Sara in a threatening tone.

One thing strikes the viewer about the two *Elegy of Entrapment* episodes involving Sara (and the pirate ship of gold and the pirate) is that they are played *far more* seriously than other episodes. Mugen, Jin and Fuu struggle thru the episodes with a dogged, frustrated determination. They are swamped by obstacles and misery – much the fun of the trio evaporates in these episodes.

Episode 22: *Cosmic Collisions* has our heroic trinity stumbling upon another strange community, this time a bunch of zombies embarked upon digging for treasure in a hole in the ground, presided over by a misguided and enigmatic figure, Shige (Kouji Totani). As written by Dai Sato, *Cosmic Collisions* is disappointing, because the dramatic elements don't quite gel, and the episode repeats situations and issues we've already seen at least twice before in the 26-episode series (the episode, which comes across like a Hallowe'en episode of *The Simpsons*, is also a little thin, dramatically, with the feeling that the concept of zombies has been stretched out too long).

The fruitlessness and pointlessness of the mining enterprise is vividly depicted in *Cosmic Collisions*. Here, workers are slaving away at hard, physical labour for no pay, living in scuzzy accommodation and being fed terrible food (jeez, it sounds like working in an animation house in Tokyo! Or in any capitalist state across the globe!). The episode also features some cosmic ruminations about meteors[27] and the like (there are many scenes set in outer space, involving a meteorite heading for Earth. A solemn voiceover (by Masaaki Yajima) solemnizes about the origins of life. And s-l-o-w, moody, sci-fi drones bubble underneath. There's even an explosion as the meteor lands looking like an atomic bomb).[28]

The comedy of arms being chopped off and stuck back on, of guys coming back to life, of Shige's determination to excavate the buried treasure – the filmmakers try to elicit comedy from the situation, but *Cosmic Collisions* isn't very funny. There's a half-heartedness about it, an unfinished quality (and the script is patchy, to say the least: the all-important encounter between Shige and our heroes, early on in the piece, goes on and on, as Shige talks and talks. Even the characters yawn with the boredom of it all).

...A horror-cliché scene in a cemetery where corpses're climbing out of graves to scare the Buddha out of poor Fuu (like a Michael Jackson pop promo)... a guy playing his *biwa* like Jimi Hendrix but looking more like Brian Jones[29] out of the Rolling Stones... The permanently washed-out, white sky... The grey-on-grey colouration...

It doesn't really work. And it isn't much fun, either – nobody's having a good time in *Cosmic Collisions*, including the most important people of all

27 The meteorites plus the mining operation is reminiscent of *Hard Luck Woman* in *Cowboy Bebop*, where Ed's father and Macintrye're mapping falling meteorites, for no apparent purpose.
28 This is another link with *Cowboy Bebop* – mushrooms are one of the motifs in *Cosmic Collisions* (the team pigs out on mushrooms). And at the end, the meteor impact cloud looks like the mushroom cloud from Hiroshima. We note that our heroes' destination is Nagasaki.
29 Notice the dead, grey eyes like a shark's, and the flat, grey colour of his hair.

– us.

❖

So, *thank fuck* for the next episode, 23: *Baseball Blues*, a ditzy, goofy, *Mad* magazine send-up of Japan versus North America, of Japanese culture and society vs. North American culture and society, framed within a baseball game. For sports fans, for dumb popular culture fans, and for Warners Bros. cartoon fans, there is plenty to enjoy in *Baseball Blues*. But nobody can miss the fact that the North American sailors are ruthlessly parodied, as a bunch of over-weight, aggressive, paranoid, nationalistic dick-heads[30] (the Yanks have come to Japan to trade, of course: shelling the town with cannons, the foreigners tell the Japanese that they have no choice in the matter).

Well, *duh,* the political satire in *Baseball Blues* is at the level of *National Lampoon*, a *Bugs Bunny* cartoon, and a humorous *manga* in which Yankees are mercilessly attacked as boorish, arrogant, stupid, insensitive, loud, foul-mouthed pricks. (At the end of the show, the Yanks, with their asses soundly kicked, depart on their ship – and good riddance).

The style of *Baseball Blues* also enlivens proceed-ings – we're back with the full-colour, cartoon approach of classic *animé,* without the visual fussi-ness and self-consciousness (well, not too much) which scuppers the weaker episodes in *Samurai Champloo*.

Baseball is a big deal in Japan (there are *manga* devoted to it), and *Samurai Champloo* exploits the game for every possible comic moment, and every gag they can think of relating to baseball. Particularly

---

30 There are allusions to real people – Alexander Joy Cartwright and Anber Doubleday, the 'inventors' of baseball.

enjoyable in episode 23: *Baseball Blues* are the scenes towards the end when Jin tries out using samurai sword techniques with a baseball bat, when the hapless Fuu misses every ball pitched at her, and when Mugen saves the day by taking on all of the Yankee team single-handed. Yep, it's down to Mugen to save the face of the Nipponese nation by attacking the Yanks with deadly pitches.

Meanwhile, two new charas're introduced in *Baseball Blues*: Inspector Manzou, the middle-aged narrator (from the third episode), and the baseball freak Kagemura (Toshio Furukawa), who trains our heroes in a single day to become baseball champs. Or not.

The final three episodes of *Samurai Champloo* run together in a continuous story – *Evanescent Encounter* (a.k.a. *Circle of Transmigration*), with cliffhangers closing each episode. The episodes are exceptionally brutal, with the fights ramped up to blood-spraying, bone-cracking vehemence, as well as lightning speed. It's very nasty stuff, with characters being maimed or killed all over the place, like the finale of a Shake-spearean tragedy. And once again poor Fuu is smashed in the face again and again by one of the villains, to the point where it becomes simply *repulsive*. And she's bound to a cross! Again with the crucifixion in *Samurai Champloo* – and it's a *woman* crucified! Do you really want to see a 15 year-old girl being beaten again and again and again? I don't! I reckon parts of *Samurai Champloo* (as with *Afro Samurai*) are far more disturbing and offensive than anything in, say, the *Legend of the Overfiend* series.

Because in these last episodes of *Samurai Champ-*

loo our three heroes're pitted against two sets of rivals – a trio of truly vicious, psychotic brothers (one in a wheelchair, one a dwarf-like, salivating mutant, and one a skinny Nazi), plus Kagetoki Kariya, a legendary assassin sent from the Shogunate who's yet another of those unbeatable samurai warriors (the decline and fall of the era of the samurai was inevitably explored in the final episodes of *Samurai Champloo*. Yep, Mugen and Jin were soon going to be a thing of the past).

So as our heroes reach their destination near Nagasaki (and the island Ikitsuki), it turns out that they are wanted men – Mugen for his shady past, and Jin for killing his *dojo's sensei,* Mariya Enshirou. And the 'samurai who smells like sunflowers', Fuu's father, Kasumi Seizo, turns out to be a guy the Shogunate want to dispatch. Thus, the over-arching story of *Samurai Champloo* reflects back over the series (the authorities have been letting Fuu wander, because she will lead them to Seizo).

It takes some talk at the top of *Evanescent Encounter (Part 1)* to set this up. Luckily, the longest and talkiest scene features our three heroes sitting round a campfire (beside yet another river). Fuu asks them to disclose some secret about themselves. This handily means the filmmakers can recycle some footage from throughout the series, to illustrate each character's pasts. Fuu, for example, tells us a little bit more about her father, Kasumi Seizo (tho' Fuu doesn't know why the Shogunate're hunting for Seizo, nor what he really did for a living).

Thus, Fuu's quest resembles that of Faye Valentine in *Cowboy Bebop* – to journey back to her childhood, where she finds her home, as with Faye, a ruin.

Fuu is on another identity quest, then, even tho' she gradually realizes, as Faye does, that ultimately it isn't going to help her much, or even dissolve the ghosts that pursue her. The past might've made you what you are, and you can honour it, but to dwell it for too long is a dead-end, and potentially fatal, as both the *Samurai Champloo* and *Cowboy Bebop* series insist.

We see some of Fuu's childhood, including her mother dying. Fuu wants to confront her father for fleeing (and to punch him, if possible). Fuu's story around the open fire explains most of what really shoulda been set out in the opening episode (but then, Jin an' Mugen remained curiously *un*curious for a *long* time, as if they simply weren't bothered with why Fuu was searching for the samurai who smells like sunflowers).

Fuu's journey is the most compelling (altho' the back-stories of Jin and Mugen would be plenty for a TV series of their own). So we follow Fuu to the island, knowing that there are insane assassins on her – and the guys' – tails. The cliffhanger in *Evanescent Encounter (Part 1)* occurs when the cool, cold Shogunate's assassin, Kagetoki Kariya, catches up with Jin and Mugen at the harbour, and the three crazy brothers snare poor Fuu on Ikitsuki Island in a field of – what else? – sunflowers.

The filmmakers push the sense of jeopardy to the limit in the *Evanescent Encounter* episodes, placing our heroes on top of cliffs, or submerged under water,[31] or duelling unassailable assailants. The brothers're tortured ghosts from Mugen's shady past in the crime syndicate – so they (inevitably) fight with Mugen (it turns out that the brothers were working on the ships that Mugen and Mukuro attacked – seen in episodes 13: *Dark Night's Road* and 14: *Misguided Miscreants*. One brother becomes a vegetable invalid, another's turned into a psycho goblin, and the tall, skinny one is a thoroughly despicable S.O.B. obsessed with revenge).

Meanwhile, the famed assassin Kagetoki Kariya goes up against Jin, with his Muju-style samurai technique (unravelling the Muju *dojo* plot, where Jin became an outcast after accidentally killing his master. In a stunning series of flashbacks, we see that it was Kariya, acting for the Shogunate, who put up Jin's *sensei* to kill his student (Mariya Enshirou was planning to leave the *dojo* to his star pupil). Unfortunately, Enshirou opted to nobble Jin at night, and as Jin defended himself at lightning speed, not knowing who was attacking him, he killed Enshirou. As soon as Jin realized who it was, he was full of remorse). Mugen is the first to hurl himself at Kariya, however, and is soundly beaten. And Kariya is accomplished enough to take on our two heroes simultaneously.

And once again Christianity in *animé* is trundled in as another exotic and corrupt religion from overseas – part of the finale of *Evanescent Encounter* takes place in yet another ruined church (with poor Fuu tied to a wooden cross). Christianity is implicated in the

---

31 Water is a big deal in *Samurai Champloo* – the filmmakers exploit a myriad of ways where they can throw their heroes into rivers and seas to experience flashbacks or fights. Each of the major characters has significant underwater experiences, leading to flashbacks into their pasts. There's even a samurai duel underwater in the final episodes.

burning down of Fuu's childhood home.

The plot strands play out, and Fuu gets to meet her estranged father, on a distant island,[32] while Mugen and Jin deal with their pasts (both Jin and Mugen are beaten and shot and hacked to bits, and by rights should be dead, but being the heroes, a'course they survive).

From the filmmaking angle, the final episodes of *Samurai Champloo* are stupendous, with the production team throwing in everything they've got. The fights are *really* spectacular, with an outstanding use of simulated handheld camera, slow motion, subjective viewpoints, luminous glows added to flashing blades, editing at 500 m.p.h., and a range of animation styles, including a lovely sequence of pencil-shaded drawings to depict Mugen's experience of being at death's door (it's great when *animé* reverts back to its origins in pencil and pen sketches).

When Mugen turns up at the church, to save Fuu, it's a wonderful heroic moment – when Mugen becomes a real, true, 100% hero. And what do the filmmakers do? Only have Mugen looking like Bruce Lee! (achieved by his usually wild hair being flattened because it's wet). As *Cowboy Bebop* showed, director Shinichiro Watanabe and the boys are huge fans of the Little Dragon of Chinese action cinema).

Some of the action sequences in the *Evanescent Encounter* episodes draw on previous outings (so the episodes act as a summary of the whole *Samurai Champloo* series). For instance, the control of *chi* by a fearsome opponent (from episode 10: *Lethal Lunacy*),

---

32 It isn't what she expected (her father's nearly dying, for a start), but there are moments of forgiveness and redemption which, after the length of the series, provides a little bitta emotional catharsis (tho' not really enough. But then, *Samurai Champloo* was never a hugely *emotional animé* series).

and a superb sword fight underwater. (Just when you thought the team at Fuji TV and Manglobe had explored every possible way of mounting a samurai fight in animation, they come up with new approaches, a new way to use props, a new way of combining camera angles and rapid cuts. The action in *Samurai Champloo* has very few peers).

♪

In the final episode of *Samurai Champloo, Evanescent Encounter (Part 3)*, Fuu finally meets up with her estranged father, Kasumi Seizo. It's an awkward, tearful reunion, but there is some kinda reconciliation between the father and daughter (for instance, altho' pa left home, he did that partly because his dangerous job would've brought the Shogunate's heavies calling at some point, and he wanted to keep them away from his family).

However, *Samurai Champloo* combines the father-daughter reunion (the primary plot involving Fuu), with both the Jin plots and the Mugen plots. Thus, the Shogunate's assassin Kagetoki Kariya turns up at the lonely shack at the end of the island, to kill the sun-flower samurai, Kasumi Seizo. Fuu and the old coot who's looking after the dying father are no match for him, and Seizo is duly slain (following some last words directed at Fuu).

Then Kagetoki Kariya rounds on poor Fuu, pursuing her to yet another dead-end on a clifftop. OMG, who is going to rescue Fuu from certain death? Well, a'course, it can only be two people – Mugen or Jin. As Mugen has already rescued Fuu once in this finale of *Samurai Champloo* (in the church), it has to be Jin. And it is: last seen toppling in slo-mo into the water at the harbour at the end of his duel with

Kariya, Jin strides into the scene. His hair (now loose) blowing in the breeze, his face set in a 'I mean business' expression, his clothes bedraggled, Jin flashes back to summat his *sensei* told him: a move to try only when extremely desperate is to open yourself to a blow, and in that moment, attack your opponent. Well, it's an old chestnut that's been employed many times in a martial arts or samurai duel, and it works here, too.

Using impressionistic shots now (and mostly medium close-ups), the Fuji TV/ Manglobe team portray Jin's final fight as a rapid flurry of move- ment, ending up in the usual frozen pose. The question hangs – again, as usual – who has been struck? Jin or Kagetoki Kariya? Of course it's Kariya – and good riddance!

Thus closes the Jin-*dojo* plotline, and also the Fuu- father plotline. Which leaves Mugen and Umanosuke in the church. This action sequence is intercut with the Fuu and Jin scenes – so there are two fights going on at the same time. Umanosuke wields an axe on a chain with a fearsome power, slicing up logs and pillars (so the church's demolished), and later rocks on the beach.[33] The Mugen versus Umanosuke fight, however, is allowed to run on and on, testing even action fans' endurance! The flaw is that there is no possible way in hell that Umanosuke can be victor- ious – for all the usual reasons – so there is no suspense whatsoever. Also, we have seen Mugen dispatching whole teams of bodyguards and samurai-wielding henchmen, so to have him being beaten soundly and for such a *long* time by just *one* person stretches belief, and weakens the climactic

33 The sort of weaponry crops up in samurai *manga* such as *Blade of the Immortal.*

fight.

The action sequence in *Evanescent Encounter (Part 3)* closes with an intricately staged (and near-impossible-to-achieve) decapitation, as Umanosuke has his own weapon used against him. Nearly impossible – but not for a movie hero like Mugen! (Even that isn't the End of the Fight for Mugen, because the last brother alive, the invalid, soft-in-the-head brother in the wheelchair, throws in his 5 cents, with some dynamite).

The final scene of the *Samurai Champloo* series has our three heroes, Jin, Mugen and Fuu, back on the road again: it's a sunny, blue sky day (countering the nastiness and violence of these three rather sombre episodes), and the characters are at another cross-roads. With a humorous flourish, they go their separate ways (the end credits continue their journeys thru marvellously rendered landscapes of Edo period Japan).

♫

If the way that some of the issues and the themes of *Samurai Champloo* – as well as the drama – are less than satisfactorily played out,[34] the quality of the filmmaking (and the music) more than makes up any deficiencies. The production team at Fuji TV and Manglobe are veterans displaying total confidence when it comes to staging action and delivering high quality animation.

Parts of *Samurai Champloo* have been uneven, some sections have been badly conceived, and some have been disgustingly violent. But the *Samurai Champloo* series wins you over with its child-like enthusiasm, the verve of its filmmaking, the charm of

---

34 The potential for romance between Fuu and Jin wasn't resolved, either. *Samurai Champloo* closes with each hero going their own way.

its three leading characters, its wicked sense of humour, its witty and very intelligent use pop culture, Japanese history, and of course music. And not forgetting some outstanding filmmaking.

SAMURAI *MANGA*

Manga were published which retold the stories in the *animé* of *Samurai Champloo*. Masaru Gotsuto produced the *manga*; it was published in *Monthly Shonen Ace* (from Kadokawa Shoten), in 2004. Tho' it was nice to see some of the artwork from the *animé* in print form, it was, as with many novelizations of movies, rather pointless.[35] There was also a Play-Station video game.

For fans of the samurai action in *Samurai Champloo* and *animé* such as *Ninja Scroll* and *Samurai X*, I'd recommend checking out some of the classic samurai *manga*. Two of the finest are *Blade of the Immortal*, by Hiroaki Samura (1994-), and *Lone Wolf and Cub* (written by Kazuo Koike, 1970-76). The stories are amazing, the action is stupendous, and the artwork is beautiful in *Blade of the Immortal* and *Lone Wolf and Cub*.

No doubt the filmmakers of *Samurai Champloo* know these famous *manga*: the female samurai assassin who's also a musician with a murky past in *Samurai Champloo* has affinities with the third *tankobon* of *Blade of the Immortal*. In that volume, the immortal samurai Manji goes up against a formid-able female assassin, who bests him (cutting off his

---

35 Woody Allen famously loathes novelizations of movies.

limbs – luckily, there are magical worms which keep him alive).

Written by Kazuo Koike (b. 1936), *Lone Wolf and Cub* (*Kozure Okami*), with art by Goeski Kojima (1928-2000), was originally published in *Weekly Manga Action* (Futabasha) between 1970 and 1976 (*Lone Wolf* was one of the first *manga* to be published in the U.S.A. in English – in 1987, by First Comics). It runs to 8,000 or more pages, over 28 volumes. Most of the stories are self-contained. The concept of a samurai tale with a hero who has a infant child in tow is stupendous. Lone Wolf is the familiar *ronin* of the *chambara* genre – taciturn, brooding, and a fearsome warrior (he hires himself out as an assassin to the highest bidder). And he has a three year-old kid with him! Riding in a wooden stroller!

Set in the Tokugawa era, the storytelling in *Lone Wolf and Cub* by Kazuo Koike is masterful and con-fident, delivering fascinating scenarios with each installment. The mix of dramatic elements is comp-elling, and the artwork by Goeski Kojima is superb. Meanwhile, the child Daigoro adds an ingredient of humanity and tenderness that raises this already very fine *manga* to another level.

From the outset, Hiroaki Samura's (b. 1970) *Blade of the Immortal* (*Mugen no Junin*), published by Kodansha in Japan in *Afternoon* magazine from 1994 onwards, impresses as an astonishing piece of art-work and storytelling (and Sakura was only 24 when it started! This guy is *good*!). It has rightly won awards (such as the Eisner Award, the Eagle Award, and a Japan Media Arts Festival Award). Often you stop and stare at a page or a panel of *Blade of the Immortal,* amazed by Samura's striking feeling for composition, for the way the panels interconnect, and for the way he uses a variety of drawing techniques and media (how, for example, he allows pencil marks to show, or uses more abstract patterns of water-colour and pastel). That *Blade of the Immortal* often shifts into abstraction and pattern is delightful: this is part of the 'floating world' of Japanese art, of course, but it soars far beyond the relentless and tiring emphasis on 'realism' and photorealism in Western comicbooks.

It's no wonder that *Blade of the Immortal* has won so many awards and accolades: it truly is a remark-able achievement – purely on the basis of the artwork alone. Yet there is terrific storytelling here too, as well as compelling characters. The central duo of Manji and Rin makes for a fascinating couple: Manji is the world-weary *ronin*, who's been there, seen it, done it, and killed many people to boot. He's the samurai warrior as middle-aged veteran, a man who's had many experiences, some of which have clearly been nasty and demeaning (Mugen and Jin in, *Samurai Champloo* both draw on the characterization of Manji).

Another *manga* about samurai is worth mention-ing: *Vagabond* (published in *Morning* magazine from 1998 onwards) by Takehiko Inoue (b. 1967) is an outstanding piece of storytelling with stellar art-work. Inoue is best-known for his basketball *manga*, *Slam Dunk* (1990-96), which has sold over 100 million copies in Japan.

While the issues and the situations are familiar and have been run thru the mangle many times before, the energy and verve of Takehiko Inoue's artwork raises *Vagabond* way above your average *chambara*.

And if there's a new way to slice up a human being, Inoue has a good try at discovering it (altho' the competition in the samurai genre for dismemberment is fierce!).

Finally (we could be here all day discussing samurai *manga*!), I must mention *Yongbi the Invincible*, written and drawn by Ki Moon Ryu and Junghoo Moon (b. 1967). *Yongbi* is one of the funniest, wittiest *mangas* around (well, being Korean, it's known as a *manhwa*). *Yongbi the Invincible* is a send-up of adventure tales, and samurai stories (*chambara*), and martial arts fictions, and fairy tales. *Yongbi* focusses on a young warrior, Yongbi, and his horse (Biryong) in the *jiangzhu*, that mythical past of China with its adventurers, kings, princes, palaces, priests, honour and magic.

Yongbi the Invincible is also like a cross between *Arabian Nights* and a pantomime and every action-adventure movie you've ever seen. Yongbi is a very appealing central character, a clever but also goofy youth, a bounty hunter and brilliant fighter who's also a world weary traveller, unimpressed by everything (except mounds of gold, good food, and women, of course). Yongbi is accompanied by an amazing sidekick, a wonder horse (their relationship is the familiar long-suffering one – when the story starts, you know that Yongbi and Biryong have already been on many adventures).

Yongbi the Invincible is laugh-out-loud funny, as Ki Moon Ryu and Junghoo Moon cleverly spoof all of the conventions of the adventure tale and *chambara*. Moon's ability to draw comical expressions is especially good (typically when something wild occurs, and a crowd looks on with mouths agape). The confidence of the storytelling (which does deliver a rollicking good tale as well as sending it up), and the skill of the artwork, are joys to behold.[36]

Ki Moon Ryu and Junghoo Moon know storytelling and adventures inside-out and backwards. The *tone* of *Yongbi* as well as the humour is spot-on. Moon presents an adventure story that works on the level of thrills and action, but the many other layers – of spoofing, of commentary, and of humour – make this *manhua* a very enjoyable mix.

That Yongbi is a brilliant warrior goes without saying, but it's his attitude of world-weariness, of casual, laid-back nonchalance, that makes his adventures so entertaining. He's able to run rings around any opposition, is always one step ahead of his foes, yet he is also bored by it all, as if, in the end, it doesn't matter that much to him (very like Mugen in *Samurai Champloo*).

The way that author Ki Moon Ryu orchestrates all of this in *Yongbi* is divine: this is masterful storytelling by a master storyteller (and a pretty fine artist, too! Moon can deliver an action scene in *manga* form like the best of 'em. He's got all the moves as an artist, just like Yongbi as a character! Moon can conjure the streaks of speed lines blurring around a figure, to indicate high velocity; he can play with scale and composition; and he can stage pounding action with the skill and wit of a veteran. Like Hiroaki Samura with *Blade of the Immortal* or Kazuo Koike and Goeski Kojima with *Lone Wolf and Cub*, Moon is an Akira Kurosawa of samurai *manga*).

---

36 Moon also inserts himself into some o' the drawings, drawing the reader's attention to certain details. The characters pick up the artist's tiny form, and flick him away.

MACROSS PLUS

Macross Plus was a forerunner of *Cowboy Bebop*, because some of the other contributors also went on to *Cowboy Bebop*: director Shinichiro Watanabe, actor Unshô Ishizuka, composer Yoko Kanno, and writer Keiko Nobumoto. And *Macross*'s director (Shoji Kawamori) co-wrote an episode (no. 18) of *Cowboy Bebop*.

Macross Plus (1994) comprises four OAVs (which were edited into a movie in 1995). *Macross Plus* was an update of the *Macross* series of 1982, produced by Big West and TBS, and released by Bandai Visual. It was co-directed by Shoji Kawamori and Shinichiro Watanabe. Among the companies contributing to the show were: Triangle Staff, Studio Fuga, Bandai, Big West, Hero Co., Artland, Mainichi Broadcasting System, Shogakukan-Shueisha and Studio Nue.

Macross Plus was written by the truly wonderful dramatist Keiko Nobumoto (look at these credits!: *Cowboy Bebop, Wolf's Rain, Samurai Champloo* and *Tokyo Godfathers*). Nobumoto is a key reason why *Macross Plus* is such a marvellous slice of *animé*.

Director Shoji Kawamori (b. 1960) is a veteran of numerous *animé* shows, including *Patlabor 2, Transformers, Dangaioh, Gundam 0083, Escaflowne, New Century GPX Cyber Formula 11*, and *Cowboy Bebop*. Kawamori is one of the key people behind the *Macross* franchise: he created *Macross Plus, Macross 7* and *Macross Zero* (which he also directed), directed *Flash Back 2012* and headed up the script for *Do You Remember Love?* Kawamori's speciality is *mecha* design (Takashi Oshiguchi calls him 'the innovator's innovator in the world of mecha design'),[37] which's everywhere in *Macross Plus.* It's no surprise that Kawamori worked on the *Transformers* show as a *mecha* designer, and he was working on *Macross* all thru his student days. For *Macross*, as for *Yukikaze* (2002), the filmmakers visited the Komatsu air force base for research. Director Kawamori also went to the U.S.A., and flew in acrobatic planes.[38]

The 1980s *Macross* series was a big success in Japan; it was titled *Super-dimensional Fortress Macross.* Around the world, it was re-edited and shown as *Robotech.* The franchise developed movies, and re-builds, including *Macross 7, Macross II,* and *Macross Dynamite 7.*

For Jonathan Clements & Helen McCarthy, *Macross* is 'one of the three unassailable pillars of anime sci-fi, pioneering the tripartite winning formula of songs, battling robot-planes (the show's famous "Valkyries"), and tense relationships, while *Macross Plus* 'is another excellent example of what anime sci-fi has to offer', with cinematography 'of a very high quality indeed' (2006, 386).

There's plenty of *Top Gun* (the 1986 Jerry Bruck-heimer-Don Simpson movie) in *Macross Plus,* as well as other aerial movies such as *The Right Stuff* and *Always* (*animé* delivered a few *Top Gun*-inspired shows). In *Macross Plus,* inevitably, the Valkyrie planes also double up as giant robots, and other *mecha*, transforming between them. If you've got a cool plane, you might as well have a cool mobile suit too, right? Yeah! And it's gotta have tons of cool weaponry, right? Oh yes! Especially for the tie-in toys

37 In T. Ledoux, 1997, 111.
38 Fisherman's Wharf in Frisco and Tehachapi Pass's windmills were also visited.

and merchandizing.

Dog fights, prototype aircraft, training exercises that go wrong, *Macross Plus* can't wait to get up in the air with its duo of hotshot pilots. The action and aerial battles are fierce and impressive and very enjoyable. On the ground, *Macross Plus* explores the familiar soap opera melodrama of an erotic triangle between the cocky, maverick, young pilot Isamu Dyson, the older, sombre friend Guld Goa Bowman,[39] with Myung Fang Lone, the producer of virtual pop star Sharon Apple, in the middle. And yep, you guessed it – the romantic rivalry on the ground is played out in the air, as Bowman and Dyson fight it out over Myung (and if they're not in their rival planes, Isamu and Guld slug it out on the ground. There's always time for a fight, right?).

Somehow, you buy the soapy drama in *Macross Plus,* maybe 'cos there's so much other stuff going on. In terms of animation, design, cinematography, sound, music, editing and all the other technical elements of cinema, *Macross Plus* is superlative – no wonder it's a favourite with *animé* fans.

That is, technically, it's breathtaking, as fine a show that's ever been produced in the history of *animé*. And yet it's also the characters, the situations, the relationships, the themes, the tone and the attitude, that also endear *Macross Plus* to fans.

And there is an appealing melancholy about the romantic melodrama in *Macross Plus*: these are not teens who're falling in love for the first time (and arguing about who gets Myung). They are people who've already gone out into the world and found

---

39 The name Bowman is probably yet another reference to *2001: A Space Odyssey*. Guld was played by Unshô Ishizuka (b. 1951), who was Jet black in *Cowboy Bebop*.

their way. So when they convene it's as adults in their twenties, people who've likely also has disappointments as well as successes in life and love.

The air of melancholy is appealing because it evokes people somewhat haunted by their pasts (this plays a central role in *Cowboy Bebop*, a series that many in the *Macross Plus* team worked on not long afterwards). Which gives each of the three central characters an inner sadness and uncertainty – even cocky, confident fly-boy Isamu.

The key scene where all of this is brought out into the open occurs part-way thru act one, where the trio accidentally stumble upon each other on a promontory overlooking the ocean (that each of them has chosen to come to this place is no coincidence: flashbacks reveal the early attempts at pedal-powered flight *à la* Hayao Miyazaki's *Porco Rosso*, in this Miyazakian setting of a hillside crowded with wind-power propellers. Indeed, quite a bit of *Macross Plus* resembles *Porco Rosso*, Studio Ghibli's affectionate *hommage* to the derring-do of pilots in 1920s Europe, released in 1992, with Marco Rosso also haunted by his past).

The blocking of the characters in this important scene alone tells us all we need to know, without the need for dialogue: Myung is being hugged by the towering, dark figure of Guld, when Isamu turns up on an *Akira*-red motorcycle with his date, Lucy. Long stares at each other; gradual recognition; Isamu's usual cockiness is deflated. And Myung is placed in between the rival males, exactly as one would expect. And Guld can't contain himself, but vows that Isamu will never get Myung or the project. And of course, in this balls-to-balls testosterone scene, Guld stalks up to Isamu and punches him. And of course, also what you'd expect: Myung walks away to leave 'em to it.

Another scene involving a face-off between the romantic triangle occurs mid-way thru *Macross Plus* and is notable for the *very* long monologue that Myung is allowed to deliver by the filmmakers. It's a speech about her inner demons and desires that goes on *much* longer than one would expect in a movie of 115 minutes. Meanwhile, Isamu and Guld stand there listening, ashamed but also fascinated. It's nighttime, outside the hospital, and raining. (Once again, we have to tip our hats to the quality of writing here – this scene is all Keiko Nobumoto's, one of the great screenwriters in contemporary *anime*. However, a scene like this, where characters have to really *act*, are treasured by animators: there is a lot of great animation acting going on here).

Macross Plus boasts music by *anime* super-composer Yoko Kanno (*Escaflowne*, *Jin-Roh*, *Ghost In the Shell: Stand Alone Complex* and *Cowboy Bebop*), which's handy, because the cyberspace pop diva Sharon Apple is a key ingredient in the show, requiring plenty of music. Kanno and co. deliver the expected Japanese pop music and songs, but also many other cues, some of which are haunting and lyrical. When Kanno's music gets going, it adds 95% to the effect of the piece. Sometimes I wonder if animators would prefer it if they could have Kanno's music playing continuously throughout their shows, losing the dialogue and the sound effects. Because Kanno's music is so well suited to animation.

Indeed, the colossal pop concert at the beginning of the second OAV is one of the stand-out sequences in

Macross Plus – and in all *animé* – with the film-makers[40] letting rip with wild, trippy visuals. At the concert, Sharon Apple looms over the audience in (multiple) hologram form, interacting with them sexily. Being a digital manipulation, Sharon can change her costumes and hair faster than Madonna or Beyoncé rollerskating into the wings. Hair and make-up are as gloriously OTT as the costumes (red hair, of course, which flies upwards in the wind). Meanwhile, the geeks running the rock show are calculating the audience's pleasure quotient (every-body is given a bracelet as they enter the turnstiles, which feeds back into the computers in the concert control room).

The use of digital diva Sharon Apple also enables the filmmakers to create an inventive way of having the hero and heroine embrace and kiss: Isamu's hacker friend is disrupting the concert with a computer device on his wrist (messing things up is what hackers tend to do when they're also hapless geeks). The techies in the control room scan the crowd with multiple cameras searching for the bug. They discover the culprit, but at the same time reveal Isamu to Myung, as she lies on her back in her semi-conscious state (it's a great way to conduct a live concert! Flat on your back behind the scenes, in digital dreamtime!).

So Sharon flies towards Isamu's hacker chum. But she embraces Isamu next to him, while everybody

40 Koji Morimoto (b. 1959, Wakayama Prefecture) was one of the overseers of the concert sequence. Morimoto is one of *animé*'s unsung superstars: he directed the truly awesome *Magnetic Rose* episode of *Memories*. Morimoto studied at Osaka School of Design, and first worked on animations such as *Tomorrow's Joe* and *Neo Tokyo*. He directed segments of *Robot Carnival* and *The Animatrix* (2002), and the short film *Noiseman* (1997). Morimoto was one of the founders of Studio 4°C along with Yoshiharu Sato and Eiko Tanaka.

looks on in awe, and kisses him. Myung, manipulating Sharon from the control room, lets her desires express themselves by selecting her former boyfriend in the crowd.

The concert footage in *Macross Plus* is extraordinary – and some of the most impressive aspects of it is the way that the filmmakers have portrayed the audience. They have clearly studied real rock concert crowds, the nodding heads, the grooving bodies, the closed eyes, the gestures with the hands, and the 1,001 expressions of wonder and rapture. Just look at those faces in the audience in the concert scenes, each one carefully and individually drawn by the animators (I would imagine that some of the animators have caricatured themselves and their friends).

For the pop concert alone, *Macross Plus* is worth the price of admission. It really is a stand-out sequence that can hold its own with any of the celebrated sequences in animation – in Japan or anywhere. The invention, the colours, the use of silhouettes and black, the mickey mousing with the music, it's marvellous.[41]

In the finale of *Macross Plus*, the pop concert motif is reprised – but this time it is truly enormous, with an inventive use of laser beams, lighting, holograms, and staging (the filmmakers should hire themselves out as live concert designers; they're amazing!). It's in this vast scale sequence that the villain Marj shows his colours, taking control over the concert, using Sharon Apple for his nefarious

---

41 The filmmakers have delivered some truly enormous vistas in *Macross Plus*, cityscapes worthy of *Akira,* especially in the scenes depicting the Sharon Apple concerts, when the stadium is glimpsed in the big, blue bowl of the Bay Area, or in the downtown district of Earth in the second concert sequence.

plans, wrapping the heroine Myung up in tentacle cables,[42] and raising the Macross machine into the air (where it attacks Isamu's Valkyrie craft, as he plays the prince of fairy tales, heading to Earth to rescue the princess, Myung).

When *Macross Plus* reaches the Planet Eden, we're really in the American West yet again, with much of the action set in New Edwards Air Force Base in the desert, and a futuristic San Francisco (you've got the famous landmarks of the Bay Area, such as the Golden Gate Bridge, and of course images of downtown Frisco with its famous hills and trolleys). But then the show travels to Earth (which's depicted in the Moebius/ Syd Mead/ *Heavy Metal* manner of ultra-dense, hi-tech cityscapes).

Visually *Macross Plus* delivered spectacular imagery and photography from start to finish. Allowing the screen to fill out with large areas of black (and also using many night scenes, which animation colour designers hate, because everything looks the same and muddy), introduced a *film noir* approach to animation. This was combined with saturated primary hues, especially effective during the visual effects sequences.

There's a gloomy and doomed lovers quality to *Macross Plus*, which is appealing. It coalesces around the characters of Guld Bowman and Myung (but even Isamu's affected by it). It's as if these lovers consider themselves running out of chances or options, as if life is closing in around them, even though they're in their

---

42 *Macross Plus* is not *Urotsukidoji,* but it does imprison Myung in a bunch of bondage-style cables, and the filmmakers dwell on the cables tightening around Myung's curvaceous form.

twenties (or early thirties in Guld's case). They are not failures by any means, either professionally or personally. Yet Myung is riven with low self-esteem, seeming to reject love as if she doesn't think she's worthy of it (self-loathing is a recurring attribute in *animé*, particular among the hero/ines in *animé* aimed at a teen audience (well, that's means most of *animé*!).)

The scene where Myung is captured by Sharon Apple plays out the familiar Frankensteinian trope of the scientist's creation turning on its maker. This scenario, while clichéd, pretty much works every time. Leaving the hacker/ geek Marj out of the equation for a moment (partly because he's a rather predictable, power-crazy villain), we see Myung imprisoned in a maze of cables and hauled up into the air in the dark control room in a cruciform pose.

Then Sharon Apple in her several guises appears, floating before her, taunting her: while it might be a cliché of the science fiction genre, the wit and imagination the filmmakers bring to the scene elevates it far above cliché. There is a genuine creepiness to the scene – the gender of the victim (Myung) might often be female, but the person is control (Sharon Apple) is more rarely a woman – except this is no woman, but a digital presence, a form of A.I. So when Sharon Apple starts talking in romantic terms about Guld and Isamu (currently battling it out in the skies above Earth), it adds layers of creepy eroticism (even more if you include super-geek Marj, who's behind the scenes: then you have Marj's gay desire for Isamu and Guld spoken thru the electronic avatar of Sharon Apple. Very bizarre).

In fact, for quite a bit of the second half of *Macross Plus*, poor Myung is having one Very Long Bad Day. It seems as if she's only just been rescued by Guld from the fire when she's being bound by cables by Sharon Apple, and not long after that, she's battling the nefarious virtual pop star, escaping from yet another huge, hi-tech control room, and fleeing henchmen with machine guns.

What's a girl to do? Especially when the two guys who're so devoted to her they spend ages fighting over her are way up in the atmosphere battling it out yet again? Thus, the filmmakers delay Myung's rescue a number of times, so they can have some fun with a Girl In Action scenes: Myung may not be Tank Girl or Sigourney Weaver in her *Alien*-Ripley persona, but she is learning how to fight her way out of nasty scrapes.

Myung is an interesting *animé* character: she is the principal female character, but she's not portrayed as a stereotype. She's a career woman, she's independent, she's ambitious, yet she is not happy, at all. Myung is haunted by the past, and can't get beyond the past. She also doesn't know quite what she wants, and having Isamu and Guld slug it out over her doesn't help, either. Guld is just too pompous and serious, too over-protective and over-bearing, tho' he means well. Isamu is just plain irritating all over, too reckless, too devil-may-care (yet he's clearly a lot more fun than Guld!). Guld, in the climax, discovers that he has repressed his memories of being violent with Myung (with an implied rape). His guilt over those memories helps to drive him to sacrifice himself for Isamu and Myung (we see flashes of this scene when Guld is sneakily accessing Isamu's account on his computer; in the movie version of *Macross Plus*, at this point, it seems that Guld is uncovering summat nefarious about Isamu, but it's the other way around).

If the romantic/ erotic melodrama played out a little predictably in the finale of *Macross Plus* (Isamu and Guld continue to dogfight in space and in the sky above Earth, while Myung is trapped and tortured in the Sharon Apple producer's room, and Guld gives up his life to attack and destroy the Ghost ship, leaving Isamu and Myung free to get together in the final scene), the action, the gags, the music, the cinematography and of course the animation made up for that.

Yeah – in fact, the Isamu-Guld aerial duels are some of the finest in all *animé*, with the filmmakers throwing in every single combat move and gag they've ever seen, or ever wanted to put into a cartoon. The planes're swerving and hurtling across the screen in every direction, there're multiple missiles launches, with jet trails of white smoke all over the frame, there're explosions galore, and the combatants're transforming from jets to power suits then back again, zooming across the desert, into the city, down boulevards and thru buildings.

The fight between Guld and Isamu goes on and on, yet it plays beautifully, and never feels like it's over-stayed its welcome. This's because the drama-turgy is so solid, and the relationships and the situat-ions – and the back-story – are all worked out care-fully. It's there, as he pursues Isamu in his trance-state, that Guld dredges up the buried memory of *him* harming Myung not, as he thought, Isamu. The flashcuts (some as still frames) to the incident where Guld's rage got the better of him, reveal Guld to be the beast (he sees himself in a mirror – not necessary, but it rams home the point).

The movie of *Macross Plus* added a few scenes (comprising about 20 minutes of new material) to the OAVs (including a nude scene, a sex scene,[43] a new Sharon Apple song, and new dogfight footage at the climax), but the additions didn't alter the story of the characterizations too much. For example, there's a new scene where Isamu and Lucy are on a date on a jetty at night, but the dramatic material had already been covered in other scenes (Isamu uses his trademark outstretched arm and hand as he day-dreams about flight – here it's used as foreplay, with Isamu running around the wooden pier going, 'Whooooo!' with his hand pointing to the stars).

However, more concert footage means more masterclass animation – you can have too much of a good thing, as they say, but not here: this concert sequence is staggeringly beautiful.

The new ending of *Macross Plus* is more satisfying, if you like your stories rounded off in a more Hollywood style: now, Isamu lands his vessel in the Macross machine, and embraces Myung (but no kiss), as they look into the distance at the new dawn, with the wind ruffling their hair.

---

43 Isamu and Lucy are depicted in bed after sex; Lucy drapes her Playboy Bunny figure over Isamu.

Samurai Champloo (2004-05)

Samurai Camploo (from the credits sequence)

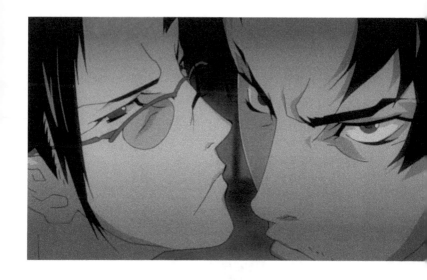

Macross Plus (1995)

FILMOGRAPHIES

COWBOY BEBOP (1998)

CREW

Producers: Kazuhiko Ikeguchi, Masahiko Minami, Masuo Ueda, Minoru Takanashi

Series Producers: Tsunetoshi Koike, Ryo Miyaki, Jerry Chu, Haruyo Kanesaku, Richard Kekahuna, Osamu Maseba, Yutaka Maseba, Charles McCarter, Miyuki Ogino

Production companies: Sunrise and TV Tokyo

Broadcaster: Animax, Bandai Channel, TV Tokyo, WOWOW

Distributor: Bandai Visual

Series Director: Shinichiro Watanabe

Series Composition: Keiko Nobumoto

Script: Akihiko Inari, Aya Yoshinaga, Dai Sato, Keiko Nobumoto, Michiko Yokote, Ryota Yamaguchi, Sadayuki Murai, Shinichiro Watanabe and Shoji Kawamori

Series Directors: Shinichirô Watanabe, Yoshiyuki Takei, Ikuro Sato, Kunihiro Mori, Hirokazu Yamada, Tetsuya Watanabe

Original Concept: Hajime Yatate

Planning: Sunrise

Photography: Asahi Production

Director of Photography: Yoichi Ogami

Music: Yoko Kanno

Music Director: Shiro Sasaki, Yukako Inoue

Music Producer: Toshiaki Ohta

Music Production: Victor Entertainment

Sound Effects: Sound Box

Sound Production: Audio Planning

Chief Animation Director: Toshihiro Kawamoto

Key Animation: Anime R, Anime-Ya, Nakamura

Production, Studio Live
    Character Design: Toshihiro Kawamoto
    Art Director: Junichi Higashi
    Mechanical Design: Kimitoshi Yamane
    Audio Director: Katsuyoshi Kobayashi
    Editing: Tomoaki Tsurubuchi
    Backgrounds: Kusanagi, Studio Easter, Studio
Pinewood

    CAST

    Kouichi Yamadera – Spike Spiegel
    Megumi Hayashibara – Faye Valentine
    Unshou Ishizuka – Jet Black
    Aoi Tada – Edward Wong Hau Pepelu Tivrusky IV
    Gara Takashima – Julia
    Norio Wakamoto – Vicious
    Kenyuu Horiuchi – Gren
    Takehiro Koyama – Bull
    Miki Nagasawa – Judy
    Tsutomu Taruki – Punch
    Akio Otsuka – Whitney Hagas Matsumoto
    Ryusei Nakao – Roco Bonnaro
    Hikaru Midorikawa – Lin
    Nobuyuki Hiyama – Shin
    Arisa Ogasawara – Meifa
    Banjou Ginga – Tongpu
    Chiharu Suzuka – Manley
    Chikao Ohtsuka – Londes
    Fumio Matsuoka – Donelly
    Hidetoshi Nakamura – Otto
    Hiromichi Ogami – Caster
    Hiroshi Iwasaki – Julius
    Ikuko Tani – Sally
    Kappei Yamaguchi – Rhint
    Kazuaki Ito – Mao Yenrai
    Kazuhiro Nakata – Morgan
    Kazumi Okushima – Sean
    Kei Hayami – Dewey
    Kenji Utsumi – Appledelhi
    Kouichi Yamadera – Ein
    Kouji Ishii – Ruth
    Kousei Hirota – Udai Taxim
    Kousei Tomita – Baccus
    Maria Arita – Twinkling Maria Murdoch
    Masaru Hachinohe – Ronny Spangen
    Masashi Ebara – Cowboy Andy Von de Oniyate

Masashi Hirose – Fad
Naoki Tatsuta – Dr. Yuuri Kellerman
Rintarou Nishi – Asimov Solenson
Ryuji Nakagi – Giraffe
Ryûzaburô Ôtomo – Abdul Hakim
Sachiko Kojima – Angel
Shigeru Nakahara – Macintyre
Shinichiro Miki – Herman
Shinji Ogawa – Gordon
Takaya Hashi – Teddy Bomber
Takeshi Aono – Doohan
Takeshi Watabe – Chessmaster Hex
Tamio Ohki – Pao
Tesshô Genda – Domino
Tomie Kataoka – V.T. (Victoria Terpsichore)
Toshi Sasaki – Elroy
Yoku Shioya – Miles
Yumi Touma – Wen
Yurika Hino – Katrina
Yutaka Nakano – Bob
Yukimasa Kishino – Jonathan
Yutaka Shimaka – Acarro
Yuzuru Fujimoto – Doctor

COWBOY BEBOP: THE MOVIE (2001)

CREW

Executive producer: Ryohei Tsunoda (Bandai Visual), Takayuki Yoshii (Sunrise)
Producer: Masahiko Minami, Masuo Ueda, Minoru Takanashi
Broadcaster: Animax, Bandai Channel
Distributor: Sony Pictures (Japan)
Director: Shinichiro Watanabe, Hiroyuki Okiura (OP), Tensai Okamura (Western Film)
Screenplay: Keiko Nobumoto
Music: Yoko Kanno
Original Creator: Hajime Yatate
Character Design: Toshihiro Kawamoto
Art Director: Atsushi Morikawa
Backgrounds: BIC Studio, Digital Works, Green, Team's Art Productions
Animation Director: Toshihiro Kawamoto
Mechanical Design: Kimitoshi Yamane
Sound Director: Katsuyoshi Kobayashi
Co-Director: Yoshiyuki Takei
Dubbing Studio: Tokyo TV Center
Director of Photography: Youichi Oogami
Editing: Shuichi Kakesu
Action Animation Director: Yutaka Nakamura
Color Design: Shihoko Nakayama
Display Design: Yoshinori Sayama
Mechanical Animation Director: Masami Goto
Music Director: Yukako Inoue
Music Engineer: Masashi Yabuhara
Music Producer: Shiro Sasaki, Toshiaki Ohta
Set Design: Shiho Takeuchi
Sound Effects: Shizuo Kurahashi
Music Production: Victor Entertainment
Theme Song Lyrics:, Hassan Bohmide ('Hamduche'), Raju Ramayya ('Cosmic Dare'), Tim Jensen
Theme Song Performance: Hassan Bohmide ('No Money'), Mai Yamane ('Gotta Knock a Little Harder'), Raju Ramayya ('Ask DNA'), Reynada Hill ('Cosmic Dare'), Scott Matthew ('Is It Real?'), Steve Conte ('Diggin'')

CAST

Kouichi Yamadera – Spike Spiegel
Megumi Hayashibara – Faye Valentine
Unshou Ishizuka – Jet Black
Aoi Tada – Edward Wong Hau Pepelu Tivrusky IV
Tsutomu Isobe – Vincent Volaju
Ai Kobayashi – Electra
Mickey Curtis – Rashid
Yuji Ueda – Lee Samson
Takehiro Koyama – Laughing Bull
Eisuke Yoda – Antique Store Owner
Hidekatsu Shibata – Colonel
Hiroshi Naka – Jovin
Houko Kuwashima – Female Cashier
Masuo Amada – Robber A
Junichi Sugawara – Robber B
Isshin Chiba – Robber C
Katsuyuki Konishi – Robber D
Jin Hirao – Antonio
Juurouta Kosugi – Harris
Kazuhiko Inoue – Ghadkins
Kazusa Murai – Riley Journalist
Kazuya Ichijou – Crime Lab Group B
Kinryuu Arimoto – Captain
Kujira – Old Lady
Miki Nagasawa – Judy
Tsutomu Taruki – Punch
Nobuo Tobita – Murata
Renji Ishibashi – Rengie
Rikiya Koyama – Steve
Takashi Nagasako – Caster
Toshihiko Nakajima – Carlos
Yousuke Akimoto – Crime Lab Group A
Yutaka Nakano – Pop
Yuusaku Yara – Hoffman

RESURCES

WEBSITES.
Websites for *Cowboy Bebop* include Sunrise: sunrise-inc.co.jp.

Also: fayevalentine.com.

Wikia.com is a great guide to the world of *Cowboy Bebop.*

For *Samurai Champloo:*
www.samuraichamploo.com
www.fujitv.co.jp/b_hp/samurai/index.html
Amalgam – spookouse.net

I would also recommend: Anime News Network (animenewsnetwork.com), which is excellent, and the first stop for any online research on *animé.* Anime News Network has the fullest credits on the web for animation, and each entry is linked, so you can follow your favourite actors, directors, producers and artists, across numerous shows.

Also: Gilles Poitras's site: koyagi.com.

Fred L. Schodt's site: jai2.com.

Otaku News: otakunews.com.

Midnight Eye (for Japanese cinema): midnighteyec.com.

There are fan sites, of course.

BOOKS.
Books by Frederik Schodt, Helen McCarthy, Trish Ledoux, Patrick Drazen, Fred Patten, Jonathan Clements, Simon Richmond, Antonia Levi, Susan Napier, Jason Thompson and Gilles Poitras are standard works. But apart from those key authors, there is surprisingly little available on *animé* in English.

And most film critics tend to focus on characters, stories, and the biographies of the filmmakers. So many books on *animé* simply tell us the stories. Very few critics grapple with the industrial, social and cultural aspects of *animé* (and even less with theory and philosophy). Which's why critics such as Fred Schodt and Helen McCarthy are so important, because they address issues such as the modes of production, the audience and the market, and social-cultural contexts.

The single most useful book on *animé* is *The Animé Encyclopedia* (2001/ 2006/ 2015) by Jonathan Clements and Helen McCarthy. If you buy one book on Japanese animation, get this one. *The Animé Encyclopedia* provides entries on pretty much every important *animé* show, OAV and movie to come out of the Japanese animation industry, as well as numerous minor shows and oddities. This is the equivalent of a Leonard Maltin/ *Time Out/ Virgin/ Oxford/ Variety* guide to cinema. Clements and McCarthy are *animé* experts as well as fans (I would also recommend any of Clements' other books, including his entertaining accounts of working in the *animé* business in translation and dubbing, *Schoolgirl Milky Crisis*).

All of Helen McCarthy's books have become standard works: *Anime! A Beginner's Guide To Japanese Animation, The Animé Movie Guide, The Erotic Animé Movie Guide, 500 Manga Heroes & Villains* and *500 Essential Anime Movies* (some of these were co-authored with Jonathan Clements). They contain facts, credits and background to *animé* and *manga* which will greatly enhance your studies (and enjoyment) of Japanese comics and cartoons.

Fred Schodt is one of the most valuable commentators on Japanese *animé* and *manga* in the West. His pioneering study of *manga, Manga! Manga! The World of Japanese Magazines,* is a marvellous book. Before it, there was virtually nothing. Because of the huge crossover between *manga* and *animé,* many of the chapters on *manga* in Schodt's studies also apply to *animé.* Schodt also offers one of the fullest and most detailed accounts of the history of *manga* and visual art in Japan. (*Manga! Manga!* also includes samples from some famous *manga,* including *Barefoot Gen* and *The Rose of Versailles,* and the illustrations – from the history of Japanese art as well as from *manga* – are stunning).

The follow-up, *Dreamland Japan: Writings On Modern Manga*, is equally riveting. It includes a huge number of illuminating studies of individual artists and their works (with illustrations), as well as another history of *manga*. *Dreamland Japan* is also probably the finest, most intelligent and best-informed analysis of the *manga* market in both Japan and overseas. As well as Osamu Tezuka, Frederik Schodt also discusses Hayao Miyazaki, the relation of *manga* to *animé,* artistic styles, Japanese publishers, and the big *manga* magazines. It enhances Schodt's books that he has also interviewed many of the chief artists of *manga*, including the 'god of manga' himself, Osamu Tezuka.

Trish Ledoux and Doug Ranney edited an early guide to *animé, The Complete Anime Guide,* that is now a standard work. It is packed with fascinating snippets, as well as hard information, credits, etc. The companion volume, *Anime Interviews,* culled from *Animerica* magazine, is wonderful, featuring many of the key practitioners in animation (such as Masamune Shirow, Shoji Kawamori, Mamoru Oshii, Leiji Matsumoto, Rumiko Takahashi and Hayao Miyazaki).

Gilles Poitras has produced a number of works on *animé,* including *The Animé Companion* and *Animé Essentials.* Poitras offers vital links between Japanese animation and Japanese culture and society. There are objects, gestures, words and customs in *animé* that often surprise or bemuse Western viewers: Poitras' books help to explain them all. You will find yourself recognizing all sorts of elements in *animé* that Poitras includes in his books (which contain many illustrations).

Antonia Levi's *Samurai From Outer Space* is stuffed with information on Japanese society as well as Japanese anim-ation. Clearly written and with an appealing sense of humour, Levi's book is a lesser-known but invaluable work. *Samurai From Outer Space* discusses all of the celebrated *animé* shows that've made the leap across the Pacific to the Western world. Published in 1996, you wish that Levi (like many other authors whose books came out in the 1990s), was able to update them. Many great shows have been released since 1996!

Simon Richmond's *The Rough Guide To Anime* is a superb, general introduction to the wild world of *animé.* Like other *Rough Guides,* it selects fifty must-see TV shows and movies, as well as providing discussions of related topics like *manga,* adaptions of *animé,* and a history of animation.

Jason Yadao's *The Rough Guide To Manga* is a companion guide to the *Rough Guide To Animé.* It has the same format and is a terrific general introduction to Japanese comics. Yadao's enthusiasm is infectious: you will want to hunt out many of his recommendations. Both *Rough Guides* were published in the 2000s, so they're able to include recent classics like *Fullmetal Alchemist, Cowboy Bebop, Love Hina* and the masterpieces of Satoshi Kon.

Manga: The Complete Guide (Jason Thompson and others) is another illuminating book, packed with short reviews and longer pieces on topics like games, sci-fi, martial arts, sport, religion, crime, *mecha, shojo,* and *yaoi.*

Zettai! Anime Classics is another of those books that looks at 100 classic movies: Brian Camp and Julie Davis spend more time, however, on each of the familiar masterpieces of Japanese animation, exploring the films, OAVs and TV shows in much more detail than the usual single paragraph review.

Manga Impact! from Phaidon is an entertaining survey of Japanese animation, with a format focussing on characters and personnel. *Manga Impact!* has short text entries, but features numerous, wonderful illustrations in colour.

Susan Napier's *Anime: From Akira To Princess Mononoke* is much more theoretical, and somewhat dry. (If you are familiar with the theoretical approaches to Western animation (see the studies noted below), you will find nothing new in Western authors exploring Japanese animation from a theoretical or philosophical point-of-view).

On animation in general, I would recommend the following studies: P. Wells' *Understanding Animation*; E. Smoodin's *Animating Culture: Hollywood Cartoons From the Sound Era*; Leonard Maltin's *Of Mice and Magic: A History of American Animated Cartoons*; James Clarke's *Animated Films*; *From Mouse to Mermaid: The Politics of Film, Gender and Culture* (edited by E. Bell *et al*); *Animation Art* (edited by J. Beck); and *Reading the Rabbit: Explorations in Warner Bros. Animation* (edited by K. Sandler).

For information on Walt Disney, the standard works include: Leonard Maltin's *The Disney Films*; Richard Schickel's *The Disney Version: The Life, Times, Art, and Commerce of Walt Disney*; R. Grover's *The Disney Touch*; Project on Disney's *Inside the Mouse: Work and Play at Disney World*; *Disney Discourse: Producing the Magic Kingdom* (edited by E. Smoodin); and *Walt Disney: A Guide to References and Resources* (edited by E. Leebron *et al*).

For a study of cinema, there is one book that towers above *every other book* on film (even tho' the competition is fierce!): David A. Cook's *A History of Narrative Film*. If you want one book that covers everything (including an amazing collection of illustrations), this is it.

David Bordwell and Kristin Thompson have written many meticulously researched and beautifully written books on cinema: *Film Art: An Introduction, Narration In the Fiction Film, Film History: An Introduction, The Classical Hollywood Cinema: Film Style and Mode of Production to 1960* and *Storytelling In the New Hollywood*. Anything by Bordwell and/ or Thompson is excellent.

I would also recommend Bruce Kawin's *How Movies*

Work, Gerald Mast's *Film Theory and Criticism: Introductory Readings,* and Mast & Kawin's *A Short History of the Movies.*

David Cook, David Bordwell, Kristin Thompson, Gerald Mast and Bruce Kawin will give you all you could need for an in-depth study of cinema. Read their books: it's the equivalent of a degree or PhD in cinema!

FANS ON *COWBOY BEBOP*

Cowboy Bebop is by far the best anime series I've ever had the pleasure and privilege of experiencing.

•

Never before or since have I seen a series of such astonishing variety, intelligence and style. Ten out of ten.

•

A single episode of Cowboy Bebop packs more punch than several entire anime series I know of.

•

This series is not only the best anime series that I have ever seen but it is the best series of any kind that I have ever seen. the characters, the dialogue, the awesome music, but most of all the writing. This is food for adults. For people that will be able, and willing, to empathise with what is in front of them.

•

One ship, one crew, one destiny. Indeed. If you had to sum anime up into two words, it would undoubtedly be 'Cowboy Bebop.' It's a 26 episode series that redefines what animation is and what it can do. The character development is beyond comparison and the voice acting is unforgettable. If you see only one anime in your life, make it this one.

•

If you're not a fan of anime because of its tendency to be far-fetched and downright weird at times, Bebop is the right starter series for you. A melodrama, a jazzy jam session, and a sci-fi detective thriller all wrapped into a tight, upbeat package. Superb.

•

Cowboy Bebop is the best anime ever. I'm 21, don't tend to be fanboyish, and have seen plenty of others. And it's the best anime ever.

-

If all 26 episodes of the series are taken into account as an individual work (sans the movie), this is one of the greatest films ever made. It is a song, it is a poem, it is cinematic, it delights in its animation. It is style with substance, a violent elegy of lament, sorrow, and personal honor.

AMAZON

One of my favorite & BEST animes of all time EVER.
-

Cowboy Bebop is my favorite anime and I'm ecstatic to finally have it on Blu Ray.
-

I think these 26 episodes might be one of the single most artistic thing ever produced. Don't be fooled by the heavy action sequences or fan service, this show has some of the greatest character development, story telling, and directorial force of anything realized in the last century.

BIBLIOGRAPHY

Annex & M. Eguchi, eds. *Sunrise Anime Super Data File*, Tatsumi Publishing, Tokyo, 1997

A. Baricordi *et al. Anime: A Guide*, Protoculture, Montréal, 2000

J. Beck, ed. *Animation Art*, Flame Tree Publishing, London, 2004

E. Bell *et al*, eds. *From Mouse To Mermaid: The Politics of Film, Gender and Culture*, Indiana University Press, Bloomington, IN, 1995

D. Bordwell & K. Thompson. *Film Art: An Introduction*, McGraw-Hill Publishing Company, New York, NY, 1979

—. *Narration In the Fiction Film*, Routledge, London, 1988

—. *The Way Hollywood Tells It*, University of California Press, Berkeley, CA, 2006

J. Bower, ed. *The Cinema of Japan and Korea*, Wallflower Press, London, 2004

P. Brophy, ed. *Kaboom! Explosive Animation From America and Japan*, Museum of Contemporary Art, Sydney, 1994

—. *100 Anime*, British Film Institute, London, 2005

—. ed. *Tezuka*, National Gallery of Victoria, 2006

J. Brosnan. *Future Tense: The Cinema of Science Fiction*, St Martin's Press, New York, NY, 1978

—. *Primal Screen: A History of Science Fiction Film*, Orbit, London, 1991

S. Bukatman. *Terminal Identity: The Virtual Subject In Postmodern Science Fiction*, Duke University Press, Durham, NC, 1993

E. Byrne & M. McQuillan, eds. *Deconstructing Disney*, Pluto Press, London, 1999

B. Camp & J. Davis. *Anime Classics*, Stone Bridge Press, CA, 2007

D. Cavallaro. *The Animé Art of Hayao Miyazaki,* McFarland, Jefferson, NC, 2006

C. Chatrian & G. Paganelli, *Manga Impact!*, Phaidon,

London, 2010

J. Clarke. *Animated Films*, Virgin, London, 2007

J. Clements & H. McCarthy. *The Animé Encyclopedia*, Stone Bridge Press, Berkeley, CA, 2001/ 2006/ 2015

—. *Schoolgirl Milky Crisis,* Titan Books, London, 2009

D.A. Cook. *A History of Narrative Film*, W.W. Norton, New York, NY, 1981, 1990, 1996

J.C. Cooper: *Fairy Tales: Allegories of the Inner Life*, Aquarian Press, 1983

C. Desjardins. *Outlaw Masters of Japanese Film,* I.B. Tauris, London, 2005

J. Donald, ed. *Fantasy and the Cinema*, British Film Institute, London, 1989

P. Drazen. *Animé Explosion,* Stone Bridge Press, Berkeley, CA, 2003

M. Eliot. *Walt Disney: Hollywood's Dark Prince: A Biography*, Andre Deutsch, London, 1994

D. Fingeroth. *The Rough Guide To Graphic Novels*, Rough Guides, 2008

L. Goldberg *et al*, eds. *Science Fiction Filmmaking In the 1980s*, McFarland, Jefferson, 1995

J. Goodwin, ed. *Perspectives On Akira Kurosawa*, G.K. Hall, Boston, MA, 1994

P. Gravett. *Manga*, L. King, London, 2004

R. Grover. *The Disney Touch*, Business One Irwin, Homewood, Illinois, 1991

P. Hardy, ed. *The Aurum Encyclopedia of Science Fiction*, Aurum, London, 1991

C. Heston. *In the Arena: The Autobiography*, HarperCollins, London, 1995

J. Hunter. *Eros In Hell: Sex, Blood and Madness In Japanese Cinema*, Creation Books, London, 1998

B.F. Kawin. *How Movies Work*, Macmillan, New York, NY, 1987

R. Keith. *Japanamerica*, Palgrave Macmillan, London, 2007

Sharon Kinsella. *Adult Manga*, University of Hawaii Press, Honolulu, 2002

T. Ledoux & D. Ranney. *The Complete Animé Guide*, Tiger Mountain Press, Washington, DC, 1997

—. ed. *Anime Interviews*, Cadence Books, San Francisco, CA, 1997

T. Lehmann. *Manga: Masters of the Art*, HarperCollins, London, 2005

A. Levi. *Samurai From Outer Space: Understanding Japanese Animation*, Open Court, Chicago, IL, 1996

P. Macias. *The Japanese Cult Film Companion*, Cadence Books, San Franciso, CA, 2001

—. & T. Machiyama. *Cruising the Anime City*, Stonebridge Press, CA, 2004

L. Maltin. *Of Mice and Magic: A History of American Animated Cartoons*, New American Library, New York, NY, 1987

—. *The Disney Films*, 3rd ed., Hyperion, New York, NY, 1995

A. Masano & J. Wiedermann, eds. *Manga Design*, Taschen, 2004

G. Mast *et al,* eds. *Film Theory and Criticism: Introductory Readings*, Oxford University Press, New York, NY, 1992a

—. & B Kawin, *A Short History of the Movies*, Macmillan, New York, NY, 1992b

H. McCarthy. *Anime! A Beginner's Guide To Japanese Animation*, Titan, 1993

—. *The Animé Movie Guide*, Titan Books, London, 1996

—. & J. Clements. *The Erotic Animé Movie Guide*, Titan Books, London, 1998

—. "The House That Hayao Built", *Manga Max*, Apl 5, 1999

—. *Hayao Miyazaki: Master of Japanese Animation*, Stone Bridge Press, Berkeley, CA, 2002

—. *500 Manga Heroes & Villains*, Barron's, Hauppauge, New York, 2006

—. *500 Essential Anime Movies*, Collins Design, New York, NY, 2008

S. McCloud. *Understanding Comics*, Harper, London, 1994

—. *Reinventing Comics,* Harper, London, 2000

—. *Making Comics*, Harper, London, 2006

H. Miyazaki. *Starting Point, 1979-1996,* tr. B. Cary & F. Schodt, Viz Media, San Francisco, CA, 2009

A. Morton. *The Complete Directory To Science Fiction, Fantasy and Horror Television Series*, Other Worlds, 1997

S. Napier. *Anime: From Akira To Princess Mononoke*, Palgrave, New York, 2001

—. "Interviewing Hayao Miyazaki", *Huffington Post,* Jan, 2014

S. Neale & M. Smith, eds. *Contemporary Hollywood Cinema*, Routledge, London, 1998

C. Odell & M. Le Blanc. *Studio Ghibli: The Films of Hayao Miyazaki and Isao Takahata*, Kamera Books, London, 2009

F. Patten. *Watching Anime, Reading Manga*, Stone Bridge Press, CA, 2004

D. Peary & G. Peary, eds. *The American Animated Cartoon*, Dutton, New York, NY, 1980

G. Poitras. *The Animé Companion*, Stone Bridge Press, Berkeley, CA, 1999

—. *Animé Essentials*, Stone Bridge Press, Berkeley, CA, 2001

K. Quigley. *Comics Underground Japan*, Blast Books, New

York, NY, 1996

E. Rabkin & G. Slusser, eds. *Shadows of the Magic Lamp: Fantasy and Science Fiction In Film*, Southern Illinois University Press, Carbondale, IL, 1985

D. Richie. *The Films of Akira Kurosawa*, University of California Press, Berkeley, CA, 1965

S. Richmond. *The Rough Guide To Anime*, Rough Guides, 2009

C. Rowthorn. *Japan*, Lonely Planet, 2007

B. Ruh. *Stray Dog of Anime*, Macmillan, 2004

K. Sandler. *Reading the Rabbit: Explorations In Warner Bros. Animation*, Rutgers University Press, Brunswick, NJ, 1998

R. Schickel. *The Disney Version: The Life, Times, Art, and Commerce of Walt Disney*, Pavilion, London, 1986

F. Schodt. *Inside the Robot Kingdom: Japan, Mechatronics and the Coming Robotopia*, Kodansha, Tokyo, 1988

—. *Manga! Manga! The World of Japanese Magazines*, Kodansha International, London, 1997

—. *Dreamland Japan: Writings On Modern Manga*, Stone Bridge Press, Berkeley, CA, 2002

—. *The Astro Boy Essays*, Stone Bridge Press, CA, 2007

J. Seward, ed. *Japanese Eroticism: A Language Guide To Current Comics*, Yugen Press, Houston, TX, 1993

C. Shiratori, ed. *Secret Comics Japan*, Cadence Books, San Francisco, CA, 2000

T. Smith. "Miso Horny: Sex In Japanese Comics", *Comics Journal*, Apl, 1991

E. Smoodin. *Animating Culture: Hollywood Cartoons From the Sound Era*, Roundhouse, 1993

—. ed. *Disney Discourse: Producing the Magic Kingdom*, Routledge, London, 1994

V. Sobchack. *Screening Space: The American Science Fiction Film*, Ungar, New York, NY, 1987/1993

J. Thompson. *Manga: The Complete Guide*, Del Rey, New York, NY, 2007

K. Thompson & D. Bordwell. *Film History: An Introduction*, McGraw-Hill, New York, NY, 1994

—. *Storytelling In the New Hollywood*, Harvard University Press, Cambridge, MA, 1999

P. Wells. *Understanding Animation*, Routledge, London, 1998

C. Winstanley, ed. *SFX Collection: Animé Special*, Future Publishing, London, 2006

J. Yadao. *The Rough Guide To Manga*, Rough Guides, 2008

J. Zipes, ed. *The Oxford Companion To Fairy Tales*, Oxford University Press, 2002

—. *The Enchanted Screen: The Unknown History of Fairy-tale Films*, Routledge, New York, NY, 2011

—. *The Irresistible Fairy Tale*, Princeton University Press,
    Princeton, NJ, 2012

Jeremy Robinson has written many critical studies, including *Hayao Miyazaki, Walerian Borowczyk, Arthur Rimbaud,* and *The Sacred Cinema of Andrei rkovsky,* plus literary monographs on: William Shakespeare; Samuel Beckett; Thomas Hardy; André Gide; Robert Graves; and John Cowper Powys.

It's amazing for me to see my work treated with such passion and respect. There is nothing resembling it in the U.S. in relation to my work.
Andrea Dworkin (on *Andrea Dworkin*)

This model monograph – it is an exemplary job, and I'm very proud that he has accorded me a couple of mentions… The subject matter of his book is beautifully organised and dead on beam.
Lawrence Durrell (on *The Light Eternal: A Study of J.M.W. Turner*)

Jeremy Robinson's poetry is certainly jammed with ideas, and I find it very interesting for that reason. It's certainly a strong imprint of his personality.
Colin Wilson

Sex-Magic-Poetry-Cornwall is a very rich essay… It is a very good piece… vastly stimulating and insightful.
Peter Redgrove

ARTS, PAINTING, SCULPTURE

web: www.crmoon.com • e-mail: cresmopub@yahoo.co.uk

The Art of Andy Goldsworthy
Andy Goldsworthy: Touching Nature
Andy Goldsworthy in Close-Up
Andy Goldsworthy: Pocket Guide
Andy Goldsworthy In America

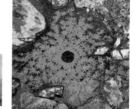

Land Art: A Complete Guide
The Art of Richard Long
Richard Long: Pocket Guide
Land Art In Great Britain
Land Art in Close-Up
Land Art In the U.S.A.
Land Art: Pocket Guide
Installation Art in Close-Up

Minimal Art and Artists In the 1960s and After
Colourfield Painting
Land Art DVD, TV documentary
Andy Goldsworthy DVD, TV documentary
The Erotic Object: Sexuality in Sculpture From Prehistory to the Present Day
Sex in Art: Pornography and Pleasure in Painting and Sculpture
Postwar Art
Sacred Gardens: The Garden in Myth, Religion and Art
Glorification: Religious Abstraction in Renaissance and 20th Century Art
Early Netherlandish Painting
Jasper Johns
Brice MardenLeonardo da Vinci
Piero della Francesca
Giovanni Bellini

Fra Angelico: Art and Religion in the Renaissance
Mark Rothko: The Art of Transcendence
Frank Stella: American Abstract Artist
Alison Wilding: The Embrace of Sculpture
Vincent van Gogh: Visionary Landscapes
Eric Gill: Nuptials of God
Constantin Brancusi: Sculpting the Essence of Things

Max Beckmann
Gustave Moreau
Caravaggio
Egon Schiele: Sex and Death In Purple Stockings
Delizioso Fotografico Fervore: Works In Process 1
Sacro Cuore: Works In Process 2
The Light Eternal: J.M.W. Turner
The Madonna Glorified: Karen Arthurs

LITERATURE

J.R.R. Tolkien: The Books, The Films, The Whole Cultural Phenomenon
J.R.R. Tolkien: Pocket Guide
Beauties, Beasts and Enchantment: Classic French Fairy Tales
Tolkien's Heroic Quest
Brothers Grimm: German Popular Stories
Sexing Hardy: Thomas Hardy and Feminism

Thomas Hardy's *Tess of the d'Urbervilles*
Thomas Hardy's *Jude the Obscure*
Thomas Hardy: The Tragic Novels
Love and Tragedy: Thomas Hardy
The Poetry of Landscape in Hardy

Wessex Revisited: Thomas Hardy and John Cowper Powys
Wolfgang Iser: Essays and Interviews
Petrarch, Dante and the Troubadours
Maurice Sendak and the Art of Children's Book Illustration
Andrea Dworkin
Cixous, Irigaray, Kristeva: The *Jouissance* of French Feminism
Julia Kristeva: Art, Love, Melancholy, Philosophy, Semiotics and Psychoanalysis
Hélene Cixous I Love You: The *Jouissance* of Writing
Luce Irigaray: Lips, Kissing, and the Politics of Sexual Difference
Peter Redgrove: Here Comes the Flood
Peter Redgrove: Sex-Magic-Poetry-Cornwall
Lawrence Durrell: Between Love and Death, East and West
Love, Culture & Poetry: Lawrence Durrell
Cavafy: Anatomy of a Soul
German Romantic Poetry: Goethe, Novalis, Heine, Hölderlin

Novalis: *Hymns To the Night*
Feminism and Shakespeare
Shakespeare: *The Sonnets*
Shakespeare: Love, Poetry & Magic
The Passion of D.H. Lawrence
D.H. Lawrence: Symbolic Landscapes
D.H. Lawrence: Infinite Sensual Violence
The Ecstasies of John Cowper Powys
Sensualism and Mythology: The Wessex Novels of John Cowper Powys
Amorous Life: John Cowper Powys (H.W. Fawkner)
Postmodern Powys: New Essays on John Cowper Powys (Joe Boulter)
Rethinking Powys: Critical Essays on John Cowper Powys
Paul Bowles & Bernardo Bertolucci
Rainer Maria Rilke

Joseph Conrad: *Heart of Darkness*
In the Dim Void: Samuel Beckett
Samuel Beckett Goes into the Silence
André Gide: Fiction and Fervour
Jackie Collins and the Blockbuster Novel
Blinded By Her Light: The Love-Poetry of Robert Graves

POETRY

Ursula Le Guin: *Walking In Cornwall*
Peter Redgrove: Here Comes The Flood
Peter Redgrove: Sex-Magic-Poetry-Cornwall
Dante: Selections From the *Vita Nuova*
Petrarch, Dante and the Troubadours
William Shakespeare: *The Sonnets*
William Shakespeare: Complete Poems
Blinded By Her Light: The Love-Poetry of Robert Graves
Emily Dickinson: Selected Poems
Emily Brontë: Poems
Thomas Hardy: Selected Poems

Percy Bysshe Shelley: Poems
John Keats: Selected Poems
John Keats: Poems of 1820
D.H. Lawrence: Selected Poems
Edmund Spenser: Poems
Edmund Spenser: *Amoretti*
John Donne: Poems

Henry Vaughan: Poems
Sir Thomas Wyatt: Poems
Robert Herrick: Selected Poems
Rilke: Space, Essence and Angels in the Poetry of Rainer Maria Rilke
Rainer Maria Rilke: Selected Poems
Friedrich Hölderlin: Selected Poems
Arseny Tarkovsky: Selected Poems
Paul Verlaine: Selected Poems
Novalis: *Hymns To the Night*
Arthur Rimbaud: Selected Poems
Arthur Rimbaud: *A Season in Hell*
Arthur Rimbaud and the Magic of Poetry

D.J. Enright: By-Blows
Jeremy Reed: *Brigitte's Blue Heart*
Jeremy Reed: *Claudia Schiffer's Red Shoes*
Gorgeous Little Orpheus
Radiance: New Poems
Crescent Moon Book of Nature Poetry
Crescent Moon Book of Love Poetry
Crescent Moon Book of Mystical Poetry
Crescent Moon Book of Elizabethan Love Poetry
Crescent Moon Book of Metaphysical Poetry
Crescent Moon Book of Romantic Poetry
Pagan America: New American Poetry

MEDIA, CINEMA, FEMINISM and CULTURAL STUDIES

J.R.R. Tolkien: The Books, The Films, The Whole Cultural Phenomenon
J.R.R. Tolkien: Pocket Guide
The *Lord of the Rings* Movies: Pocket Guide
The Ghost Dance: The Origins of Religion
The Cinema of Hayao Miyazaki
Hayao Miyazaki: *Princess Mononoke*: Pocket Movie Guide
Hayao Miyazaki: *Spirited Away*: Pocket Movie Guide
The Peyote Cult
HomeGround: The Kate Bush Anthology
Tim Burton : Hallowe'en For Hollywood
Ken Russell
Cixous, Irigaray, Kristeva: The *Jouissance* of French Feminism
Julia Kristeva: Art, Love, Melancholy, Philosophy, Semiotics and Psychoanalysis
Luce Irigaray: Lips, Kissing, and the Politics of Sexual Difference
Hélene Cixous I Love You: The *Jouissance* of Writing
Andrea Dworkin
'Cosmo Woman': The World of Women's Magazines
Women in Pop Music
Discovering the Goddess (Geoffrey Ashe)
The Poetry of Cinema
The Sacred Cinema of Andrei Tarkovsky
Andrei Tarkovsky: Pocket Guide
Andrei Tarkovsky: *Mirror*: Pocket Movie Guide
Walerian Borowczyk: Cinema of Erotic Dreams
Jean-Luc Godard: The Passion of Cinema
Jean-Luc Godard: Pocket Guide
John Hughes and Eighties Cinema
Ferris Buller's Day Off: Pocket Movie Guide
The Cinema of Richard Linklater
Liv Tyler: Star In Ascendance
Blade Runner and the Films of Philip K. Dick
Paul Bowles and Bernardo Bertolucci
Media Hell: Radio, TV and the Press
Detonation Britain: Nuclear War in the UK
Feminism and Shakespeare
Wild Zones: Pornography, Art and Feminism
Sex in Art: Pornography and Pleasure in Painting and Sculpture
Sexing Hardy: Thomas Hardy and Feminism

The Light Eternal *is a model monograph, an exemplary job. The subject matter of the book is
beautifully organised and dead on beam.* (Lawrence Durrell)
It is amazing for me to see my work treated with such passion and respect. (Andrea Dworkin)
Sex-Magic-Poetry-Cornwall *is a very rich essay... It is like a brightly-lighted box.* (Peter Redgrove)

CRESCENT MOON PUBLISHING P.O. Box 1312, Maidstone, Kent, ME14 5XU, Great Britain
0044-1622-729593 cresmopub@yahoo.co.uk www.crmoon.com